PUBLIC RAPE

Second-wave feminism's mission was to end the blanket silence shrouding rape and bring it to public attention. Now feminist critics must confront a different issue. In *Public Rape: Representing Violation in Fiction and Film*, Tanya Horeck considers the public investment in images of rape and the figure of the raped woman.

Introducing the idea of 'public rape', Horeck looks at how images of rape – from news stories to Hollywood films and popular fiction – serve as cultural fantasies of sexual, racial and class difference. *Public Rape* argues that the concept of fantasy, while much maligned in traditional feminist writing on sexual violence, is the key to understanding the investment in narratives of rape.

Topics addressed include the use of rape as an origin story in the work of classic feminist writers such as Susan Brownmiller and Marilyn French, the infamous New Bedford 'Big Dan's' gang rape case, rape in films such as *The Accused, Strange Days, Boys Don't Cry* and *Raw Deal: A Question of Consent*, and the controversy surrounding Sarah Dunant's feminist sex thriller *Transgressions*.

Horeck takes an interdisciplinary approach that works between the fields of gender, film and cultural studies to reveal how representations of rape raise vital questions about the relationship between reality and fantasy, and between violence and spectacle.

Tanya Horeck is Lecturer in Communication Studies in the School of Arts and Letters at Anglia Polytechnic University.

SUSSEX STUDIES IN CULTURE AND
COMMUNICATION
Series Editor: Jane Cowan
University of Sussex

Books in this series express Sussex's unique commitment to interdisciplinary work
at the cutting edge of cultural and communication studies. Transcending the
interface between the social and the human sciences, the series explores some of
the key themes that define the particular character of life, and the representation of
life, at the end of one millennium and the beginning of the next.

Our relationship to each other, to our bodies and to our technologies are
changing. New concepts are required, new evidence is needed, to advance our
understanding of these changes. The boundaries between disciplines need to be
challenged. Through monographs and edited collections the series will explore
new ways of thinking about communication, performance, identities and the continual refashioning of meanings, messages and images in space and time.

PUBLIC RAPE

Representing violation in fiction and film

Tanya Horeck

Routledge
Taylor & Francis Group

LONDON AND NEW YORK

First published 2004
by Routledge
11 New Fetter Lane, London EC4P 4EE

Simultaneously published in the USA and Canada
by Routledge
29 West 35th Street, New York, NY 10001

Routledge is an imprint of the Taylor & Francis Group

© 2004 Tanya Horeck

Typeset in Bembo by
Newgen Imaging Systems (P) Ltd, Chennai, India
Printed and bound in Great Britain by
Antony Rowe Ltd, Chippenham, Wiltshire

British Library Cataloguing in Publication Data
A catalogue record for this book is available from the British Library

Library of Congress Cataloging in Publication Data
A catalog record for this book has been requested

ISBN 0–415–28855–X (hbk)
ISBN 0–415–28856–8 (pbk)

CONTENTS

PREFACE

This book is about the cultural representation of rape in feminism, literature, film and popular culture. It explores the prevalence of images of rape, and the figure of the raped woman, across a range of texts. Above all, it is a book about public fantasies of rape that dramatize collective fears and fascinations.

During the years I have researched and written on rape, people have frequently asked whether it is upsetting to study such a horrific subject. Often, the assumption is that I am writing about rape from a sociological perspective – collating case studies of rape, speaking to victims, looking at rapists' profiles. In fact, as I would explain, my subject is the cultural representation of rape, the depiction of sexual violation. It is an important distinction to make. This book is not about the physical crime of rape *per se*, but the ways rape is thought about, and used, in cultural texts, as a scene for working through questions regarding reading and spectatorship. It is also about sexual politics, ethnic and racial tensions, and the contested boundary between the real and the imaginary. Images of rape often make us self-consciously aware of our position in relation to the text. What are the ethics of reading and watching representations of rape? Are we bearing witness to a terrible crime or are we participating in shameful voyeuristic activity? These questions form the key preoccupation of this book, linking my discussion of texts from the fields of political theory, popular media, contemporary fiction and Hollywood film.

Inspired by, yet critical of, the groundbreaking feminist work on rape during the 1970s and 1980s, I explore the relevancy of that work to a present day critical reading of rape. Nearly thirty years after Susan Brownmiller brought rape to international attention with her pioneering treatise *Against Our Will: Men, Women and Rape* (1975), we are faced with a continuing proliferation of images of rape in the public domain. Susan Griffin's call to break the 'conspiracy of silence' (1982: 4) surrounding rape was once feminism's goal; it now seems that the main challenge facing feminist cultural critics approaching the topic of rape in the twenty-first century is how to deal with the intense publicity trained on the crime.

From the eighteenth-century onwards, it has been perceived as a crime 'in its nature commonly secret' (cited in Ferguson 1987: 91), but it is my contention that rape has increasingly become the most 'public' of crimes. From literary texts to popular films; to talk shows and reality crime television; to magazines and newspapers; representations of rape permeate every aspect of cultural life. In the chapters that follow, I explore what I call 'public rape'. By this I mean something more than simply the publicized controversies surrounding stories of sexual violence, though these will also be discussed. Rather, I want to use the term public rape to refer to the idea of rape as an event that relates to the affairs of a community or a nation.

To explore 'public rape' is not to ignore the personal tragedy that victims of rape suffer; it is to examine and interrogate the collective investment in narratives of rape. Stories of rape are essential to the way in which the body politic is imagined, serving as a site for cultural conflict and the embodiment of public concerns. As will emerge throughout this book, the question of who is represented by, and excluded from, the terms of the body politic, is made plain through images and stories of rape.

This book began life in an English Literature department, was completed at an interdisciplinary institution where it circulated between the fields of English, Critical Theory and Media Studies, and was finally finished in its present form in a Communication and Film Studies department. I was attracted to the subject of rape and representation precisely because it troubles the boundaries between literature, politics, law, popular culture, film studies and feminism. Rape is a topic relevant to many disciplines, and much of the excitement of this project has come from finding salient similarities and provocative disjunctions among different representations of sexual violation. Through exploring images of rape across a range of fields, I have been forced to continually reappraise my understanding of the very concept of representation, and its relationship to reality. The aim of the Sussex Studies in Culture and Communication Series – 'to explore new ways of thinking about communication and the continual refashioning of meanings, messages and images' – is one to which I remain committed, and is one that the topic of rape and representation exemplifies. I hope that my reading of public fantasies of rape demonstrates the promise and the possibility of interdisciplinary studies, raising critical questions about our relationship to representations of violence.

ACKNOWLEDGEMENTS

Thanks first of all to the British Council, which funded three years of my research on this project at the University of Sussex. The idea for this work first came into being at Carleton University in Ottawa where I was lucky enough to be taught by three wonderful professors, Priscilla Walton, Barbara Leckie and Brenda Carr. Their help in putting together a proposal was invaluable. My supervisor at the University of Sussex, Vicky Lebeau, deserves special thanks. I am deeply grateful to Vicky for her careful supervision of my work, her many detailed comments on various versions of the manuscript, and her generous intellectual and emotional support. Thanks to Suzy Gordon and the students of the Sussex MA seminar 'Feminism and Film Theory' (1998, 1999) for their interest in my work. Their useful comments are reflected in my writing, particularly on *The Accused*. I would also like to thank Lyndsey Stonebridge and Lindsay Smith for their enthusiasm about this project and their encouragement that it should be turned into a book. Their suggestions were incisive and enormously helpful. I am grateful to my colleagues in the Communication Studies Department at Anglia Polytechnic University for providing me with intellectual advice. An earlier version of Chapter 4, 'They did worse than nothing': Rape and Spectatorship in *The Accused* appeared in *Canadian Review of American Studies*, University of Toronto Press 2000; Chapter 5, 'More Intimate Than Violence': Sarah Dunant's *Transgressions* was previously published in *Women: A Cultural Review*, Taylor & Francis 2000; and sections of Chapter 1 pertaining to Dorothy Allison were first published as 'Let Me Tell You a Story': Writing the Fiction of Childhood in Dorothy Allison's *Bastard Out of Carolina* in *New Formations*, Lawrence and Wishart 2001. My thanks to the journals and publishers for permission to reprint revised versions of these articles. Finally, I am incredibly fortunate to have had the unflagging support and loving encouragement of my family. I would like to extend my gratitude to my parents Ron and Lynita Horeck. Heartfelt thanks to Hugh Perry for his unswerving belief in this work, his tireless help with editing, and his perceptive suggestions and comments. His love and support guided me through the ups and downs of the writing process and made the experience worthwhile. This book is dedicated to him.

INTRODUCTION
Rape and public fantasy

On 15 November 1993, a book review resulted in the 'public rape' of Catharine MacKinnon, the American feminist lawyer and anti-pornography campaigner.[1] One of the common critiques of MacKinnon's work is that she blurs the line between real and represented rape. Responding to this perception of her work in a review written for US weekly *The Nation*, Carlin Romano began with a shocking suggestion: 'Suppose I decide to rape Catharine MacKinnon before reviewing her book' (1993: 563). The outcry that ensued as a result of this review has since become part of the mythology surrounding MacKinnon's persona as the 'lodestar of the feminist anti-pornography movement' (Brown 1995: 78).

At a National Press Club conference, MacKinnon described the review as 'public rape' (cited in Hentoff 1994: 17). It was the extremely public nature of this bizarre controversy, as much as the incident itself, which caught the national media's attention. *Time* covered the 'war of the words' under the headline, 'Assault by Paragraph: Catharine MacKinnon, legal theorist and anti porn activist, says she was raped by a book review'. *The Nation* was deluged with letters denouncing the 'wrongness of the use of rape as a tool for the conduct of criticism' ('Words' 1993: 786) and a furious Jeffrey Masson – author of *The Assault on Truth: Freud and Child Sexual Abuse* and MacKinnon's then partner – told Romano: 'I want you to know, if there is ever anything I can do to hurt your career, I will do it' (cited in Angelo 1994: 37).

This 'public rape' is fascinating for the way it lays bare fiercely debated questions in feminist, literary and cultural studies regarding the links between violence and representation, and fantasy and reality. The idea of 'public rape' is an unusual but powerful way of thinking about how sexual violation circulates in the public domain as a culturally invested issue. It provokes and horrifies, but also engages and fascinates. Paradoxically, while rape has been understood as the most private and shameful of crimes, it has always had a high profile in Western public life, with a rapt public following for famous cases and trials, as well as controversial literary and filmic depictions of sexual violation.

By way of introduction to this book and its exploration of rape, representation and fantasy, I'd like to discuss the 'public rape of Catharine MacKinnon' in greater detail to further explore its very public exposure of what is at stake in reading and writing about rape. The first question that comes to mind is: why would Romano include such a scene in his book review? At issue, writes Romano, is MacKinnon's controversial view that pornography is 'an act of violence against women' (1993: 564). To dispute this point he begins his book review with the following:

> Suppose I decide to rape Catharine MacKinnon before reviewing her book. Because I'm uncertain whether she understands the difference between being raped and being exposed to pornography, I consider it required research for my critique of her manifesto that pornography equals rape and should be banned. I plot and strategize, but at the last minute, I chicken out. People simply won't understand.
>
> (ibid.: 563)

So Romano decides to 'do the next best thing': he imagines the act through 'fantasy'.

> Not having raped before, I'm caught off guard by her fury, her indefatigable effort to talk me out of it, her insistence that pornography would be just as effective, the wrenching final expression of disgust and despair on her face and my own self-revulsion – even if it is just fantasy research.
>
> (ibid.)

At this point in his increasingly elaborate fantasy, Romano imagines *The Nation* publishes his piece, which was written for 'literary reasons', a 'thought experiment' (ibid.).

'Across town', Romano writes, 'another critic who's been assigned to review *Only Words* – call him Dworkin-Hentoff – reads my piece and concludes that he too needs to rape Catharine MacKinnon before properly evaluating her book' (ibid.). The composite rapist constructed by Romano is a tongue in cheek reference to Ronald Dworkin and Nat Hentoff, First Amendment champions who are recognized opponents of MacKinnon's anti-pornography battle. Unlike Romano, who only 'fantasized' the act, Dworkin-Hentoff 'acts on the idea' and 'really' rapes MacKinnon. Afterwards, Dworkin-Hentoff publishes a book review in *The New York Review of Books*, describing 'his rape of MacKinnon in long-winded, pornographic detail, arguing that she does not really equate rape with pornography, that the claim in her book is a wild intellectualization' (ibid.). Police charge both Dworkin-Hentoff and Romano with rape. 'Not fair', Romano writes. 'What I did was different' (ibid.). But evidently not, according to MacKinnon: 'He had me where he wanted me. He wants me as a violated woman with her legs spread. He needed me there before he could address my work' (cited in Angelo 1993: 37). Columnist Nat Hentoff was asked by MacKinnon to 'disavow this rape of me in your name' (cited in Hentoff 1993: 16). In response to this request, Hentoff published an article in *Village Voice* that strongly criticized Romano for the dehumanizing nature of his review: 'The rape – hypothetical or fantasy or whatever – was a rape. An invitation to the reader to imagine the actual Catharine MacKinnon being overpowered and stripped of her physical integrity' (1993: 17).

Editorial staff at *The Nation* took issue with readers who declared Romano's review to be 'misogynous', 'morally offensive', 'dangerous' and 'sickening', on the grounds that they were ignoring an important distinction between fantasy and reality ('Words' 1993: 786). 'Fantasy' was not even the appropriate word, they argued: 'The thought experiment – which is not the same as a sexual fantasy – is a familiar technique in philosophical writing. Romano made clear that he despises rape, and while the tone of his essay was fervently opposed to one woman, it did not seem to us to be anti women' (ibid.). For his part, Romano defended his review: 'I *despise* real rape and didn't rape anyone by writing *about* rape (an old-fashioned distinction, I'll admit, but there you are)...At the same time I think it's MacKinnon who trivializes real rape by equating it with everything from *Playboy* to graffiti' (ibid.).

But what constitutes 'real rape' in this dispute? More specifically, what is Romano trying to communicate or preserve with this idea of 'real rape'? Ostensibly, in using this phrase he is attempting to reiterate the point that there is a difference between fantasy and the 'real thing', between figural and literal rape. But by producing a fictionalized, composite figure, I would argue that Romano 'chickens out' from his fantasy rape as if he too suddenly loses the distinction he has been attempting to assert. As Hentoff asks: 'Even in protected fantasy, why step back from the act by making Dworkin and me the rapists?' (1993: 17) The answer, it would seem, is that Romano requires this idea of 'real rape' in order to put his fantasy into place.

I begin with the uproar surrounding Romano's book review in order to give an example of the violent debates that attend the attempt to determine the link between real and represented rape. In the book that follows I explore the phenomenon of what I call public rape – representations of rape that serve as cultural fantasies of power and domination, gender and sexuality, and class and ethnicity. Prior to the feminist politicization of the crime in the 1970s, there was a shroud of silence surrounding rape: a 'cultural cover-up' (Higgins and Silver 1991: 4). The feminist goal, as Linda Alcoff and Laura Gray attest, was to make rape public, to 'reposition the problem from the individual psyche to the social sphere where it rightfully belongs' (1993: 261). In contemporary popular culture, the silence on rape has been broken with an outburst of discourse. As Alcoff and Gray suggest, the worry for feminists now concerns the extraordinary publicity swirling around rape and the fact that 'the media...often eroticize the depictions...of sexual violence to titillate and expand their audiences' (ibid.: 262). Moreover, while the phrase 'breaking the silence' remains an important articulation of the difficulty victims of rape have in speaking out about their violation, it no longer has the same force when it comes to talking about what Ken Plummer refers to as the 'overload of stories' of rape in the public sphere (1995: 79).[2] As Plummer concludes, where in previous times the narrative of rape 'hardly existed except in private, often hidden, form' now 'such stories are everywhere' (ibid.: 78).

Instead of decrying the publicity surrounding rape, I am interested in interrogating the nature of its public status. Public rape: at first glance, the term seems paradoxical. How can rape, generally thought of as the most personal and private of crimes, be considered a public event? Yet as my reading of a variety of literary, filmic and media representations of rape will reveal, cultural images of rape serve as a means of forging social bonds, and of mapping out public space. It is a crime that has a pervasive effect on the life of the community and the workings of the body politic. And it is a crime that dominates public fantasies regarding sexual and social difference.

Where the term 'public rape' sounds paradoxical, the phrase 'public rape fantasies' seems positively scandalous. Indeed, this introduction self-consciously brings together two terms rarely seen in feminist writing on sexual violence: fantasy and rape. When these two terms do appear in feminist discourse it is usually only to violently denounce their association. As is illustrated dramatically in the above case of 'rape by book review', rape fantasy is an explosive subject, particularly for feminism. There are important historical explanations for feminism's distrust of fantasy in relation to the issue of sexual violence. For many feminists, the conjunction of fantasy and rape has meant one thing only: the disavowal of women's experiences of sexual violence. According to this understanding of the term, fantasy means the opposite of reality; the fantastic, the untrue ('she made it up', 'she really wanted it'). Historically, the idea that women secretly fantasize about sexual violation has been grounds for dismissing women's charges of rape in the legal arena. Following this patriarchal use of the term, the expression 'rape fantasy' has generally been understood in two ways in feminist discourse: in the first instance, 'rape fantasy' refers to lurid male fantasies of violating helpless women. In the second instance, the term refers to the troubling 'female rape fantasy', in which women fantasize about being sexually violated by men (a prevalent subject in popular female romance and a thorn in feminism's side). Both, according to important feminist writers such as Susan Brownmiller, Andrea Dworkin and MacKinnon, are patriarchal fantasies, designed to tyrannize women. As is made clear in political writing from the 1970s, which I will discuss in Chapter 1, feminism's moral and political imperative has been to destroy fantasy in order to bring home the horror of rape to a culture that is either indifferent or hostile to stories of sexual violation.

But is this the only way to think about the idea of fantasy in relation to rape? If fantasies of rape, both individually and collectively, are a potent force in culture, as most second-wave feminists acknowledge, then is fantasy something to be forsaken in our discussions of rape? In her important book *States of Fantasy* Jacqueline Rose argues that 'fantasy is not antagonistic to social reality; it is its precondition or psychic glue' (1996: 3). According to Rose, there is 'no way of understanding political identities and destinies without letting fantasy into the frame' (ibid.: 4). Following Rose's argument, I will argue that the concept of fantasy is necessary for an understanding of the representational politics of rape.

Given the controversial history behind the term 'fantasy' and its relation to rape, it is important to specify my use of the term. My approach to fantasy is strongly influenced by psychoanalysis, including the important re-reading of Freud's work by J Laplanche and J-B Pontalis, but also, in particular, the engaging psychoanalytic work on fantasy conducted by literary and film theorists such as Rose, Elizabeth Cowie, John Fletcher and Vicky Lebeau. Significantly, the psychoanalytic understanding of fantasy refuses the everyday notion of the term as the opposite of 'reality'. Psychoanalysis is concerned with the internal world of imagination (Burgin 1992: 84–86). The term that repeatedly crops up in psychoanalytic discussions of fantasy, and which is especially vital to my exploration of rape and representation, is that of 'scene'. Fantasies, as Laplanche and Pontalis point out, are 'scripts of organized scenes which are capable of dramatization – usually in a visual form' (1988: 318). The subject is 'invariably present in these scenes', even if only in the part of a spectator or an observer; it is not an object *per se* that the subject imagines, but a sequence of events offering up a number of different roles and positions (ibid.). Fantasy, therefore, is not only about fulfilling wishes in imagined scenarios; in Freudian psychoanalysis, fantasy is the 'arranging of, a setting out of, desire' (Cowie 1997: 133). In the analysis of representations of rape to follow, my interest is in looking at how rape is structured as a scene through which a multitude of conflicts are staged.

Fantasies are not unique, individual phenomena. Freud discovered this through his clinical work with patients. He observed that the same fantasies occur over and over again, leading him to conclude that there are 'types' of collective scenarios that are shared by members of a culture (Lebeau 2001: 6). One of these collective scenarios is the primal scene. Freud contended that behind every individual postulation of fantasy there lay an original, 'primal fantasy' (Laplanche and Pontalis 1986: 17). Described most famously in his 'Wolf Man' case study, the original Freudian primal scene is the child watching his parents engage in sexual intercourse. It is an act the child perceives as violent, 'a primal rape or wounding of the mother by the father' (Fletcher 1986: 113). The primal scene is ambivalent, however, because the child is confused by the 'expression of enjoyment' on the mother's face, which appears to contradict the perception of the act as violent (Freud 1979: 277). This 'primal rape', an act in which sex is indissociable from violence, came to be designated as '*the* primal scene', not only in psychoanalysis, but in a range of cultural narratives (Fletcher 1995: 343). As Mandy Merck has noted, representations of rape, 'in which sex is not so much coupled with violence as equated with it', are present in many contemporary artistic works, as well as in many feminist critiques of heterosexuality (2000: 255). Moreover, the position of the child, watching an illicit scene of sexualized violence in a darkened room, is, as film theorist Christian Metz suggested, similar to the audience's voyeuristic position in relation to the cinema screen. In the second half of the book, when I explore the idea of rape as public media spectacle, I look at how cinematic scenes of sexual violence call into question the activity of spectatorship.

Of course, to draw on the Freudian notion of fantasy to discuss rape is not without its problems. Psychoanalysis has always been seen as inimical to the subject of rape. As Margaret Whitford suggests: 'The psychoanalytic account of violence and aggression is not thought to be adequate to deal with the many different forms which violence may take, nor to tackle the specificity of rape as a social and cultural phenomenon' (1992: 366). One of the main reasons why many feminists consider psychoanalysis inadequate in this regard, is Freud's so-called abandonment of the 'seduction theory' and his turn to the world of fantasy.[3] Fuelled by Jeffrey Masson's 'exposé' of Freud as a coward who 'turned his back on reality' (*The Assault on Truth: Freud and Child Sexual Abuse* 1992), many feminists continue to repudiate Freud on the grounds that he covered up his discovery of the pervasiveness of child sexual abuse. Psychoanalysis' alleged 'betrayal' of female patients has become one of the keynote stories about rape within the feminist movement. Masson's pejorative definition of fantasy has set the tone for the debate: 'Fantasy – the notion from Freud that women invent allegations of sexual abuse because they desire sex – continues to play a role in undermining the credibility of victims of sexual abuse' (1992: xxiii). Here fantasy is understood as the opposite of reality. Those who are interested in the psychoanalytic understanding of fantasy are seen to be denying the 'truth' and colluding with those who sexually victimize children. However, as many critics have argued (see Fletcher 1986; Laplanche and Pontalis 1986; Rose 1989; Brown 1993; Lebeau 1995; Scott 1996), it is not accurate to say that Freud turned away from the 'real event'. In fact, the question of the relationship between fantasy and the 'real event' was one he grappled with throughout his career.

It is not my intention to revisit the exhaustive debates over Freud and the seduction theory. A great deal of time has been spent trying to rescue Freudian theory from those who would reject it purely on the grounds of Masson's argument. It is time to move past the well-worn debate over whether Freud turned his back on 'the reality of sexual abuse' in order to explore what significance the concept of fantasy may hold for a consideration of representations of rape. Where the debate over Freud's so-called abandonment of the seduction theory pits 'reality' against 'fantasy' and assumes their fundamental incompatibility, psychoanalytic theory, by contrast, sees 'reality' and 'fantasy' as involved with each other in uncomfortable but nonetheless fascinating ways. As Laplanche and Pontalis note, 'the use of the term "phantasy" cannot fail to evoke the distinction between imagination and reality' (1988: 315). Psychoanalysis recognizes that the question of what was real and what was imagined is often difficult to determine, particularly in regard to traumatic events. The internal mind does not make a clear distinction between the two. As Ann Scott puts it: 'In psychoanalysis all events become invested with fantasy, conscious and unconscious, and may on occasion be potentiated by fantasy' (1996: 6). It is the question of how the event of rape becomes invested with fantasy that fascinates me. The subject of rape forces us to a new understanding of the critical communication between the real and the imaginary.

In my reading of rape and its representation in a number of texts, both written and visual, my interest in this book is to explore what Elizabeth Cowie calls 'public fantasies', those collective or typical fantasies found in the 'creative writing' of novels and films (1997: 137). In exploring the 'public circulation of fantasies', it is fascinating to see how the same scenarios reveal collective wishes that 'devolve, as in the original fantasies, on positions of desire: active or passive, feminine or masculine, mother or son, father or daughter' (ibid.: 137, 143). In looking at public fantasies of rape designed for cultural consumption, I consider what sort of wishes or desires are being played out in and through these texts. Why do the same stories about rape get told and retold? What is the mythic status of rape in popular culture?

The other key term in this book is representation. According to WJT Mitchell, representation takes two forms: 'aesthetic or semiotic (things that 'stand for' other things) and political (persons who 'act for' other persons)' (1995: 11). Rape exposes the double meaning of representation in so far as it is often made to serve as a 'sign' for other issues, and as it is also frequently used as a means of expressing ideological and political questions concerning the functioning of the body politic. Representation, the attempt to open the 'lines of communication with others', is also, as Mitchell argues, always a misrepresentation. 'As soon as we begin to use representations in any social situation ... then representation begins to play a double role, as a means of communication which is also a potential obstacle to it' (ibid.: 13). As I will demonstrate, depictions of rape bear out this 'double role' of representation, in which representation is at once a means of, and an obstacle to, communication. For example, in my discussion of Rousseau's story of rape and revenge, *Le Lévite d'Ephraim*, in Chapter 2, I reveal how the raped woman is the figure that negotiates the link between semiotic and political representation. While she is an obstacle to social and political unity – it is the discovery of her raped and mutilated body that initiates untold suffering and warfare – she is simultaneously the means by which the dispersed people come together and originate the social contract. In this story of the origins of the social–sexual contract, we also see how the decision to have rape stand in for something or somebody is done by 'virtue of a kind of social agreement' (Mitchell 1995: 13).

In the representations of rape I examine, the raped woman is not only a sexual other. She is also often marked out as other by dint of her ethnic and class positioning. From the Levite's 'concubine', a woman who is 'virtually a slave, secured by a man for his own purposes' (Trible 1984: 66); to the real life New Bedford rape victim, a woman from a working-class immigrant community; to the representation of the raped woman in *The Accused* as 'white trash'; to the labelling of the woman at the centre of the controversy in the documentary *Raw Deal: A Question of Consent* as a 'low-class whore', the figure of the raped woman stirs up fears about sexual and social distinction.

Just as I provide readings of diverse texts from different media, so too, my reading of texts employs a wide range of critical theory and approaches, from psychoanalytic film theory, to black cultural studies, to deconstruction. In examining how rape is always a problem of representation, just as the problem of representation is constantly revealed through the issue of rape, my aim is to disturb a positive-images approach to the question of violence. Discussions of literary and filmic depictions of rape have been particularly prone to pivot on the question of whether a depiction of sexual violence is 'positive' or 'negative', 'good' or 'bad'. This is perhaps because of the high emotional and political stakes involved in reading and watching rape in contemporary culture, particularly in the wake of feminist consciousness-raising on the subject. Much of my interest in the topic derives from the charged discussion around depictions of rape in the cultural arena. Tracking the issues that get thrown up in the wake of cultural panics surrounding representations of rape is one of the preoccupations of this book.

This study can be situated in relation to a growing body of feminist cultural criticism on rape and representation initiated by the influential anthology *Rape and Representation* (Higgins and Silver 1991). The key questions emerging from this body of work concern the proliferation of representations of rape in both 'high' and 'low' culture, the cultural fixation on the figure of the violated woman, and finally, and perhaps most critically, the question of feminism. As both Jacinda Read (2000) and Sarah Projansky (2001) note, representations of rape are one of the prime locations for determining popular ideas about femininity, feminism and post-feminism. A second related issue tackled by these writers concerns the direction feminist criticism should take in regard to dealing with cultural images of rape. For the contemporary feminist, analysing depictions of sexual violence necessarily brings self-reflexive questions about feminist politics and feminist interpretation to the foreground.

From the beginning, this study presented me with a challenge: how to retain the important insights of second-wave feminism on rape, while resisting some of the more programmatic aspects of that work. Like many other feminist cultural critics influenced by post-structuralist theory, I am concerned about some of the rigid conclusions drawn by the major feminist thinkers on rape (Brownmiller, Dworkin and MacKinnon notably). In the script of gender relations offered by these thinkers, there is often a disheartening repetition of the male as the abuser, the female as the victim. In her engaging essay, 'Fighting Bodies, Fighting Words', Sharon Marcus notes that traditional feminist discourse takes 'violence as a self-explanatory first cause and endows it with an invulnerable and terrifying facticity which stymies our ability to challenge and demystify rape' (1992: 387). In order to avoid such a debilitating view of violence, Marcus proposes that we understand rape as a 'scripted interaction' (ibid.: 390). A script involves a narrative, and the 'concept of a narrative avoids the problems of the collapsed continuum ... in which rape becomes the inevitable beginning, middle, and end of any interaction. The narrative element of a script leaves room and makes time for revision' (ibid.: 391). According to Marcus, 'rape is not only scripted – it also scripts' (ibid.). The question is how narratives of rape position men and women in particular ways, and to what cultural uses narratives of rape are being put.

While I draw on post-structuralist theory to critique certain limitations of what can be called 'radical feminism', this is not to say that I dismiss second-wave feminist discourse on rape entirely. I would argue that some critics are too quick to reject that work as irrelevant or outdated. This is especially true of the popular 'post-feminist' response to rape, as expressed by critics such as Katie Roiphe. Described on the dust-jacket of her book, *The Morning After: Sex, Fear and Feminism* (1993) as the 'first of her generation to speak out publicly against the intolerant turn the women's movement has taken', Roiphe's cynical book inspired angry debate amongst feminists, in large part because of the dismissive tone she takes towards the feminists who preceded her.[4] Like Marcus, Roiphe worries about the view of gender relations being offered in much feminist discourse: 'Rape-crisis feminists reinforce traditional views about the fragility of the female body and will' (1993: 66). But Roiphe takes this point even further. She suggests that 'rape is a natural trump card for feminism' and that 'arguments about rape can be used to sequester feminism in the teary province of trauma and crisis' (ibid.: 57). Roiphe writes that Susan Brownmiller, one of the 'prophets of the rape-crisis movement', uses 'grand, sometimes paranoid strokes' to describe rape as 'something originary, something that defines relations between men and women' (ibid.: 56).

Rather than discarding founding feminist texts such as Brownmiller's for the perceived limitations of their vision, I suggest that we need to explore how second-wave feminism casts rape 'as something originary'. It is important to inquire into the kind of work rape has performed for feminism not so we can conclude, as Roiphe does, that the views of 'rape-crisis feminists' are outdated and puritanical, but so we can understand the role that rape plays in feminism as a scenario through which questions are posed about masculine and feminine identity, sexuality and sexual difference, and the origins of culture. Beginning with a re-reading of Brownmiller's *Against Our Will: Men, Women and Rape* (1975), I want to retrieve what I see as the most forceful aspect of her argument: her conception of rape as an act that renders something explicit about the workings of what I will call the socio-sexual contract. One of my interests in this book is to look at the ways the theory of rape attributed to Brownmiller has been taken up in the years following *Against Our Will*.[5] As I will demonstrate throughout, Brownmiller's exemplary vision of rape, and its relation to the socio-sexual contract, plays an animating role in a number of different cultural productions. Though its meaning will emerge more gradually through my discussion of cultural objects and texts, it is necessary to define here what I mean by the 'socio-sexual contract'. A social contract is the agreement between individuals that constitutes an organized society. The sexual contract, which tells the story of how women become excluded from public life, is, according to feminist political theorists such as Carole Pateman, what gets omitted from masculine stories about the foundations of modern civil society. Representations of rape, and the figure of the raped woman, I will argue, operate as the ground over which the terms of the social – and the sexual – contract are secured. As I will have occasion to illustrate in a number of different ways throughout this book, images of rape function as the site of collective identification, what Rose refers to in a different context as the 'emotive binding […] of social groups' (1996: 3). As Rose suggests, 'fantasy surely ceases to be a private matter if it fuels, or at least plays a part in, the forging of the collective will' (ibid.). Here the idea of public rape is given an added resonance. It is in the literary, media and filmic depictions of rape that these public, collective fantasies take hold.

Visual images of rape have always been especially contentious. This book seeks not only to reconsider some of the more notorious cinematic images of sexual violence, as in *The Accused* (1988) and more recently in *Strange Days* (1995), *Boys Don't Cry* (1999) and *Raw Deal: A Question of Consent* (2001), but also to inquire more broadly into the relationship between images of sexual violation and anxiety about spectatorship and visual technology. Graphic images of rape in visual culture have long played a significant role in debates regarding what it is acceptable to watch. Films featuring rape are routinely singled out as objects of moral outrage. Critics such as Christopher Goodwin worry about the 'dangerous devaluation of sexual violence' at the movies and suggest that rape by its 'very ubiquity has begun to seem like a mere sensational device', a public spectacle (1996: 10 March). But more often than not, the worry is that images of rape are something more than 'mere sensational devices'. Arguments about screen violence tend to turn around the question of whether or not images of rape on television and at the cinema are directly related to real-life violence. What I find worthy of note about these arguments is that while critics battle over the question of reality and representation, they do not really consider the issue of rape. It is thus important to ask: What might it be about rape that expresses an anxiety about the relationship between fictional and actual violence? How is rape being used to communicate ideas about the relationship between audiences and texts?

Considering controversial visual depictions of rape, I set out to re-evaluate a long-running debate about the association between reality and representation, a debate that has hinged on the radical feminist slogan: 'Pornography is the theory; rape is the practice'. The idea that there is a tie between the reality of rape and its representation, made most famously by MacKinnon and Andrea Dworkin, has been much criticized. Though many of the criticisms of the MacKinnon–Dworkin position on pornography are useful and valid, important questions about the negotiation between the reality of rape and its representation have been overlooked in the clash between anti-pornography and anti-anti-pornography feminists. To avoid the generalities that have mired debates about screen violence, I engage in a close reading of media texts and controversies, arguing that it is important to re-examine the connection between the violence of representation and the violence of rape.

Organization and structure

Rape sparks discussion across a number of fields, including criminology, film and media studies, art history, literature, anthropology and evolutionary biology. Prevalent in an array of fields and intellectual disciplines, rape is a subject that needs to be approached from an interdisciplinary standpoint.

This book is divided into three main sections. Part I of the book, 'Primal Scenes', develops the question of rape and its relation to the socio-sexual contract and lays the theoretical foundation for my examination of public rape in popular culture. Chapter 1, 'Origin Stories: Rape, Fantasy and the Foundations of Feminism', begins by looking at how rape is cast as the originary moment of the social contract in two of the best-selling Anglo-American feminist texts of the 1970s – Brownmiller's *Against Our Will* (1975) and Marilyn French's novel *The Women's Room* (1977). These texts offer an epic reading of rape as the origin of patriarchal culture. But I also want to examine how the narratives they provide function as origin stories of feminism, considering how an image of rape as primal scene secures feminism's own foundations.

The images of original rape found in these best-selling feminist books, I contend, generate subject positions predicated on race and gender. Exploring the critique of Brownmiller's work by black feminists such as Alice Walker, Angela Davis and Jacquelyn Dowd Hall, I consider how, to borrow Marcus' phrase, 'rape is not only scripted – it scripts', when it comes to imagining sexual and racial difference (1992: 391). To open up a question about the status of rape as private and public fantasy, I turn to two novels: Gayl Jones' *Corregidora* (1988) and Dorothy Allison's *Bastard Out of Carolina* (1993). These novels call attention to how rape operates as fantasy and narrative, a recognition missing from Brownmiller and French.

Chapter 2, 'Body Politics: Rousseau's *Le Lévite D'Ephraim*', puts the question of rape and its relation to the social contract in a historical context by looking at a violent prose poem by the eighteenth-century political philosopher Jean-Jacques Rousseau. Remarking on the curious absence of this story in feminist accounts of rape, I argue that Rousseau's story of rape, murder and mayhem brings into graphic focus what Carole Pateman calls the 'lost story of the sexual contract' (1988: 19), the dark and murderous underpinnings of the social contract. Moreover, in its subplot of homoerotic desire, the story calls attention to a subject largely ignored by traditional feminist accounts of sexual violence: male-on-male rape. Rousseau's prose poem also reveals the way rape is turned into a 'civic crime', raising questions about the links between violability, citizenship and a fantasy of the body politic. The raped woman becomes 'public property', with her dismembered body serving as a sign over which men initiate then resolve war. In addition to exploring how rape gets re-written as 'love' and marriage in Rousseau, this chapter asks why Jacques Derrida's reading of Rousseau's *Essay on the Origin of Languages* fails to discuss his use of the Levite story, choosing instead to discuss the example of 'love'. A story of rape and revenge, *Le Lévite D'Ephraim* brings into focus the argument at the heart of this book: that rape is at once essential, yet disruptive to, the social order.

In its exploration of the raped woman as a grotesque means of communication, the *Lévite* sets the stage for Part II of this book: public spectacles of rape. 'The Spectacle of Rape' examines representations of rape in popular media and film. I explore how images of rape have come to serve as public spectacles *par excellence*. The emphasis here is on how public desires and anxieties about the links between violence and spectatorship find expression in visual representations of rape. Here, I seek to reveal how the politics of rape exists in what one can call the violence of civic identification, which is in turn propped up by technologies of news and entertainment.

A particular interest in this section of the book is the tension between 'reality' and 'spectacle' and the possibility of mistaking one for the other. My key case study of public rape in this section is the Big Dan's gang rape, one of America's most sensational rape cases. Chapter 3, 'Rape is Not a Spectator Sport: The New Bedford "Big Dan's" gang rape', examines the public fascination with the 'reality' of rape, and considers how this fascination is tied to the reproduction of rape as spectacle. What is both compelling and unsettling, is that a rape case that exposes a communal failure to 'witness' a woman's gang rape, becomes the first ever televised rape trial, which, in turn, is justified on the grounds that it serves the ends of public justice. Continuing the previous chapter's discussion of how the violated female body is made to trope the body politic, this chapter also explores how the story of a woman's gang rape is transformed into the story of the violation of a city. As the first criminal trial ever to be televised by CNN, I argue that the Big Dan's rape case, which turns on the difficult relations between sexuality, class, ethnicity and nationality, demands to be recognized as the inaugural moment for the network's new style of broadcasting.

Chapter 4 pursues the question about the relation between rape and new technologies of vision in regard to Hollywood cinema. Turning to *The Accused*, the fictionalization of the Big Dan's rape case, I explore what happens in the shift from the real event to cinema. In particular, I examine how one of the most infamous representations of rape in popular culture re-writes the historical record to construct a public fantasy of white social justice. Re-reading the white feminist acclaim of the film, this chapter considers how *The Accused* functions as feminist wish fulfillment. That the feminist reception of the film is wishful, and at key moments blind, to the film's coded storyline of race, nationality and civic justice, points to the exclusionary violence of attempts to universalize the white woman's experience of violation.

Part III, 'Rewriting Rape', focuses on two contemporary public controversies. A literary scandal over a feminist writer's depiction of female sexual arousal in a rape scene forms the basis of Chapter 5, an exploration of what is at stake in the recurring use of rape as a storyline in feminist fiction of recent times. This literary sex scandal raises questions about the responsibility of feminist authors regarding the public circulation of images of rape. In this chapter I employ the controversy over Sarah Dunant's 1997 thriller *Transgressions* as a way into a consideration of the feminist uses of fiction in relation to sexual violence. Returning to questions raised in Chapter 1 concerning the role of rape stories in feminism, I draw links between the controversy regarding *Transgressions* and the critical debate around Andrea Dworkin's *Mercy* (1990), a text many consider to be the paradigmatic feminist representation of rape, but which has been criticized for its fantastic descriptions of sexualized violence and the sexually violated woman. Moving beyond the controversy over *Transgressions*, I provide a close reading of Dunant's novel and its central scenario of sexual danger and female empowerment, one that, I suggest, is found throughout the burgeoning arena of female crime writing. Discussing a range of feminist crime thrillers, including work by Barbara Wilson, Elisabeth Bowers, Barbara Neely, Jenny Diski and Susanna Moore, I assert that, far from being a mere plot device, stories of rape are integrally linked to the rise of the feminist crime thriller.

My concluding chapter, 'Rape on Tape?' examines the American documentary *Raw Deal: A Question of Consent* (2001), which includes footage of a woman's alleged rape, and which, in its difficult dealings with the interaction between reality and representation, brings new and disturbing meaning to the term 'public rape'. In this final chapter, I consider the implications of the increasing trend towards ever more explicit and 'authentic' cinematic scenes of sexualized violence, and interrogate what these images have to tell us about the act of spectatorship. Though popular discussion of *Raw Deal* has focused on the idea of truth and the question of who to believe – the woman who says she was raped, or the fraternity brothers who say she wasn't – I argue that what is most interesting about the documentary is the way in which it shows how rape is a battle over the ownership of meaning and of reality. With *Raw Deal* we find an especially graphic example of how cultural ideas about rape and sexualized violence are used to voice public fantasies about masculinity and femininity and the positions that men and women should take in regard to the body politic. The need to examine how images of rape are employed in the public domain is intensified here by the fact that, in this particular case, the spectacle of sexualized violence replaces the legal forum altogether, with videotape recordings of the incident open to all as a 'public record'.

Building on the insights of second-wave feminism, *Public Rape: Representing Violation in Fiction and Film* seeks to open up the debate about representations of rape. The concept of fantasy in this book does not undermine feminism's efforts to make known the realities of violence. Rather, an exploration of the enduring force and intensity of public fantasies of rape can help us better understand the depth and the extent of that violence.

Part I

PRIMAL SCENES

1

ORIGIN STORIES

Rape, fantasy and the foundations of feminism

> The search for origins, especially when it takes the form of reconstructing a hidden or forbidden scene, is one of the most seductive of all narratives.
>
> John Fletcher

Rape reached widespread public attention with Susan Brownmiller's best selling study *Against Our Will: Men, Women and Rape* (1975). Credited as the book responsible for 'uncovering the existence of rape as an important element in world history, one which historians have ignored or trivialized', *Against Our Will* was one of the first feminist texts to attain great mainstream success (Hartmann and Ross 1978: 932). In 1976, *Time* selected Brownmiller as one of its ten 'women of the year', summarizing her contribution to the women's movement as follows: 'Four years ago, Susan Brownmiller, one of feminism's most articulate and visible activists, disappeared into the library stacks. She surfaced last fall with *Against Our Will: Men, Women, and Rape*, the most rigorous and provocative piece of scholarship that has yet emerged from the feminist movement' ('A Dozen' 1976: 20).

In this chapter, I want to return to Brownmiller's work in order to question the role that rape plays in establishing and grounding feminist discourse. There is little doubt that rape is central to the feminist attempt to trace the origins of women's oppression. If 'all questions relating to the role and position of women in society...founder on the bed-rock of "When did it all start?"' twentieth-century feminism has tended to pose the question of origins through an image of rape as primal scene (Mitchell 1974: 364).[1] The 'Founding Mother of the anti-rape movement'[2] in America, Brownmiller provides feminism's classic, paradigmatic representation of rape as the primal scene of culture. 'Rape is nothing more or less than a conscious process of intimidation by which *all* men keep *all* women in a state of fear'. The conclusion to the first chapter of *Against Our Will*, this is one of feminism's most famous declarations.[3] Brownmiller's provocative, if problematic, text deals with the question of origins; it seeks to reveal how an original scene of rape recurs throughout history and throughout culture, determining the present-day treatment of women.

Moreover, Brownmiller's book is itself a point of origin, the beginning of an era of new critical thinking on rape. *Against Our Will* is the text used by theorists to mark the point when rape begins to be thought of as a 'major social force' that 'must be understood in terms of gender relations and sexual politics' (Porter 1986: 216).

Sylvana Tomaselli and Roy Porter, editors of the anthology *Rape*, situate the book's importance as follows:

> *Against Our Will* proved a turning-point by focusing public attention upon rape, by demonstrating the seriousness of the problem and by demanding a rethink of the crime: after reading her book, and others like it, no one can continue to see rape as an isolated incident, simply as one man – a "sex maniac" – sexually assaulting one woman.
>
> (1986: xi)

Brownmiller's book is not just a historical relic; in its construction of a universal story about rape, and in its exposure of how social bonds are established through sexual violation, *Against Our Will* has continuing critical relevance.

Recently Brownmiller has re-evaluated the status of her work and its contribution to a wider public understanding of rape. *In Our Time: Memoir of A Revolution* (1999), Brownmiller's account of the Women's Liberation Movement in America, states that 'rape theory was conceived of and developed by the American movement' and remains one of radical feminism's most important and 'successful contributions to world thought' (194). Brownmiller's memoirs provide us with an engaging account of how she came to write *Against Our Will*, and of how the women's movement came to fight against rape. However, there is little sense of how her argument that rape is a 'process of intimidation' impacted upon the understanding of sexuality, gender and race in feminism. By this I mean that while there is a strong sense of rape as a real event that feminism was forced to respond to, as well as of the important, concrete changes made in the way cases of sexual violence are handled by legal and social authorities, there is little sense of how feminism itself structures rape.[4]

It is significant that two issues return to haunt Brownmiller in her account of the experience of writing *Against Our Will*. The first, and the most upsetting for Brownmiller, which I will discuss in some detail later, is the question of race; specifically, the accusation that her text contains racist elements. The second has to do with the complaint that her work portrays all women as victims. According to Brownmiller, this criticism is over-simplified. She explains:

> Our goal in politicizing rape had been to illuminate the role of the male aggressor, not to train a perpetual spotlight on women as victims. Of course, the political explication of male violence proved infinitely harder to keep in the public eye than the victimization of women, but the failure to do so wasn't the movement's fault.
>
> (1999: 251)

Reference to 'failure' and 'fault' is significant here. The question of who is to blame, and Brownmiller's attempt to exonerate feminism on the ground of its good intentions gone awry in the face of the media's 'own agenda and interests when it came to rape' (ibid.: 250), once again overlooks an important and politically pertinent question – about how rape is constructed by feminism.

In his discussion of Brownmiller as the writer who 'first mobilized the imaginative power of rape for a significant spectrum of feminism', William Warner suggests that 'in Brownmiller's hands, the scene of rape, like the primal scene in Freud, becomes self-constituting for her feminism at the moment it is uncovered and projected back as the moment of an original wounding or trauma' (1983: 26). Against what he sees as Brownmiller's restrictive focus on 'reality', Warner calls for work that recomposes this 'founding myth' and addresses how rape has an 'important role in individual and collective life, as myth, imagination, and fantasy' (ibid: 13). But what does Warner mean by fantasy? It is worth noting that one of the writers he holds up as exemplary is Helen Hazen, author of the anti-feminist tract, *Endless Rapture: Rape, Romance, and the Female Imagination* (1983). 'Fantasy' in Hazen's work translates loosely as 'romance': her argument is that a woman's desire to be sexually dominated by men is, in fact, biological. Hazen attacks feminism for confusing a distinction between violent crime and women's wish-fulfilment and argues that the feminist critique of rape ignores women's true masochistic sexuality.

In his rather reductive reading of what he calls Brownmiller's 'little narrative of rape', Warner tellingly neglects to mention that the idea of 'fantasy' is present in a great deal of second-wave feminist work. In *Sexual Politics* (1970), Kate Millett refers to the 'sadistic character of such public fantasy as caters to male audiences in pornography or semi-pornographic media', and writes that a publicized rape case elicits a 'collective *frisson*' not unlike that that occurs in racist society when its members have 'perpetrated a lynching': 'unconsciously, both crimes may serve the larger group as a ritual act, cathartic in effect' (1977: 45). Brownmiller uses the term 'public fantasy' in a similar way, with her discussion of the prevalence of images of rape in popular culture focusing attention on the 'private and public fantasies of the men who dominate and define the culture' (1991: 288). Far from being understood as make-believe or harmless sexual role-playing, fantasy is understood in both its private and public dimensions, as a potent psychic and social force. In both Millett and Brownmiller public fantasy is a male concern, and fantasy is something to be abolished on the way to attaining greater knowledge about reality and political consciousness.

The problem is not that fantasy is thus ignored by second-wave feminist discourse on rape but that it is seen as something that comes from masculine culture. As Jacqueline Rose argues, radical feminism's discarding of the concept of fantasy locates violence solely on the outside – 'an outside that then turns into man posed in his immutable and ahistorical essence as man' (1989: 31–32). This is most clearly evidenced in Brownmiller's call for the destruction of the female rape fantasy: '*The rape fantasy exists in women as a man-made iceberg. It can be destroyed – by feminism*' (1991: 322, her italics). As Brownmiller continues: 'Our female sexual fantasies have been handed to us on a brass platter by those very same men who have laboured so lovingly to promote their own fantasies' (ibid.: 323). Speaking about such retrograde masculine fantasies is seen to be a thoroughly uncomfortable matter, with potentially dangerous consequences. As John Forrester observes:

> Many feminists have written as if the very *existence* of rape fantasies were an embarrassment, a collective shame of women, as if admitting their existence might give hostile men, or even simple sceptics, cause for returning to one of the male myths that all women (or, more moderately, those women who have rape fantasies) want to be raped.
>
> (1986: 63)

According to Forrester, the difficulty with the feminist response to rape fantasy, as epitomized by the above statement from Brownmiller, is that it repeats 'the disowning of the responsibility that lies at the heart of the rape fantasy itself' (ibid.). In other words, if the appeal of the rape fantasy is that it affords pleasure while at the same time freeing the individual of responsibility for her desire (which is attributed wholly to the active other), then to say that this fantasy is itself an imposition from the external world is to perpetuate, rather than explore 'the common fantasy that sexuality is introduced into the woman from "the outside", by an external force ("man-made")' (ibid.).[5] It is to put women on the 'outside' of fantasy.

Psychoanalytic feminists have challenged the traditional feminist view of fantasy, arguing that to talk about fantasy and violence is not to weaken feminism's political struggle. Rather, as Rose suggests, to discuss the psychoanalytic understanding of fantasy and the unconscious is 'a way of allowing that women might be mentally playing out, or with, the positions that they are simultaneously condemning and trying to exclude' (1993: 239). Rose takes this point even further when she argues that it is 'precisely *because* it is so clear that in certain contexts women are the victims, this, then, should be seen as releasing a permission internal to the discourse of feminism to talk about fantasy' (ibid.: 240). For the purposes of my examination of rape as an imaginary within feminism, what is most suggestive and meaningful about Rose's argument is her idea that we need a 'language' in which we can talk about women's oppression and, at the same time discuss the complicated and contradictory aspects of women's fantasy lives (ibid.). Part of my concern in this book is to reappraise the separation between reality and fantasy in feminist discourse on rape in order to tackle the difficult question of how we can approach these two matters – the reality of woman's victimization and the ambivalence and complexity of fantasy. For feminism is not – however much some feminists might wish to be so – on the 'outside' of public fantasies or narratives of rape.

In what follows, I want to look at how rape functions as what John Fletcher calls the 'mise-en-scene of stories of identity, desire, and death' in a selection of American feminist and female-authored texts (1995: 341). The subject of rape serves as a focal point for a range of disputes at the heart of the women's movement. What does it mean to think of rape as the primal scene of feminism? In their influential discussion of 'primal phantasy' in Freud, J Laplanche and J-B Pontalis suggest that fantasies or myths of origins claim 'to provide a representation of, and a solution to, the major enigmas which confront the child. Whatever appears to the subject as something needing an explanation or theory, is dramatized as a moment of emergence, the beginning of a history' (1986: 19). Hence, in 'the primal scene, it is the origin of the subject that is represented; in seduction phantasies, it is the origin or emergence of sexuality; in castration phantasies, the origin of the distinction between the sexes' (ibid.). Drawing on this discussion, I want to examine the myth of origins found in two of the best-selling white American feminist texts of the 1970s: *Against Our Will* (1975) and Marilyn French's novel *The Women's Room* (1977). In both of these founding feminist texts, a mythic scenario of rape as primal scene figures the origins of the social contract. But how has an image of rape as primal scene worked to secure feminism's own foundations?[6] I would suggest that the images of rape found in these commercially successful and widely read feminist texts function as origin stories of feminism, figuring the origins of the female subject, the origins of sexuality, and finally, the origin of the relations between the sexes.

The 'Question of Race', to borrow the title of Brownmiller's controversial chapter on the subject, is another key feature of the origin stories in these founding feminist texts. In the scenarios of rape offered by Brownmiller and French, the story of white feminist origins is secured through an elision of concern for racial issues. Exploring the criticism of Brownmiller by Angela Davis and Jacquelyn Dowd Hall, among others, I want to suggest it in this body of writing on rape and lynching by black feminist thinkers, that we can begin to locate a politics of fantasy in feminism. What emerges through these accounts of the interrelation of rape, race and gender, is an understanding of sexual violence as a fantasy formation; a scene through which images of femininity and masculinity and racial and gendered identity are imagined.

I conclude this chapter with a discussion of two novels that further problematize second-wave feminist founding narratives on rape – Gayl Jones' *Corregidora* (1988) and Dorothy Allison's *Bastard Out of Carolina* (1993).[7] Originally published in the same year as *Against Our Will*, *Corregidora* tells the story of a black female blues singer and her struggle to come to terms with a legacy of slavery and sexual abuse. More recent is Allison's novel, which tells the story of Bone, a young girl who comes from a poor Southern 'white trash' family, and who is sexually abused by her stepfather. In acknowledging how fantasy is constitutive of woman's identity, these texts reveal how the ' "real world" is not all that is real for us' (Burgin 1992: 87). They challenge the idea of a simple origin in which woman is cast as the eternal victim, left in what Mandy Merck has referred to as 'an immutable present of male oppression' (1993: 214). While both Jones and Allison have been criticized for bringing together sexuality and violence, and desire and sexual victimization, my argument is that these texts raise politically relevant questions for feminism about the need to include fantasy in our discussions of rape.

Against Our Will

Re-reading Brownmiller after nearly thirty years of feminist thinking on rape, there is a strong sense that the force of her work derives from what has been perceived as its central weakness: its tendency to list unremitting examples of rape, without considering how the discursive construction of 'rape' has developed.[8] I agree with Ken Plummer when he accounts for the wide-reaching significance of Brownmiller's work in the following terms:

> Synthesising the stories of rape of Huguenot woman in sixteenth-century France, the rape of the Sabine women in early Rome, the rape of black women slaves on plantations in the southern United States, the gang-bang of the modern Hell's Angels and the mass rape-murders of a psychopathic Boston strangler, she constructed the large-scale grand historical narrative so necessary for the telling of a major new rape story. Her book brings together a past, provides a collective memory and sets an agenda for sexual politics.
>
> (1995: 68)

It is precisely the epic quality of Brownmiller's narrative that serves as the enabling condition for what Plummer calls the 'modern rape story' (ibid.: 63). And it is this quality that goes some way to accounting for why *Against Our Will* has acquired landmark status in feminist thought. While this status is partially attributable to the fact that it is the first book of its kind to seriously address rape as a historical phenomenon, I would suggest that the reason *Against Our Will* retains its critical force, resides more fundamentally in its vision of rape as an act that renders something explicit about the workings of what can be described as the socio-sexual contract. The question that agitates beneath her work is fundamentally important: why is rape such an integral part of culture?

Although Brownmiller mentions the term 'social contract' just once, her book provides a detailed exploration of the essential role rape plays in establishing patriarchal culture. The original and radical contention of *Against Our Will* is that rape is essential to, and constitutive of, the social bonds of patriarchy. Crucial to this thesis is the idea of rape as the primal scene of culture:

> In the violent landscape inhabited by primitive woman and man, some woman somewhere had a prescient vision of her right to her own physical integrity and in my mind's eye I can picture her fighting like hell to preserve it.
>
> (1991: 14)

As much as it is a story of the origins of patriarchal culture, this is a story of the origins of feminism. Brownmiller is inviting the female reader to visualize her feminist forebears' defiant resistance. In this account of an originary rape, it is notably the woman, and not the man, who starts the first war:

> After a thunderbolt of recognition that this particular incarnation of hairy, two-legged hominid was not the Homo sapiens with whom she would

like to freely join parts, it might have been she, and not some man, who picked up the first stone and hurled it. How surprised he must have been, and what an unexpected battle must have taken place. Fleet of foot and spirited, she would have kicked, bitten, pushed and run, but she could not retaliate in kind.

(ibid.)

This description of primal woman's resistance, her prescient vision of her right to say 'no', kicking, biting and screaming, is a key paradigm for the vision of organized feminist resistance to rape that lies at the heart of *Against Our Will*. As Brownmiller concludes: 'That women should *organize* to combat rape was a women's movement invention' (ibid.: 397).

Licence to read *Against Our Will* as an origin story for feminism is included in its opening pages.[9] In 'A Personal Statement', Brownmiller gives the reader an account of her coming to consciousness about rape. Intriguingly, particularly in light of the internal divisiveness the issue would come to hold for feminism, Brownmiller explains: 'rape has been a theme of mine since 1968 when I wrote a piece for a magazine about an interracial rape case with political ramifications' (ibid.: 7). Brownmiller recalls she wrote the story from 'the perspective of a woman who viewed a rape case with suspicion ... I did not seek out nor did I attempt to speak with the victim. I felt no kinship with her, nor did I admit, publicly or privately, that what had happened to her could *on any level* happen to me' (ibid.: 8). It is her identification with the raped woman, her recognition that rape can happen to any woman, however 'combative, wary and verbally aggressive', that leads to Brownmiller's 'moment of revelation' – when she connects the individual experiences of women to their situation in the society at large:

Something important and frightening to contemplate had been left out of my education – a way of looking at male–female relations, at sex, at strength, and at power. Never one to acknowledge my vulnerability, I found myself forced by my sisters in feminism to look it squarely in the eye ... I wrote this book because I am a woman who changed her mind about rape.

(ibid.: 9)

The story of her coming to consciousness about rape is one that Brownmiller tells and re-tells in her discussions of the origins of *Against Our Will*.

Out of man's prehistoric rape of woman, Brownmiller derives the 'creation of a male ideology of rape' (ibid.: 14). For 'if the first rape was an unexpected battle founded on the first woman's refusal, the second rape was indubitably planned' (ibid.). What was 'an accommodation requiring the locking together of two parts, penis into vagina', becomes transformed into a 'mass psychology' of rape:

> One of the earliest forms of male bonding must have been the gang rape
> of one woman by a band of marauding men. This accomplished, rape
> became not only a male prerogative, but man's basic weapon of force against
> woman, the principal agent of his will and her fear. His forcible entry
> into her body, despite her physical protestations and struggle, became the
> vehicle of his victorious conquest over her being, the ultimate test of his
> superior strength, the triumph of his manhood.

(ibid.)

Communal bonding through gang rape leads to the idea of collective male ownership of women as property and Brownmiller hypothesizes that man's rape of the
female led 'sometime later to the full-blown male solidification of power, the patriarchy' (17–18). The raped woman was, she writes, 'the original building block, the
cornerstone, of the "house of the father"' (ibid.). It is important to note the idea
of the raped woman as the foundation of culture, the object over which men
organize. Throughout the text, Brownmiller returns to an idea of gang rape as the
site of collective identification: 'The act of group rape forges an alliance among
men against the female victim who becomes, for their purposes, Anonymous
Woman' (ibid.: 187–188). This vision of the symbolic force of group rape runs
counter to Brownmiller's reliance elsewhere in the text on a theory of biological
determinism.[10] Brownmiller's conjectural history forcefully demonstrates how,
with the planning and communion between men, rape becomes cultural.

One of the most important questions addressed in Brownmiller's opening
chapters is: if patriarchal power is based on the sexual violation of women, then
how do we understand the seriousness with which rape has been treated by the
legal system through the ages? Brownmiller cites several examples of gruesome
punishment for convicted rapists: the loss of both eyes, castration, drowning. Her
answer to this apparent paradox – the punishment of what is in fact the foundation of male power – is that rape is treated as a crime against the male estate. The
only reason rape is a state concern is because of a contract between men regarding their mutual property rights: 'Criminal rape, as a patriarchal father saw it, was
a violation of the new way of doing business' (ibid.: 18).

Brownmiller's documentation of rape in war remains one of the most powerful and
convincing demonstrations of her thesis that there is something basic in culture that
supports violence against women. In 'Making Female Bodies the Battlefield' (1993),
Brownmiller returns to the theme of rape in war through her discussion of the mass
rape of women in the war-torn former Yugoslavia. The first thing to notice about this
account is that her analysis of rape as the integral act of masculine identity and culture is not amended by the debate over the role ethnic tensions and religious differences played in the mass rape. 'Balkan women, whatever their ethnic and religious
background, and in whatever fighting zone they happen to find themselves, have been
thrust against their will into another identity. They are victims of rape in war' (1992:
180). To those who call the mass rape in the former Yugoslavia 'unprecedented',

Brownmiller refers to an overwhelming series of historical examples – examples which she had already recounted two decades earlier in *Against Our Will*: the rape of Belgian women by German soldiers in the First World War; the rape of Russian, Jewish and German women in the Second World War; mass rapes committed by Pakistani soldiers in newly independent Bangladesh in 1971; and the 'sporadic cases of gang rape' committed by American soldiers during the Vietnam war. Whatever the arguments made about national and religious pride, the horrific, and inescapable fact of the matter, is that 'women are raped in war by ordinary youths as casually, or as frenetically, as a village is looted or gratuitously destroyed' (ibid.).

Brownmiller's account of the 'adrenaline-rushed' young men who 'give vent to…submerged rage against all women *who belong to other men*', returns us to *Against Our Will* and its vision of the primal scene (ibid.). In her typology, if the patriarchal fathers were the first to formulate an idea of sexual violence as a necessary tool for the domination of women, it is the sons who are responsible for carrying out this primal brutality in the present day:

> Rape is a dull, blunt, ugly act committed by punk kids, their cousins and older brothers, not by charming, witty, unscrupulous, heroic, sensual rakes, or by timid souls deprived of a "normal" sexual outlet, or by supermenschen possessed of uncontrollable lust. And yet, on the shoulders of these unthinking, predictable, insensitive, violence-prone young men there rests an age-old burden that amounts to an historic mission: the perpetuation of male domination over women by force.
>
> (1991: 208–209)

This gang of errant youths constitutes a fraternal bond to which women are denied membership but for which the violent appropriation of their bodies is necessary as a means of bolstering a notion of group masculinity and power. As Brownmiller sees it, these 'banal police-blotter rapists' function as patriarchy's 'front-line masculine shock troops, terrorist guerrillas in the longest sustained battle the world has ever known' (ibid.: 209). The collective psychology of rape gets passed down through the generations; the brothers and sons who do the 'dirty work' of violation are nothing more or less than lackeys to the greater cause of male supremacy. If rape is the origin of women's suffering, then the repeated extension of sexual violation throughout history is a perpetuation of a social order sadistically intent on the sexual and social subjugation of women.

Having established this thesis through her dramatic re-enactment of the primal scene, Brownmiller examines this through a series of historical incidents, case studies and artistic representations. In Brownmiller's account, the raped woman serves at once as the 'building block' and the 'battlefield' of a masculine social order that seeks to continually renew its authority through her violation.

The Women's Room

With Marilyn French's *The Women's Room* we find a literary staging of the theoretical issues and preoccupations at the heart of *Against Our Will*. Published three years after Brownmiller's important text, *The Women's Room* is an acknowledged feminist classic. Facing the 'truth' of women's reality is the central thematic of *The Women's Room* and it is enacted, I suggest, through three disparate, though interlocking, scenes of rape. The first is an intraracial attempted gang rape; the second, which is the centrepiece of the book, is a black man's rape of a white woman; the third, and final rape scene, a postscript to the book, involves the attempted rape of a black woman by a white man. It is through these imaginative scenarios or fantasies of rape that the novel narrativizes its radical feminist vision.

Though the first scene of the book famously begins with its female protagonist Mira cowering in a toilet in the women's room at Harvard University, the opening chapters go back to the beginning to trace Mira's passage from girlhood into womanhood. The event called upon to signal this transition is an attempted gang rape. The incident occurs in a crowded college bar; Mira gets drunk and dances while a crowd of men watch her. When a song ends, one of the men, Biff, pulls Mira out of the bar. A confused Mira tries to discover what has happened. 'At last she understood. The dancing he said, and Lanny's leaving her alone ... So those guys got the wrong impression. It was not her fault. They didn't know her innocence, her "purity" he called it' (1997: 35). Mira finally pieces together what has nearly happened: ' "All of them?" she asked, appalled ... Her mind churned that. How would they manage that? "In turns?" she asked him' (ibid.). The knowledge of what might have happened strikes Mira temporarily dumb; returning home she 'fell immediately into a deep sleep and slept for fourteen hours. The next day she did not get up at all' (ibid.: 36).

When Mira does get up, it is with the realization that she has been indoctrinated into womanhood: 'This was what it was all about, all the strange things she had been taught. Everything fell into place, everything made sense. And that everything was too big for her. Other girls went to bars, other girls danced. The difference was she had appeared to be alone' (ibid.). This realization stuns Mira:

> That a woman was not marked as the property of some male made her a bitch in heat to be attacked by any male, or even by all of them at once. That a woman could not go out in public and enjoy herself dancing without worrying what every male in the place was thinking or even worse, what they might do, seemed to her an injustice so extreme she could not swallow it.
>
> (ibid.)

Like the prehistoric woman of Brownmiller's primal scene, it is Mira's vision of her own bodily integrity that defines rape: 'She thought about what would have happened had Biff not been there and her mind went black with the horror, the blood, the desecration. It was not her virginity she treasured, but her right to herself, to her own mind and body' (ibid.). But, unlike Brownmiller's vision of the prehistoric woman's resistance, Mira doesn't try to 'bite, kick, scream, or run'. The shift from Mira's attempted rape to her imprisonment in the institution of marriage happens within the space of a few paragraphs, thus signalling the novel's bleak parody of the female *Bildungsromane*: 'Mira retreated. She was defeated ... There was marriage and there was the convent. She retreated into the one as if it were the other, and wept at her wedding' (ibid.: 37–38).

With its stress on an image of woman-as-spectacle, its setting in the male gathering-place of the tavern, and its focus on male group dynamics, the attempted rape scene in *The Women's Room* predates the rape on a pinball machine in *The Accused*, discussed in Chapter 4. In pointing out the remarkable similarity between the rape scenes in these very diverse texts, I am not suggesting that *The Accused* owes a direct debt to the depiction of rape in *The Women's Room*. What is significant to note is that the repetition between these two texts – and others as well – turns the 'drunk girl in a bar' into a mythic figure. The scene of rape offered in *The Women's Room* is one that will be worked over and over again in the years to come, suggesting that there is, in fact, something basic being worked through the scenario it dramatizes.

The scene of attempted gang rape in *The Women's Room* is an archetypal scenario of the dynamics of group identification. According to Menachem Amir's classic sociological analysis, the participants in a group rape can be typified as: 'a) the group "core" members who identify completely with the group and its aggressive climate; b) The reluctant participant who will go along after some hesitation; c) the gang member who ... refuses to participate' (1971: 192). During the scene in the bar, Mira is oblivious to the intentions of the men around her. The men who surround her see an opportunity and act (either for or against) the rape. Here the text depicts the competing fantasies of masculinity that are operative in culture and demonstrates how the protection of women can be as powerful a fantasy as the desire to rape them. According to Mira's final judgement of Biff, these fantasies amount to the same thing: 'They thought one thing or they thought another: but their thinking was all the same' (ibid.: 38).

The Women's Room self-reflexively foregrounds its status as a feminist origin story by way of a re-writing of Virginia Woolf's story of Shakespeare's sister. In one of her many asides to the reader, the first-person narrator (as yet unnamed as Mira), explains:

> Shakespeare's sister did, as Woolf thought, follow her brother to London, but she never got there. She was raped the first night out, and bleeding and inwardly wounded, she stumbled for shelter into the next village she found. Realising before too long that she was pregnant, she sought a way to keep herself and her child safe. She found some guy with the hots for her, realised he was credulous and screwed him.
>
> (ibid.: 45–46)

The narrator concludes: 'Shakespeare's sister has learned the lesson all women learn: men are the ultimate enemy ... So much for the natural relation between the sexes' (ibid.: 46). This radical feminist rewriting of Woolf's story of Shakespeare's sister, a story that has figured as a paradigm for women's exclusion from the bastion of male culture and literary tradition, clearly casts women's relation to culture as a form of rape. But this re-writing of Shakespeare's story also calls attention to an aspect of *The Women's Room* that is rarely considered in any detail: the role rape plays in establishing the idea of feminist literature.

From the start of *The Women's Room*, rape is the issue used to police the boundaries between fiction and real life. Though the text does not come right out and denounce Mira's fantasies as 'false consciousness', it is nevertheless careful to point out that there is an important distinction between Mira's fantasies and 'real life':

> She recognized that there was a large difference between her life and art. In the movies and in her fantasies, the things that were done to the heroine hurt but did not hurt. They left no scars. But that was not so in life. In life such things would hurt and scar and build up incredible hatred.
>
> (ibid.: 31)

Reflecting on how 'young men like to say that young women want to be raped', the narrator entertains the possibility that 'young women caught in psychological bonds' probably 'half welcome a violent solution to the dilemma' of whether or not to have sex:

> But the kind of rape they imagine is like the one in *The Fountainhead*: it springs from passion and love, and it has no consequences more serious than the consequences for Justine's body of all her whippings and torture. No broken bones, scars, destroyed tissue. Act without consequence, arrows with rubber tips, comedy: like the cartoons they make for children in which the cat or bear or whatever gets smashed over and over, but always rises from its own ashes.
>
> (ibid.: 30)

This passage suggests that dominant, masculine-oriented literature, here represented by Ayn Rand's *The Fountainhead*[11] and the Marquis de Sade's *Justine*, offer fictional – made-up, untrue – images of female indestructibility. It is against such a 'fictional' treatment of the abuse and violation of women that *The Women's Room* situates its brand of feminist realist literature. This passage, spoken by the novel's narrator, points to the 'truth' of its discourse:

> Do you believe any of this? It is not the stuff of fiction. It has no shape, it hasn't the balances so important in art. You know, if one line goes this way, another must go that way. All these lines are the same. These lives are like the threads that get woven into a carpet and when it's done the weaver is surprised that the colors all blend: shades of blood, shades of tears, smells of sweat.
>
> (218)

Here story is conflated with reality: *The Women's Room* is 'not the stuff of fiction'. The idea that feminist literature must represent the 'reality' of women's lives is central to a feminist debate about how best to represent the issue of sexual violence. The goal of feminist literature, like the goal of theoretical work on rape by feminists such as Brownmiller, is to make 'rape a *speakable* crime, not a matter of shame' (Brownmiller 1991: 396). As we will see in Chapter 5, where I discuss the controversy surrounding Sarah Dunant, a feminist writer who is seen to abandon the reality of rape in favour of fiction, rape brings into focus deeply contentious questions about the role of fiction in feminist writing. Before I move on to discuss the final two rape scenes in *The Women's Room* – the rape of a white woman by a black man, and the attempted rape of a black woman by a white man – it is necessary to introduce the issue of race and rape.

Race and rape

'Who knows what the black woman thinks of rape? Who has asked her? Who *cares*? Who has even properly acknowledged that *she* and not the white woman in this story is the most likely victim of rape' (1982: 93)? Taken from Alice Walker's 1971 short story, 'Advancing Luna – and Ida B. Wells', this quotation introduces the issue of race into the discussion of rape, fiction and feminism. Walker's story forces us to confront the mythic status of an idea of rape as a unifying issue for feminism. For if Brownmiller's theory of rape is to be recognized as a foundational moment for feminism, it must be remembered this foundation is based on a blind spot to racism and racial oppression. Karin Cope suggests that:

> At a point when the differentiation of concerns among women of different race and class backgrounds seemed, to some radical feminists, to threaten the cohesiveness of the women's movement, the growing consciousness that violence against women permeated almost every woman's experience and consciousness seemed to promise a more or less universal issue over which all women could be united.
>
> (1992: 389)

'Seemed' because, in the years that followed Brownmiller's famous declaration that 'rape is nothing more or less than a conscious process of intimidation by which *all* men keep *all* women in a state of fear', a number of feminists stepped forward to question what such a blanket definition of rape might mean.

Black feminist theorists were among the first, and the most cogent, of Brownmiller's critics.[12] Angela Davis, in 'Rape, Racism, and the Myth of the Black Rapist', while praising Brownmiller's book as a 'pioneering scholarly contribution to the contemporary literature on rape', concludes that 'many of her arguments are unfortunately pervaded with racist ideas' (1983: 178). In particular, the idea that the black man is 'especially prone to commit acts of violence against women' (ibid.: 177–178). Davis points to Brownmiller's example of Emmett Till, a young black

29

boy who, in 1955, was brutally murdered and then thrown into a river by two white men for whistling at a white woman. In Brownmiller's account, Till's look at a white woman is cast as part of a wider system of male domination over women, on a par with rape and sex-murder. Brownmiller writes: 'The whistle was...a deliberate insult just short of physical assault, a last reminder to Carolyn Bryant that this black boy, Till, had in mind to possess her' (1991: 247). As Davis observes, in Brownmiller's account of the Till case 'the Black youth emerges ... as a guilty sexist – almost as guilty as his white racist murderers' (1983: 179).

Over twenty-five years later, Davis' criticism of *Against Our Will* still rankles Brownmiller. In *In Our Time* (1999), Brownmiller describes Davis' charge of racism as the 'worst blow' (249). 'Nothing devastates me more,' she writes in regard to those who accused her of being a racist. She remains perplexed by the claim that she is insensitive to racial issues, while she recalls how she 'grieved' knowing that *Against Our Will* 'would never be read by a substantial number of radicals whose opinions were formed by the harmful attacks' (1999: 250). That Brownmiller still cannot countenance the problems of her discussion of race and rape in *Against Our Will* is due, I think, to her continuing failure to recognize what Kimberle Crenshaw refers to as the 'intersectionality' of race and gender.[13] 'Rape is to women as lynching was to blacks: the ultimate physical threat by which all men keep all women in a state of psychological intimidation' (Brownmiller 1991: 254).[14] Unfortunately, Brownmiller all too frequently presents the fight against rape and the fight against racism as an either/or choice – either gender *or* race. This is symptomatic of the white American women's movement's wider failure to take race on board in its account of rape as a patriarchal crime.

Brownmiller's discussion of the Till case is included in her chapter, 'A Question of Race'. It is here she begins to racially identify herself. She writes:

> I speak as a white woman whose first stirrings of social conscience occurred when I read of certain famous cases, now legend, in which black men had been put to death for coming too close to white women. Tales of Scottsboro, Emmett Till and Willie McGee were part of my formative experience.
>
> (ibid.: 210)

Brownmiller's story of how she became a feminist is staged as a break with her liberal past, a past in which she would have felt sympathy for the racist persecution of black men. The story of her feminist origins is figured against an image of the tortured and murdered black body.

> At age twenty and for a period of fifteen years after the murder of Emmett Till, whenever a black teenager whistled at me in the street ... I smiled my nicest smile of comradely equality...Did not white women in particular have to bear the white man's burden of making amends for Southern racism? It took fifteen years for me to resolve these questions in my own mind, and to understand the insult implicit in Emmett Till's whistle.
>
> (ibid.: 247–248)

Here Brownmiller puts herself in the position of Carolyn Bryant – the position of innocent and defiled white womanhood – and fails to acknowledge how the history of rape is closely bound up with the history of racism.

The Women's Room similarly secures its idea of rape as a metaphor for white women's oppression through its denunciation of sympathy for black men and racial issues.[15] The novel concludes with the rape of Val's daughter, Chris, by a black man.[16] The event is used to stage Val's complete transformation to radical feminism:

> Val sat there remembering that downstairs she had felt sorry for the black boys in the line-up, knowing that such sympathy was gone in her, and that it would never return. It didn't matter if they were black or white, or yellow, or anything else for that matter. It was males against females and the war was to the death.
>
> (1997: 469)

Sympathy for racial issues is shown as something that has to be denounced in order to become a radical feminist.

Given the novel's self-avowed focus on white middle-class femininity, it is fascinating to note that in *The Women's Room* a fantasy of feminist resistance is put into place through the trope of blackness. In the novel's conclusion, the figure of the black woman plays a decisive role, becoming the catalyst for the text's explorations of the limits of feminist resistance.[17] With the introduction of the black woman we are given the text's third, and final variation on the rape motif: the white man's rape of the black woman. It is against this particular configuration of the rape scenario, rarely discussed by the novel's critics, that the text chooses to stage the death of its white, radical feminist heroine, Val, who is murdered by the police when she and a group of 'militant feminists' attempt to rescue Anita before she is carted off to prison. The narrator explains:

> A young black woman, Anita Morrow, who worked as a domestic during the day, attended classes at Northeastern at night ... Anita had been walking from her class ... when a man attacked her. He came up behind her and put his arm across her throat and dragged her into an alley. He threw her down and pulled her skirt up, but Anita had grown up on the streets and she had a knife in her pocket. She kicked him in the chin, and got up fast, and when he grabbed her again, stabbed him. She kept stabbing him, blood and fear pounding in her ears, but the noise, her cries and his, had attracted some people. They saw her stabbing him after he had fallen, and they ran to stop her. They held on to her until the police arrived ... She was charged with murder. The man was from a respectable white family, he had a wife and six kids.
>
> (1997: 507)

31

Where the primal woman of Brownmiller's imagination *'could not retaliate in kind'*, here the woman responds to an attempted rape with murder (1991: 14). In a novel that universalises the 'plight of the middle class white woman as women's condition full stop', the sudden appearance of the black woman is significant (Lauret 1994: 104). It is as if the novel is finally compelled to reveal its own blind spot, providing the one variation on the rape motif on which it has remained silent. Sentenced to twenty years to life for first-degree murder, Anita voices the novel's radical feminist vision of rape: ' "He tried to rape me, so I stabbed him," she said incredulously to the group of women before they led her into the armed car' (1997: 508). This idea of murder as the only form of retaliation for the symbolic death of rape is the novel's concluding statement. Though she exits the text almost as soon as she is introduced, the figure of the black woman exposes the racialized foundation of the feminist attempt to articulate the origins of woman's socio-sexual subjugation.

So what of the black woman whose position in society is one of 'double jeopardy', posed between the twin concerns of race and gender (Dowd Hall 1983: 332)? It is a question left unanswered by *The Women's Room*, as well as by *Against Our Will*. While Brownmiller professes to look at how 'the white woman and the black woman' have been used as pawns 'in the cause of politics, ideology, and power', she makes it clear her particular concern is the cause of white women. 'This chapter is going to concern itself with interracial rape as a national obsession, and by that I mean the phenomenon of black men raping white women' (1975: 216). Passages like these lead Davis to conclude that Brownmiller 'sometimes boxes herself into the position of defending the particular cause of *white* women, regardless of its implications' (1983: 198).[18]

The black male rapist, the virginal white victim: these are the terms that have pervaded dominant public discourse on rape. It is within the terms of this public narrative that the pressure of fantasy emerges most clearly. 'The myth of the black rapist was never founded on objective reality', as Jacquelyn Dowd Hall writes in her discussion of the relationship between rape and lynching (1983: 335). Rather, the stories of the rape of white women used as the justification for lynching black men were significant as public fantasy:

> Rape and rumors of rape became the folk pornography of the Bible Belt. As stories spread the rapist became not just a black man but a ravenous brute, the victim a beautiful young virgin. The experience of the woman was described in minute and progressively embellished detail, a *public fantasy* that implied a group participation in the rape as cathartic as the subsequent lynching.
>
> (ibid.: 335, my italics)

This idea of public participation in a fantasy of rape is central to this book and my exploration of how rape serves as the site for individual and collective identification. What the above discussion of public fantasy describes is the way in which rape is a 'special kind of crime in relation to narrative' (Higgins 1991: 307). As legal theorist Susan Estrich, author of *Real Rape* (1987) argues, a rape is not legally considered a rape unless it conforms to preconceived notions of what counts as 'real rape'. And as Estrich notes, in the eyes of the law, 'real rape' has meant rape by an 'armed stranger jumping from the bushes' or the 'black man jumping the white woman' (1987: 8). In other words, rape cases are decided in interpretative arenas (Rooney 1991: 89).

In the next section of this chapter, I examine two female-authored texts that thematize storytelling and fantasy in their exploration of sexual violation.

Corregidora

Gayl Jones' novel *Corregidora* (1975) was published in the same year as Brownmiller's *Against Our Will*.[19] Like Brownmiller, Jones presents rape as an originary act between men and women, a primal scene of sexual relations. But it is a primal scene anchored in the American history of slavery, its story of gender, sexuality and rape inescapably linked to racial discourse. *Corregidora* is about the psychic legacy of slavery, and in particular the institutionalized rape of black women by slave masters. Unflinching in its examination of sexual cruelty, one of the reasons why *Corregidora* has not featured prominently in feminist discussions of rape, I would argue, is because it raises uncomfortable questions about woman's psychic investment in a story of sexual violence. How is the 'real event' of rape incorporated into women's psychic life? What is the relationship between sexual desire and sexual oppression?

There is one scene and one subject in *Corregidora*: the scene of sexualized violence. Resonating with Freud's definition of original phantasy, the 'primal scene' of the book is the 'wounding or rape of the mother by the father' (Fletcher 1986: 113). As in Brownmiller and French, the primal rape in question is interracial: in this case, the rape of a black woman by a Portuguese slave owner. From the time she is a young girl, Ursa Corregidora is told the story of an original trauma: the rape of her great-grandmother at the hands of Corregidora, a Portuguese seaman turned plantation owner. Made to work as a whore for Corregidora, Ursa's great-grandmother was his favourite 'little gold piece' (1988: 10). The story of her great-grandmother's sexual enslavement is told to the young Ursa 'over and over again... as if the words were helping her, as if the words repeated again and again could be a substitute for memory, were somehow more than the memory' (ibid.: 11). It is a painful story of rape and incest: 'old man Corregidora fathered my grandmama and my mama too', as Ursa tells her lover. In hearing this story from a very young age ('I was five years old then'), the child is being made to witness the scene of her own origins (ibid.: 10, 14).

The emphasis placed in *Corregidora* on the activity of listening and hearing stories of original violence corresponds to the privileged position accorded aural perception in Freudian original phantasy. Aural perception, as Laplanche and Pontalis note, is about 'the history or the legends of parents, grandparents and the ancestors: the family *sounds* or *sayings*, this spoken or secret discourse, going on prior to the subject's arrival, within which he must find his way' (1986: 19).

In *Corregidora*, Ursa must find her way through this secret family discourse of sounds and sayings, this mysterious and intimate language passed down from female generation to generation, which began long before she arrived on the scene and which is meant to continue through the imperative of 'making generations'.

The family legend of violence, a repetitive scenario of horror and violation, is to get passed down through the generations as a form of evidence. As Great Gram instructs: 'We got to burn out what they put in our minds, like you burn out a wound. Except we got to keep what we need to bear witness' (1988: 72). This complicated work of burning out the horror, but retaining it as remembrance at the same time in order to 'bear witness', constitutes Ursa's difficult inheritance. Pushed down the stairs by her partner, Mutt, Ursa has lost her womb and is thus unable to make generations, which leaves her questioning her female sexuality and her status as a woman.

A difficult relationship is established in *Corregidora* between real event and fantasy, memory and narrative, past and present, such that it is impossible to decipher any clearly defined distinction among these different categories. The novel is composed of disturbing dream sequences, interior monologues and rhythmic dialogue. Whether events are real or imagined is not significant; what matters is the psychical reality of Ursa as she struggles to forge her own existence as a woman out of the sexual trauma of her foremothers. Her dreams are often just as painful, if not more so, than any real event could ever be.

One of the central characteristics of primal phantasy is that 'the subject is present *in* the scene' (Laplanche and Pontalis 1986: 22). Ursa shifts between different subject positions in the primal scene of original violence, as in the following complex dream sequence when she imagines herself giving birth to Old Man Corregidora:

> I dreamed that my belly was swollen and restless, and I lay without moving, gave birth without struggle, without feeling. But my eyes never turned to my feet. I never saw what squatted between my knees. But I felt the humming and beating of wings and claws in my thighs.
> I felt a stiff penis inside me. "Those who have fucked their daughters would not hesitate to fuck their own mothers." Who are you? Who have I born? His hair was like white wings, and we were united at birth.
> "Who are you?"
> "You don't even know your own father?"
> "You not my father. I never was one of your women."
> "Corregidora's women. Yes, you are."
>
> (1988: 77)

In this dream Ursa shifts between the subject positions of mother and daughter, giving birth to the man who then rapes her and claims ownership of her as one of 'Corregidora's women'. It is a dream that asks: Who am I? Where do I come from? This fantasy of birth and violation is a way of identifying, and at the same time, struggling against, the terrible memories of her great-grandmother and grandmother, memories which haunt Ursa. Growing up with 'Corregidora's women', Ursa is made to live with 'their memories, never my own' (ibid.: 100). In her dreams of Corregidora, fantasy is about both reliving and containing the trauma of memory. As Vicky Lebeau writes of Freud's understanding of fantasy, there is a 'reference to *pain* which immediately complicates a familiar association between wish (fulfillment) and pleasure' (29).

Corregidora explores the question of what happens to sexual relationships between black men and women under conditions of slavery, conditions that abolish familial bonds. The position afforded the black man in the primal scene of rape is made brutally apparent in the story told by Great Gram. While the slave master, Corregidora, takes any black woman he pleases, the black male partners of these women are shipped out of their own beds and permanently displaced. If there is any form of resistance, 'it'll be your life they be wonting and then they make even that some kind of sex show, all them beatings and killings wasn't nothing but sex circuses, and all them white peoples, mens, womens, and childrens crowding around to see' (1988: 125). In *Corregidora* the act of lynching black women and black men is revealed as a form of sexualized violence. Significantly, as in other black woman's writing from the period, the black man is shown to be sexually victimized and violated by white supremacy and the system of slavery.[20] This provides a very different way of accounting for the black man's position than that found in Brownmiller and French's work, in which the only role for the black man is that of rapist or potential rapist. In *Corregidora*, the interracial rape of the black woman by the slave master results in the death of the black man. The psychosexual, racialized overtones of the slave master's desire are made clear in his order to Ursa's great-grandmother: 'Don't let no black man fool with you, do you hear? I don't wont nothing black fucking with my pussy' (ibid.: 127). Part of the homosocial pleasure of the white male ownership of the black woman is its devastating impact on the black man. As Trudier Harris notes in his discussion of lynching as 'communal rape': 'For the white males ... there is a symbolic transfer of sexual power at the point of the executions. The black man is stripped of his prowess, but the very act of stripping brings symbolic power to the white man' (cited in Wiegman 1993: 242). In *Corregidora*, a white mob goes after a black man who dares to speak to one of 'Corregidora's women', a scene of violence that is shown to afford the slave master great sexual excitement and pleasure. As Great Gram tells it: 'While he [Corregidora] was up there jumping up and down between my legs they was out there with them hounds after that boy' (1988: 127). In such a perverse economy of sexual violation and ownership, '"normal sexuality" (socially constructed or otherwise)', as Houston Baker notes, 'is subsumed by an economics, politics, and symbolic projection of rape' (1991: 207).

The question of how a black woman can carve a sexual identity out of such a troubled history of rape and sexual degradation is at the forefront of *Corregidora*. Ursa is alienated from her sexuality; from her relationship to her own body; as well as from the men in her life. The secret family discourse that Ursa most wants access to, but which is denied her in the face of the story of Corregidora, is her mother's personal story, a story which is shown to have strong links to Ursa's own disturbed history with men. According to Jones, in writing *Corregidora*, she 'was concerned with getting across a sense of an intimate history, particularly a personal history, and to contrast it with the broad, impersonal telling of the Corregidora story' (1985: 92). Following this, one could argue that *Corregidora* provides its readers with an 'intimate history' of rape, one that contrasts Brownmiller's 'epic' public history of rape.

Criticism of Jones' work has centred on her apparent failure to provide 'positive images'. In response to this complaint, Jones has said that she is not interested in 'positive' or 'negative' images, but in the complex psychology of her characters. 'I was and continue to be interested in contradictory emotions that coexist...people can hold two different emotions simultaneously' (1985: 99). One of the most captivating and disquieting things about *Corregidora*, is this attempt to explore the contradictory emotions of 'hate and desire'. 'How much was hate for Corregidora and how much was love' (1988: 131)? In looking at the links between desire and abuse, and the way this gets re-lived in the heterosexual relationships of the daughter, *Corregidora* is not suggesting, at least not in any simplistic way, that Ursa's great-grandmother and grandmother get 'pleasure' from having sex with the slave master. It may be the case, as Hortense Spillers notes, that 'whether or not the captive female and/or her sexual oppressor derived "pleasure" from their seductions and couplings is not a question we can politely ask' (1987: 76). As Spillers argues, 'sexuality, as a term of implied relationship and desire', is not really accurate to capture the familial arrangements under slavery, in which notions such as '"reproduction", "motherhood", "pleasure" and "desire" are thrown into unrelieved crisis' (ibid.: 76). *Corregidora* also makes the point that notions of agency and pleasure are foreclosed in the economy of slavery; the novel indicates that there was no alternative, other than torture and death, to submit to the sexual whims of the slave master. Nevertheless, it attempts to deal with the question of how sexuality and desire cannot be excised from the world of rape and violence by exploring how, within a scene of sexual danger, women can attain sexual agency. The novel concludes with just such a moment, a moment of 'hate and love', of 'excruciating pleasure and pain at the same time', in which Ursa fellates her lover (1988: 184).

Writing on black women's novels in the wake of the civil rights movement, Melissa Walker excludes *Corregidora* from her discussion because its 'narrative focuses primarily on personal and sexual themes divorced from larger social issues' (1991: 4). I would suggest that this statement also gives us an idea of why *Corregidora* is not generally included in feminist discussions of rape: it is seen to focus more on the personal, than the political, the intimate, rather than the public. Yet *Corregidora's* 'intimate history' is not divorced from the social issues that have dictated feminism's response to rape. On the contrary, in its attention to the psycho-sexual history of rape and slavery, and in its examination of psychic violence and fantasy, *Corregidora* fills in certain silences in Brownmiller's official feminist history of rape. That the primal scene of rape presented in *Corregidora* – the scene of a black woman being raped by the white man – is one that remains unspeakable in popular culture, is a disquieting scenario I will discuss in regard to *The Accused* in Chapter 4.

Bastard Out of Carolina

Like *Corregidora*, *Bastard Out of Carolina* is a story about a young girl who is concerned to find her way in a secret family history that exists prior to her arrival in
the world. In its examination of how female sexual identity is forged out of violence and fantasy *Bastard Out of Carolina* makes us reconsider Brownmiller's definition of the female rape fantasy as a 'man-made iceberg' to be destroyed by feminism.

From the start, *Bastard* foregrounds its status as a story concerned with the question of origins. The novel begins with the birth of Ruth Anne 'Bone' Boatwright,
the illegitimate daughter of the book's title. It is a birth from which the father, but
more curiously, the mother, is absent. When one of Bone's drunken uncles crashes
into another vehicle, pregnant fifteen-year-old Anney Boatwright flies through the
windshield of the truck and is unconscious when she gives birth to Bone a few
hours later. When she awakes it is to her undying horror to find out that, in her
absence, Bone was 'certified a bastard by the state of South Carolina' (3).[21]

As in *Corregidora*, the focus in *Bastard* is on family history and the violence of
racial, class and sexual victimization. Allison's fiction reveals how the family operates as a fantasy scenario wherein a series of interlocking roles works to produce,
justify and perpetuate a situation of childhood abuse and violation in which Bone
is beaten, molested and eventually raped by her stepfather.[22] At the same time, it is
only out of her ambivalent identification with her family, in particular the mother
who does not save her, that Bone finds the means of self-preservation.

Decisively, it is the girl's stories and sexual fantasies about the abuse, rather than the
abuse itself, that the novel spends the most time considering. For it is Bone's memory
of the trauma, and the masturbatory fantasies in which she re-enacts her violation, that
constitutes the pain of her psychic reality; she is 'more ashamed for masturbating to
the fantasy of being beaten than for being beaten in the first place' (113). When her
stepfather Daddy Glen molests her in his car, a numb and paralysed Bone is left wondering if she had 'dreamed' the whole scene (48). She is unable to represent what happened to her. The inability to represent her sexual violation brings Bone to the world
of storytelling. As Allison has suggested, in the space of fiction the child finds a place
where she can be the heroine (cited in Megan 1994: 75). To take this point even further we can say that in the realm of fiction Bone finds a space of self-preservation
where she can survive the everyday violence she must endure. For example, on the
way home from the hospital after another beating from Daddy Glen, Bone creates an
elaborate story in which she imagines an enraged doctor screaming at him:

> *"You son of bitch! You ever touch that child again and I'll grind you into meat and
> blood!"* Daddy Glen would weep tears of blood...He'd...get on his knees
> before the whole family. "I have sinned," he'd say, and hold his hands out to
> me, beg my forgiveness and cry my name. Mama would say no. My aunts
> would say no...But I would pull myself up from my sickbed. I would look
> right into his eyes...Yes, I would say. Yes. I forgive you. Then probably I would
> die...The pain was hot and I took the story away so fast I made a little sound.
>
> (116)

Here Bone dies with the martyred heroine she identifies herself with, but lives beyond her to take up her place in other heroic narratives.[23] Stories in which Bone entertains her own death thus becomes a way for her to sustain her existence.

Storytelling, of course, is something that is prohibited by Daddy Glen who refuses to allow the girls to listen to 'all those stories Granny and Aunt Alma were always telling over and over again. "I'll tell you who you are," he said. "You're mine now"' (52). The girl's relation to storytelling in the face of paternal prohibition accords with Allison's description of the feminist writer's reaction to dominant fiction that purports to represent the reality of the marginalized. For Allison, storytelling is about telling the story that 'has to be told in order not to tell the one the world wants, the story of us broken, the story of us never laughing out loud, never learning to enjoy sex, never being able to love or trust love again, the story in which all that survives is the flesh' (1996: 72). Without her angry stories of vengeance, in which she imagines horrible acts of violence befalling Daddy Glen, Bone falls into the despair of yearning for the story she knows she can never have: 'The worst thing in the world was the way I felt when I wanted us to be like the families in the books in the library, when I just wanted Daddy Glen to love me like the father in *Robinson Crusoe*' (209).

Bone's violent sexual fantasies constitute another form of storytelling, in which she is able to imaginatively re-enact, and at least momentarily, to rise above, her violation through identification with spectacle. These fantasies, in which the child imagines herself being beaten by Daddy Glen, have what Kaja Silverman calls 'a scenic quality' (1992: 160). That is to say, they are imagined as visual spectacles. The single most important element of these fantasies is being watched:

> Someone had to watch…Sometimes a whole group of them would be trapped into watching. They couldn't help or get away. They had to watch. In my imagination I was proud and defiant. I'd stare back at him with my teeth set, making no sound at all, no shameful scream, no begging. Those who watched me admired me and hated him. I pictured it that way and put my hands between my legs. It was scary, but it was thrilling too. Those who watched me, loved me. It was as if I was being beaten for them. I was wonderful in their eyes.
>
> (112)

True to the complexities of a psychoanalytic definition of fantasy as the staging of desire, such a fantasy is not about attaining a concrete object. Rather, as Lynne Segal notes, the fantasy is its 'own object, in the sense that it allows for multiple identifications across differing people and positions' (1993: 70). If storytelling fails the child at the time of the trauma, then Bone's sexual fantasies, in which she is able to identify with the various positions of spectator, victim and perpetrator, enable her to take an active part in what was a terrifyingly passive situation. Here fantasy serves a protective function. As Lebeau suggests: 'Fictions, daydreams are conjured by a subject who feels the need for protection. Fantasy intervenes. It comes between the self and its history – consciousness and reality – making use of things seen, heard, and experienced to rework the world' (2001: 29).

The novel sets out clearly why a fantasy of violation can be such a powerful scenario for the victim of sexual abuse: 'It was only in my fantasies with people watching me that I was able to defy Daddy Glen. Only there that I had any pride...There was no heroism possible in the real beatings. There was just being beaten until I was covered with snot and misery' (113). This understanding of sexual fantasy cannot be accounted for in terms of Brownmiller's view of the woman's rape fantasy as a patriarchal construct to be destroyed. The young girl may be having these fantasies because of the patriarch's abuse, but the crucial point is that she desperately needs them: 'I loved those fantasies even though I was sure they were a terrible thing. They had to be; they were self-centered and they made me have shuddering orgasms' (ibid.). Nor can they be framed in terms of a question of 'free choice' or the right of expression.[24] Bone compulsively returns to these fantasies, repeating the same scene over and over again, as in her 'dreams of fire' (63, 254).

In her representation of the sexual arousal Bone experiences from a re-engagement with the scene of her violation, Allison is working towards a more complicated understanding of sexuality than that that has generally been articulated in the context of the bitter feminist debates known as the 'sex wars'.[25] As a feminist writer and activist, Allison has long struggled against the idea that women must make a choice between pleasure and danger, between feminist politics and sexual desire. In so doing, she has been accused of being a proponent of anti-feminist sexuality and has as such been singled out by anti-pornography representatives as a sexual deviant. As one who writes essays both about her experiences as an incest survivor and as a lesbian sex radical, Allison has been criticized for the apparent incompatibility of these narratives. 'For most of my life I have been presumed to be misguided, damaged by incest and childhood physical abuse, or deliberately indulging in hateful and retrograde sexual practices out of a selfish concentration on my own sexual satisfaction' (1996: 45). But as Allison insists, sexual need cannot be so easily divorced from a context of male violence. The question posed by *Bastard Out of Carolina* is: does the story of the girl's sexual fantasies make the story of her abuse any less painful, any less horrible? That these two stories commingle in the most complex of ways is what constitutes the child's confusion and guilt (Allison 1996: 45). Like *Corregidora, Bastard* is concerned with debunking the idea that we can only 'tell one story at a time', that to tell the story of sexual desire is in some way to invalidate the story of sexual abuse.[26]

Through its representation of the girl's sexual fantasies, the novel demonstrates that violence is not only the perpetrator's domain – in other words, violence is not only something that happens to the girl – but, rather, is a 'means through which the self...is constituted and maintained' (De Vries and Weber 1997: 2). In her re-engagement with the scene of her endangerment, the young girl finds a way of preserving a relationship with her body – the body she is made to believe she should hate. Objects, often the very weapons used to torture her, become a source of the fetishistic magic she searches for, but cannot find, within herself: 'I kept looking for something special in me, something magical' (207). Bone touches the leather belts Daddy Glen beats her with as 'if they were something animal that could be tamed' (112). But the object that becomes most valuable and sacred to Bone is a hook and chain her cousin retrieves from the river. Polishing and caring for the hook, Bone turns it into an instrument of her autoeroticism.[27] Fastening the glistening hook around her body, she rocks back and forth: 'I was locked away and safe. What I really was could not be touched…Somewhere far away a child was screaming, but right then, it was not me' (185). For Bone, storytelling and fantasy is all about this moment, the moment when she feels 'locked away and safe', the moment when she is somehow removed from the horror of her violation. The satisfaction lies in the staging of a scenario. Her pleasure comes from the compulsive acting out of the scene, not from its consummation.[28] When the moment is over, Bone is still unsaved and is left with the feeling that she is 'mourning the loss of something I had never really had' (152). For, as Allison has written elsewhere, there are painful limitations to the act of storytelling: 'Imagine vengeance. Imagine justice. What is the difference anyway when both are only stories in your head? In the everyday reality you stand still. I stood still. Bent over. Laid down. "No, Daddy. I'm sorry Daddy. Don't do that Daddy"' (*Trash* 1995: 41).

Allison's recognition of her role as a storyteller emphasizes the work of fiction and fantasy in representing the complicated, and often unspeakable, reality of rape. In *Bastard Out of Carolina*, a novel about the way trauma both resists and initiates narrative, the abused girl's storytelling indicates Allison's authorial engagement with fiction as a site for re-imagining scenes of untold violation and suffering. Bone's imaginative use of narrative as a way of remaking her abusive world corresponds to Allison's description of writing as a 'process of survival, of deciding once more to live – and clinging to that decision … The stories were the blood and bone of it' (ibid.: 7, 9).

Conclusion

> Isn't storytelling always a way of searching for one's origins, speaking one's conflicts with the law, entering into a dialectic of tenderness and hatred?
>
> Roland Barthes

Stories of rape have played a powerful and important role in the search for the origins of women's oppression. The fascination that attends the uncovering of an original act of violation goes some way towards accounting for the enduring power of Brownmiller's comprehensive narrative of rape. But origin stories do not just reveal a structure of oppression. They also play a role in structuring symbolic roles and positions. In the founding feminist stories of Brownmiller and French, rape is not only a site of origins for masculine culture, it is a site of origins for feminism at which a series of battles regarding gender, sexual identity and race are fought out.

In Brownmiller and French's work, the emphasis is on revealing the reality of rape. A neglected, and compelling question – and one that I have argued is politically necessary in order to move the feminist conversation about rape forward – concerns the significance of fantasy. As the criticism of Brownmiller offered by black feminists such as Davis suggest, feminism is not, and never can be, on the 'outside' of public fantasies of race and rape. The criticism offered by black feminists in the wake of *Against Our Will* is a strong reminder of the fact that feminist stories and analyses of rape are always linked to public fantasies of not just man and woman, but white and black.

What emerges through my discussion of *Corregidora* and *Bastard Out of Carolina* is that fantasy – private and public – is not something to be destroyed on the way to greater political consciousness about rape. In their exploration of the mutual implication of sex and violence these texts undermine the distinction between reality and fantasy, demonstrating that it is possible to tell more than one story at a time. Like *Against Our Will* and *The Women's Room, Corregidora* and *Bastard Out of Carolina* are origin stories: the primal scenes of violence they provide figure the origins of the female subject, the origins of sexuality and the origins of sexual difference. But *Corregidora* and *Bastard Out of Carolina* complicate what Ned Lukacher has elsewhere called 'a simple origin' (1986: 160). As Lukacher suggests in his discussion of psychoanalytic re-readings of Freud's case history of the 'Wolf-Man', what is important for the subject is not so much the historical referent as the repetition and re-staging of the scene. As he writes: 'the analytic session itself incorporates and repeats the primal scene' (ibid.: 160). Similarly in *Corregidora* and *Bastard Out of Carolina*, the real event of an original act of rape and sexual violation is less important than the active reworking of the scene by the female subject. The significance of this narrative revision is that, while it recognizes rape as a 'process of intimidation' (Brownmiller 1991: 15) it leaves open the possibility that the story of rape may be scripted differently.

The emphasis in this chapter has been on how rape is represented and figured in selected feminist discourse and woman's writing; on how scenes of rape imagine relations between men and women and between white and black. In the next chapter, I continue my exploration of the significance of rape as primal scene, elaborating on what I see as the most important and provocative argument made by Brownmiller: far from being an act of cultural deviance, rape is central to the workings of the body politic.

2

BODY POLITICS

Rousseau's *Le Lévite d'Ephraim*

> The body of a raped woman becomes a ceremonial battlefield, a
> parade ground for the victor's trooping of the colors. The act that is
> played out upon her is a message passed between men – vivid proof
> of victory for one and loss and defeat for the other.
>
> (Susan Brownmiller, *Against Our Will: Men, Women and Rape*)

The idea that rape bolsters male power is forcefully expressed in the phenomenon
of rape in war. Once ignored or taken for granted in public accounts of warfare,
the occurrence of rape in wartime has now entered collective consciousness.[1]
In 2001 the UN war crimes tribunal enforced its ruling that rape is a crime against
humanity by convicting three Bosnian Serbs for sexual violence ('Rape War
Crime' 23 February 2001). For Brownmiller and others this was an important
recognition of a long-ignored fact: the bodies of raped women function as symbols
of violent communication between men. As Claudia Card suggests, the raped
woman in war and in peace functions as a sacrificial victim used to 'communicate,
and produce or maintain dominance' (1996: 3).

I want to shed further light on this idea of rape as a perverse and deadly form of
communication by turning to a thinker who is rarely considered in feminist discussions of rape and war. Jean-Jacques Rousseau is known as an eighteenth-century
political philosopher, of particular interest to feminists for his engagement with
the question of how sexuality and gender relates to political life. What is perhaps
less well known is that Rousseau's theories regarding the relationship between
communication, citizenship and gender, found what he considered to be their most
poetic and profound assertion through a vicious and sordid story of rape, murder
and dismemberment. *Le Lévite d'Ephraim*, a pastoral prose poem that includes overt
descriptions of both heterosexual and homosexual desire, can be considered an
early literary exploration of how rape gets used as a weapon of war. But in *Le Lévite
d'Ephraim* rape is much more than a weapon of war, it is the founding cause of
war; just as even more curiously, it is eventually the means by which the war is concluded, the community restored and the social contract initiated.

Rousseau based *Le Lévite d'Ephraim* on an Old Testament tale from the Book of
Judges. In Rousseau's *Essay on the Origin of Languages*, written in 1761, we find the
first reference to the biblical story that so fired his imagination.[2] Here Rousseau
calls upon the story of a woman's rape and murder to demonstrate his contention

42

that 'the most vigorous speech is that in which the Sign has said everything before a single word is spoken':

> When the Levite of Ephraim wanted to avenge the death of his wife, he *did not write* to the tribes of Israel; he divided her body into twelve pieces which he sent to them. At this horrible sight they rushed to arms, crying with one voice: *Never has such a thing happened in Israel, from the day when our fathers left Egypt until this day*! And the tribe of Benjamin was exterminated.
>
> (Rousseau 1990: 242)

This grotesque image of the raped female body in bits and pieces is an example of what Rousseau calls 'eloquence muette', mute eloquence (ibid.). For Rousseau the Levite's presentation of the dismembered woman's body shows the eloquent power of the 'mute sign': 'Nowadays it would have been turned into lawsuits, debates, perhaps even jokes; it would have dragged on and the most ghastly crime would finally have remained unpunished' (ibid.). There is an important lesson about visual communication to be learned from this story of a woman's rape and murder: 'Thus one speaks much better to the eyes than to the ears' (ibid.).

The story's subject matter is, as Rousseau himself acknowledged, truly 'horrible' (1996: 575). A young woman is raped and murdered by a group of men. By way of vengeance, her anguished lover cuts the woman's dead body into twelve pieces and sends her dismembered body parts throughout Israel. At the sight of this terrible spectacle, the tribes of Israel band together and seek revenge against those responsible for the woman's rape and murder. A civil war ensues that claims thousands of lives. Following this bloody carnage, the story concludes where it began: with rape. In order to reunify the decimated tribes, the rape of over six hundred virgins is authorized by the tribes of Israel. Israel is reunited.

Despite its evident interest for a feminist account of the relationship between rape and the origins of culture, Rousseau's rewriting of the Levite story is not considered in most feminist accounts of sexual violence, even those that focus specifically on the foundations of the socio-sexual contract. Brownmiller only refers very briefly and very generally to the biblical version of the Levite story in a discussion of how the 'ancient patriarchs' used the 'rape of women to forge their own male power' (1991: 18). Brownmiller's reference to the 'unfortunate lot of women caught in the middle of intertribal warfare within the twelve tribes of Israel' is part of a wider analysis of how rape is treated as a 'property crime of man against man' (ibid.). In Brownmiller's account, the biblical narrative is yet another tragic example, as noted in the epigraph to this chapter, of the way in which the raped woman's body 'becomes a ceremonial battlefield' (ibid.: 38).

Brownmiller is not the only feminist to have left Rousseau's story out of a discussion of rape's significance to masculine cultural bonds. The *Lévite* is a striking omission from political theorist Carole Pateman's *The Sexual Contract* (1988). This examines Enlightenment ideas of citizenship and contract to disclose how white male privilege has been protected by the rhetoric of the 'universal' citizen. According to Pateman, what is missing from the classic conjectural stories of the founding of civil society is the story of the sexual contract. 'The original contract is a sexual–social pact but the story of the sexual contract has been repressed' (1988: 1). Through her re-reading of the founding fathers of eighteenth-century social contract theory, among them Thomas Hobbes, John Locke and Rousseau, Pateman seeks to retrieve this 'lost' or 'repressed' story. According to Pateman, all the classic stories of political origins, including Rousseau's, are missing a 'political book of genesis'; they lack what she calls the 'story of the *primal scene*' (ibid.: 105). Her study speculates that the 'true origin of political right' is a rape.[3]

In the introduction to her book, Pateman makes a declaration: 'Let me make it clear that although I shall be (re)telling conjectural histories of the origins of political right and repairing some omissions in the stories, I am not advocating the replacement of patriarchal tales with feminist stories of origins' (1988: 18). Here she attempts to safeguard herself from the charge that, by creating her own speculative scenario of an original rape, she is offering a new feminist story of origins. Indeed, while Pateman notes the importance of stories she concludes by calling for the abolition of the social contract story: 'To change modern patriarchy, to begin to create a free society in which women are autonomous citizens, the story must be cast aside' (ibid.: 220).

But eradicating social contract stories is not the answer. As feminist philosopher Moira Gatens asks in her commentary on Pateman: 'Can we cast aside these stories? Are they simply fictions which can be neatly excised from the world of fact?' (1996: 87) As I argued in the previous chapter, the question of story and narrative is essential to a feminist analysis of rape and its representation. In calling for the story to be cast aside, I would argue Pateman is losing sight of the 'as if' of thinking. As she notes: 'The original contract … is not an actual event but a political fiction; our society should be understood *as if* it originated in a contract' (1988: 202). If correct, this becomes a matter not of throwing the story aside, but of looking at how femininity is made to figure in the 'as if' of political fictions.

I want to reconsider the importance of Rousseau's revision of the biblical story by placing it in the context of what Pateman describes as 'the grand tradition of theoretical speculation about the origins of human society, civilization, and culture' (ibid.: 112). With its depiction of rape as an originating moment of the social contract, *Le Lévite d'Ephraim* affirms the question Pateman poses in her discussion of the primal scene: 'Does the origin of political right lie in a rape?' (ibid.: 105). In fact, it is tempting to suggest that this obscure tale is the 'missing half of the story' that Pateman attempts to piece together through her re-reading of the major social contract theorists. It is tempting to suggest that the *Lévite* is the 'lost story' of the sexual contract; the dark and violent foundation of the more benevolent vision of social relations presented in Rousseau's *The Social Contract*.

Much of my interest in the *Lévite* story derives from the way in which its representation of sexual violation complicates the traditional feminist account of rape as the primal scene of culture analysed in Chapter 1. As a story about how the social contract is founded through repeated acts of rape and murder, I suggest the *Lévite* fills in certain silences found in the better known social contract stories; not only those in Rousseau's body of writing, but also those found in the conjectural histories offered by Brownmiller, French and Pateman. My argument is that Rousseau's re-writing of the *Lévite* makes explicit the demands placed on the violated female body as the image that is made to represent 'a putting into place of ... culture and, crucially, of [hetero]sexual relations' (Cowie 1990: 128).

Reading for the blind spot

In *Allegories of Reading: Figural Language in Rousseau, Nietsche, Rilke, and Proust*, Paul De Man suggests that the first task for the reader of Rousseau is 'to diagnose what, if anything, is being systematically overlooked by other readers' (1979: 136). This is a task especially relevant to the *Lévite*, a story that, as John Morley noted in 1888, 'no man has read' (69). An exaggeration, perhaps, but it is true nevertheless that the *Lévite* has long been the blind spot of Rousseau's readers.[4] Generally considered to be one of his minor works, it has been persistently ignored by critics, including De Man himself who, in *Allegories of Reading*, relegates the story to a footnote.[5] Interestingly enough, it would seem that Judges 19, the biblical story from which the *Lévite* takes its subject matter, has suffered a similar fate. As Mieke Bal remarks: 'The story is arguably the most horrible one of the entire Bible, and deserves more attention than it usually gets' (1986: 77).

Why has this spectacular, gruesome story been neglected? And does this critical neglect have something to do with the subject matter of rape? De Man's theory of reading again proves helpful. In his celebrated *Blindness and Insight: Essays in the Rhetoric of Contemporary Criticism*, De Man develops a critical approach we can call 'reading for the blind spot'. Reading the work of literary critics such as Lukacs, Blanchot and Poulet, he argues that in each of these works, critical insight seems to have been 'gained from a negative movement that animates the critic's thought, an unstated principle that leads his language away from its asserted stand' (1983: 103). Critical blindness, then, is also always a form of critical insight. De Man says it even more strongly: 'Critics' moments of greatest blindness with regard to their own critical assumptions are also the moments at which they achieve their greatest insight' (ibid.: 109). This is not an insight that can be spotted by the critics themselves. Rather, the 'insight exists only for a reader in the privileged position of being able to observe the blindness as a phenomenon in its own right' (ibid.: 106).

Treating the blindness towards the *Lévite* as a phenomenon in its own right, I want to consider why this 'has possessed the curious privilege of rendering itself invisible' (De Man 1979: 136). Jacques Derrida's exclusion of the Levite from his reading of Rousseau's *Essay on the Origin of Languages* will be central to this chapter's attempt to explore the critical blindness towards the *Lévite*. As I will argue, there is a striking coincidence between Derrida's occlusion of the Levite story in favour of a discussion of 'love', and Rousseau's re-writing of the Levite of Ephraim into a 'love story'.

De Man's observations on blindness and insight are instructive in regard not only to the *Lévite* but also to the general question of rape and representation. In the important anthology *Rape and Representation*, editors Lynn Higgins and Brenda Silver identify a pattern at work in literary representations of rape:

> Analyses of specific texts, when read through and against each other, illustrate a number of profoundly disturbing patterns. Not the least of which is an obsessive inscription – and an obsessive erasure – of sexual violence against women (and against those placed by society in the position of "woman"). The striking repetition of inscription and erasure raises the question of not only why this trope recurs, but even more, of what it means and who benefits.
>
> (1991: 2)

What unites a number of diverse literary texts on rape is this strangely suggestive repetition of presence and absence:

> Over and over in the texts explored here, rape exists as an absence or gap that is both product and source of textual anxiety, contradiction, or censorship. The simultaneous presence and disappearance of rape as constantly deferred origin of both plot and social relations is repeated so often as to suggest a basic conceptual principle in the articulation of both social and artistic representations.
>
> (ibid.: 3)

This 'rhetoric of elision', as Higgins and Silver call it, can be evinced in some of the 'most widely read white male fictions of rape', including Shakespeare's *The Rape of Lucrece*, Thomas Hardy's *Tess of the D'Urbervilles*, and EM Forster's *A Passage to India* (ibid.: 5). As a text that both inscribes and elides the scene of sexual violence, the *Lévite* can be broadly situated in this tradition of male fiction writing.[6] And yet, as I will show, the *Lévite* pushes to extremes this idea of rape as the 'product and source of textual anxiety' (ibid.: 3). That is to say, its repetition of the scene of sexual violation and murder exaggerates this motif of inscription and erasure. The *Lévite* is not a linear narrative; in the fantasy of social origins it offers, rape is called upon to cure the damage done by rape.[7] Rape and murder lead to rape and murder on an even grander scale. What does it mean that the socio-sexual contract is founded by repeating the very crime it initially denounces? And what can this structure of repetition – the process by which rape repeatedly disrupts and renews – tell us about the cultural investment in images of rape?

I also want to focus on what is perhaps the greatest blind spot of social origin stories involving sexual violence: male-on-male rape. Juliet Flower MacCannell suggests it is curious that Rousseau's major commentators, (among them Starobinski, Lacan and Derrida), have not seen fit to read him in the 'homosexual frame' (1991: 76). I want to extend this observation to the criticism of the

Lévite, a narrative that depicts the threat of male-on-male rape as the reason for male-on-female rape. Given the text's open depiction of homosexual desire it is interesting that, traditionally, critics have tended to ignore the part it may play in the fantasy of social origin at work in the text. Much more than the merely incidental status to which it has been assigned, a myth of substitution in which a woman's violable body is made to stand in for a man's is key to the story's vision of the reinscription of the civic bond.

In the *Lévite*, rape is the site where 'aesthetic or semiotic representation (things that "stand for" other things) and political representation (persons who "act for" other persons)' come together (Mitchell 1995: 11). The *Levite* begins with an example of semiotic representation, when the raped woman's body parts are sent out as 'signs' to the tribes of Israel. It concludes with an example of political representation when a young woman, Axa, sacrifices her personal desires and acts on behalf of the greater good of the community. And indeed, the semiotic use of the raped woman – the way her dead body parts are called upon to represent the crime of the Benjaminites – is related to the idea of the woman's mutilated body as a political representative, sent out to the tribes of Israel on behalf of the Levite to 'represent' the crime to the people. The role rape plays in negotiating the complex links between aesthetic/semiotic and political forms of representation has implications that extend far beyond the *Lévite*. This story, which tells the tale of how a raped woman is made to represent the violation of the body of the community, brings into relief a process that is at work more generally in cultural texts on rape. To question what is at stake in the cultural use of the raped woman's body as a representational sign is to confront one of the most important questions about representation itself. As WJT Mitchell explains: 'One crucial consideration that enters into any analysis of representation is the *relationship* between the representational material and that which it represents. By virtue of *what* "agreement" or understanding does representation occur?' (ibid.: 14). So by what agreement is a fantasy of the raped woman made to stand in for the act of semiotic and political representation?

A tale of terror

Chapters 19–21 of the Book of Judges contain the most violent set of episodes in a 'strikingly violent book' (Bal 1988: 1). 'To hear this story is to inhabit a world of unrelenting terror that refuses to let us pass by on the other side': this is the warning with which feminist biblical scholar Phyllis Trible begins her discussion of the tale (1984: 65). Here Trible's reference to another biblical story, of the Good Samaritan who refuses to 'let us pass by on the other side', urges the reader to supply the missing sympathy for the unnamed raped woman.

What was summarized in the Bible with the short sentence – 'He had taken as concubine a woman from Bethlehem in Judah' – is re-written by Rousseau in the style of a pastoral idyll.[8] As in the biblical tale, the woman is silent throughout the story. During the couple's courtship the only activity accorded to her is a smile. During the lengthy passages detailing the Levite's adoration of his young 'wife', this smile finds its parallel in the woman's tears: 'Daughter of Bethlehem, he said to her, why must you always cry for your family and your country' (1210)? Eventually, we are told that the concubine leaves the Levite to return to her family. While in the Bible it remains unclear why the woman leaves the Levite (some critics say she was unfaithful, others say she was angry), in Rousseau's version, a clear, if banal, reason is provided: the woman is simply bored, 'perhaps because he had left nothing for her to desire' (1210). This reference to the woman's boredom is not, however, as trite as it might first appear. The theme of desire, and the role that it plays in promoting or destroying the relations between the sexes, is central to Rousseau's account of sexual relations. Keeping the passions excited, fuelling the desire necessary to maintain relations between the sexes is, for Rousseau, a complex balancing act, which requires strict adherence to the roles prescribed by sexual difference. According to Rousseau, it is the role of the man to be 'audacious'; after all, 'someone has to declare' (1960: 84). Feminine modesty enflames desire.

Miserable without her, the Levite travels to her father's house to bring her back home with him. Though Rousseau refers to the concubine as a 'wife' and the Levite as her 'husband' (the Levite is also called 'son-in-law' by the concubine's father), the text nevertheless sets out precisely why the young woman cannot become the Levite's official wife. Upon meeting the young girl, the Levite declares: 'Daughter of Judah, you are not of my tribe, you do not have a brother' (1209). This idea of the woman as an exchangeable object between men offers a well-known account of the social bond as one dependent upon the relations between brothers.[9] Because the young woman is without a brother, the standard exchange between men cannot occur. But while the couple cannot marry, this does not mean that the Levite cannot have sexual access to the young woman. As the Levite tells the young woman's father, she is no longer a marketable commodity since he has claimed her virginity. He has thus ensured that she cannot become anyone else's property.

Each time the Levite attempts to leave the house with the young woman, the father urges him to stay. For though the young woman may not be a sister, she is most emphatically a daughter. Throughout Rousseau's version of the story the woman is interchangeably referred to as the 'young daughter', the 'Daughter of Judah' or the 'Daughter of Bethlehem'. As if to make the point, Rousseau provides the concubine with an entire family (in the Bible there is only a father) and creates a dramatic farewell scene in which the narrator draws attention to the 'price of this fatal separation' from the bosom of the family (1211). As the young woman leaves her father's house, it is as if she is already dead; her 'horrible fate' is foreshadowed by the father's 'convulsive' reaction to her separation from the bosom of the family. With the father's silent suffering (his 'mute embraces' [ses muettes étreintes]) we find an example of the 'mute eloquence' attributed to the young woman's dismembered body in the Essay.

In the second chant, the Levite and the concubine journey towards Ephraim and stop overnight in Gibeah, home to the tribe of Benjamin. Despite the Levite's expectations, no one offers them hospitality. As the group waits in the public square, the narrator interjects with a celebratory digression on the nature of hospitality. Addressing the 'men of our days', the narrator tells them not to judge the customs of their fathers. In these 'early times', he explains, it may be true that men did not have the same luxuries, but they had the 'feelings of hospitality that made up for this lack' (1213).[10]

Hospitality is the one code of behaviour characterizing the social organization in the *Lévite*. In his study, *Adultery in the Novel*, Tony Tanner writes:

> The conventions and rules dictating or circumscribing the practice of "hospitality" (which etymologically contains within it both guest and host, but also, from the Latin *hostis*, a stranger and potentially an enemy) were … absolutely crucial for tribes and city-states, since a mutual recognition of these rules and rituals was the key way of avoiding rupture both within the tribe or state and at its boundaries.
>
> (1979: 24)

When the Levite stops overnight in Gibeah, he is clearly marked as the 'unknown "other"' within the city walls (ibid.: 24). As the group of rapists instructs the old man: 'Hand over to us that young stranger whom, without permission, you receive within your walls; his beauty shall pay the price of his asylum' (1213). The old man refuses to hand over the Levite on two grounds: because it violates the rule of hospitality; and because the Levite's status as a priest forbids such a desecration. What becomes brutally apparent here is that the bonds of hospitality do not extend to the woman. In fact, one might turn this around and say that the forcible exclusion of the woman is precisely what constitutes the bonds of hospitality. For if, as Tanner suggests, 'the notion of a "stranger" necessarily requires, or assumes, the concept of a "friend"', the *Lévite* dramatizes the way the attempt to negotiate these two concepts relies upon and requires the violent exclusion/expulsion of the woman (1979: 25).

The *Lévite* is a story that devolves on a series of violent substitutions and repetitions: the Levite substitutes his body with that of the concubine; the dismemberment of the concubine's body leads to the slaughter of a tribe; and the rape of the concubine is repeated with the rape of over six hundred virgins. Of these, it is the first act of substitution, in which the Levite forcibly exchanges his rapable body with that of the young woman's, which most clearly sets the *Lévite* apart from the feminist origin story offered by Brownmiller. For the question immediately arises: what happens to the feminist account of rape as the paradigmatic experience of women under patriarchy when the possibility of male rape is factored into the equation?

When feminists have discussed male-on-male rape, they have tended to cast the male body as a substitute for the woman's. As Monique Plaza argues: 'Socially the anus of a man can be put in the place of "bodies of women" and be appropriated as such' (1981: 28). In other words, if men are raped, they are raped as 'women'. What the standard myth of substitution does not take into account, and what

Rousseau's story forces us to consider, is the issue of homosexual desire. In the *Lévite*, it is not the man who is a substitute for the woman, but the woman who is a substitute for the man. It is the 'young' and 'beautiful' Levite who is the object of the rapists' lust. What is at issue in this substitution, I suggest, is the attempt to distinguish self and other through the medium of the woman as rapable object. Put crudely, the young woman is raped *because* the Levite is rapable. In this instance, the possibility of male-on-male rape is what ensures heterosexual rape; the Levite defends his body from violation by putting the woman's body in his stead. With the awareness of his own rapability comes a desperate, and lethal, attempt to prove that he is the subject, rather than the object of violence, by enforcing sexual difference along the lines of violability.

When the men demand to have the Levite handed over to them, the old man proves his worth as a host by offering his virgin daughter as a substitute. Importantly, the old man does not offer the Levite's concubine as a potential substitute. The sole responsibility for that action lies with the Levite.

> But the Levite, who had been frozen by terror until this moment, regains his senses at this deplorable prospect, forestalls the generous old man, runs ahead of him, forces him to go back in the house with his daughter, and taking himself his own beloved companion, without saying a word to her, without raising his eyes to her, drags her to the door and hands her over to the accursed ones.
>
> (1214)

The young woman stands in the place of the virgin daughter of the old man, as well as in the place of the Levite, the original object of desire. She is the object of exchange not only between the old man and the Levite (my concubine, instead of your daughter) but also between the Levite and the rapists (her body instead of mine) and finally among the rapists themselves. Rousseau describes the rape in melodramatic fashion:

> They immediately surround the half-dead young girl, seize her, and carry her off without pity. In their brutal fury they are like a pack of hungry wolves as they surprise a weak heifer at the foot of the frozen Alps and throw themselves upon her.
>
> (1215)

In a further address to the rapists, the narrator condemns them for 'destroying their species' through 'the pleasures meant to reproduce it', and asks how it is possible that their ferocious desires are not arrested by the woman's 'dying beauty' (1214–1215). He then goes on to describe this '*beauté mourante*' in detail.

> Look at her eyes already closed to the light, her fading features, her darkened face; the pallor of death has covered her cheeks, livid violet has replaced

50

the roses in them, she has no more voice in which to moan, her hands have not the strength to repulse your outrages. Alas! she is already dead!

(1215)

This statement appears to add one, final twist to the biblical tale: rape has extended beyond the moment of death to become necrophilia. If one reads no further than this line, it would appear as though Rousseau has supplied a resolution to one of the most fiercely debated issues surrounding the biblical tale – the time of the woman's death.

Given the apparent finality of the statement 'she is already dead', it comes as something of a shock to read the following lines: 'The wretched woman, with her last remaining strength, drags herself to the old man's dwelling. At the door she falls face down, her arms stretched out upon the threshold' (1215). At this stage, then, she is still alive. Upon finding the woman's body on the threshold, the Levite says: '"Arise and let us be going"... But there was no answer' (1215). In the Greek Bible, this statement is accompanied by the observation 'for she was dead', a comment which confirms that the woman was, in fact, murdered as well as raped. The Hebrew text, on the other hand, is silent on the matter, allowing several commentators to surmise that the woman may still be alive (Trible 1984: 79).

Bal dismisses those who assume the woman must already be dead as 'apologists' for the figure of the Levite (1991: 369). According to Bal, there appears to be a strong desire on the part of readers to 'partake in the diegetic misreading of the Levite who wishes the woman to be dead' (ibid.). In her reading of Rousseau's version of the story, Judith Still makes an opposed argument: 'The Levite would prefer his beloved *not* to be dead if only so that he can attempt to expiate his crime towards her' (1989: 26). According to Still, the reader, like the Levite, would 'prefer the victim not to have experienced the rape, and so it is tactfully asserted that she is already dead' (ibid.). In other words, death is preferable to rape.

I would suggest that, in Rousseau's version of the story, the figure of the already dead woman is considerably more complicated than either of these readings allow. For it is never simply a question of whether the woman is literally dead or not; as Rousseau's story makes clear, the woman is symbolically dead from the moment the Levite pushes her outside to the rapists. The figure of the raped woman is caught between what Slavoj Žižek describes as 'real (biological) death and its symbolization' (1989: 135).

Upon realizing his love is dead, the Levite decides to take vengeance, resorting to the language of gesture. Without 'hesitation', the Levite, whom the narrator here describes as a 'barbarian' – a repetition of the word used to describe the rapists – cuts the woman's body into a dozen pieces. 'With a firm hand, he strikes fearlessly, cutting flesh and bones, separating head and members, and sends to the Tribes these frightful messages' [*ces envois effroyables*] (1215). In the *Lévite*, the raped woman's body parts are sent out not only as messages or missives but as representatives or envoys on behalf of the Levite. As Allan Bass explains in a different context, this second sense of the term envoy or *envoi* comes from the reflexive verb *s'envoyer*, which can mean 'to send oneself, transitively or intransitively' (cited in Derrida 1987: xxi). According to Bass, 'one might say that if one sends oneself, then one's en-voy (also *en-voi*) or representative has to be one's double or ghost' (ibid.). This idea of the woman's dead body as ghosting or doubling that of the Levite's is important, particularly in light of the way the Levite forcibly substitutes his body with that of the woman's, thereby defending himself from rape. In addition to upholding the bodily integrity of the Levite, this act of substitution serves an important symbolic function: it constructs the male body as exempt from violation (Halperin 1990: 96–97).

In the *Lévite*, which is a story about how a community bands together and re-inscribes the civic bond, the symbolic significance of rape is central to the formation of a new social order. What becomes pressing here is the question of the role rape plays in the determination of citizenship. That there may be an antithesis between rapability, citizenship and participation in the civic bond has emerged, at least implicitly, in recent political theory regarding the notion of the 'ideal citizen'. Étienne Balibar, for example, has suggested that the postulation of a concept of citizenship, as founded in the Greek *polis*, 'is dependent upon a coincident ability to identify those who are not citizens, those outside of the *filia* of male homosexual, ethical, and political bonds' (cited in Jeffords 1991: 209). In light of the representation of rape in the *Lévite*, we can rework this observation slightly to suggest that one of the ways citizenship may be defined is through identifying the rapability of the body. For is it possible to be a citizen when you are also always a potential victim of rape?

Leo Bersani has noted that 'even in cultures that do not regard sexual relations between men as unnatural or sinful, the line is drawn at "passive" anal sex' (1987: 212). For the ancient Romans and Greeks, for example, to be anally penetrated was judged to be an 'indecorous role for male citizens' (ibid.). In *One Hundred Years of Homosexuality* David Halperin similarly notes the intimate relationship between democracy, civic duty, sexual violation and the body politic. Sexual violation was the limit set to uphold 'the dignity and autonomy – the social viability, in short – of every (male) citizen, whatever his economic circumstances' (1990: 96). The sexual inviolability of the male body was the one marker that distinguished citizens from slaves and foreigners. Halperin concludes:

> To violate the bodily sanctity of a citizen by treating him as one would a slave, by manhandling him, or even by placing a hand on his body without his consent was not only to insult him personally but to assault the corporate integrity of the citizen body as a whole and to offend its fiercely egalitarian spirit.

> (ibid.)

To offend the individual body is to offend the citizen body as a whole, what Rousseau describes in *The Social Contract* as 'an artificial and collective body' known as the 'body politic' (Rousseau 1968: 61). This artificial body, like the body of the (male) individual, is sacrosanct. The *Lévite* is significant because it allows us to track the process by which women's violated bodies are made to support the 'corporate integrity' of the citizen body. In the *Lévite*, rape is not only a violation of the woman's body; nor is it simply a violation of the man's property rights. The violation is cast as a violation of Israel; the battle that follows is an attempt to restore Israel to its 'purity'.

We can clarify the logic behind this conceptualization of rape as a civic crime by turning to a consideration of the third chant, which begins with the assembled tribes, brought together by the horrible missives of the woman's dead body. When they ask, 'how was this wickedness brought to pass?' they are referring not to the rape and murder – of which they know nothing at this point – but to the act of dismemberment itself. One might say that in the *Lévite* the writing with the raped woman's body is called upon as a necessary remedy to a critical situation, while at the same time it is the critical situation for which a remedy must be sought (Johnson 1995: 45). Once the tribes are assembled, the Levite tells his version of the events:

> I entered the Benjamin city of Gibeah with my wife to pass the night; and some people from the city surrounded the house where I lodged, and wanted to offend me and to kill me; I was forced to surrender my wife; she died as she left their hands. Then I took her body, divided it into pieces and I sent them to each of you.
>
> (1216)

This scene is notably absent from Rousseau's earlier use of the story in the *Essay*. What makes the story stand out as an example in that earlier work is precisely the fact that the Levite does not need to speak. In the *Lévite* the mutilated pieces of the woman's body operate as powerful 'signs', but it is only through the use of accompanying verbal discourse that they become meaningful. Peggy Kamuf has suggested that the raped woman's body in the *Lévite* functions as a kind of advertisement: 'Like a newspaper that publishes sensationalist photographs on the front page and directs readers to an inside page for details, the Levite's publicity stunt works first of all to get everyone's attention' (1988: 93). Understood in this light, the Levite's dismemberment of the woman's body, the 'language of gesture' as Rousseau calls it in the *Essay*, can be seen as a way of 'stimulating the imagination' or 'arousing curiosity': it assembles the tribes and gains a hearing for the story (Rousseau 1990: 241).

When the Levite finishes telling his side of the story all of Israel rise together and give one great, unanimous cry: 'The blood of the young woman will fall back on her murderers ... We will not return to our dwellings ... until Gibeah is exterminated' (1216). Here the raped woman's body parts function as the site of collective identity. In keeping with his attempt to recast the biblical text as a romance, Rousseau adds a significant scene to this sequence. Whereas in the Bible the figure of the Levite exits immediately after his recounting of the event, Rousseau scripts a speech to his dead wife:

> Maiden of Bethlehem, I bring you good news: your memory shall not go unhonoured. In saying these words, he fell forward onto his face, dead. His body was accorded a public funeral. The pieces of his wife's body were brought together and placed in the same tomb. And all Israel shed tears upon them.
>
> (1216)

The bits and pieces of the raped woman's body are literally put back together again in a fantasy of reparation that shadows and anticipates the eventual reintegration of the tribes of Israel. There is a resonance between the imaging of the violability and mutilation of the female body and the violability and mutilation of the body politic. In fact, there is a correlation between the images of rape, dismemberment and reparation present in the *Lévite* and Rousseau's descriptions of the body politic in *The Social Contract*. Consider Rousseau's fanciful description of the way political theorists divide or dismember the principle of sovereignty:

> It is said that Japanese mountebanks can cut up a child under the eyes of spectators, throw the different parts into the air, and then make the child come down, alive and all of a piece. This is more or less the trick that our political theorists perform – after dismembering the social body with a sleight of hand worthy of the fairground, they put the pieces together again anyhow.
>
> (1968: 71)

Though in this instance Rousseau uses an image of dismemberment and reparation to criticize existing political theory on sovereignty, as we have just seen, he himself calls upon a related image to figure his vision of the social order in the *Lévite*. The difference is that where Rousseau's political critique acknowledges the violence done to a supporting phantasmatic body – the body politic – such a critique gives way before a romance of restoration when it comes to the woman's actual dismembered body.

Restoration

Despite having achieved their stated objective of exterminating Benjamin, the people of Israel are unhappy because they 'felt the wound that they had inflicted on themselves' (1219). Benjamin is part of a whole and the injuries they have sustained are felt by all of Israel. A cure must be found. 'After having disposed of the evil that they had in their soul, the children of Israel had to find a remedy to re-establish in its entirety the mutilated race of Jacob' (1220). Because they had vowed never to give their daughters in marriage to a Benjaminite, the tribes must find another way of securing wives for the six hundred men at Rhimmon Rock who have survived the battle. Therefore, they follow through on another oath: to exterminate anyone who failed to help them take vengeance against the Benjaminites 'with the sole exception of the virgin daughters; you will bring them to the camp, and there give them in marriage to the Benjaminites' (1220).

The narrator once more draws attention to the violent circular logic at work here: 'To repair the desolation of so many murders these fierce people go on to commit murder on an even grander scale' (1220–1221). Meanwhile, Israel sends word to the Benjaminite refugees at Rhimmon Rock and they return 'among their brothers'. But their return is 'without joy … the shame and remorse covered their faces' (1221). The remaining members of the tribe are brought back into the fold by allowing them to commit the rape for which they were initially condemned and for which they are here portrayed as mournful and ashamed.

The narrator speculates about the terrible plight of the 'timid virgins' and offers the apparently sympathetic observation: 'Slave or tyrant, the sex that man oppresses or adores, and whose happiness, like his own, he will never know without letting the sexes be equal' (1221). But in the next breath the text goes on to recount the plot for yet another collective rape. It is here that Rousseau introduces the Old Man of Lebona, a council elder who steps forward with the following suggestion:

> Say to the children of Benjamin: Go, and ambush the vineyards: then, when you see that the young girls of Silo have started to dance with their flutes, envelop them, and each of you ravish a woman; then you will return, with your wife, to establish a country in Benjamin.
>
> And when the fathers and the brothers of the young girls protest and complain to us, we will tell them; take *pity* … since … we are not able to give them our women and go against the oath, we are guilty of their ruin if we leave them to perish without descendants.
>
> (1221)

On these instructions, the Benjaminites surround the young girls who have come to Silo to dance. As with the rape of the concubine, Rousseau describes the 'ambush' of the virgin daughters with descriptive flourish. The scared young women flee as their 'dancing turns to running' (1222). As the 'ravishers' are attacking the frightened women, a crowd of angry townspeople assemble. The fathers and mothers of the girls demand freedom for their daughters. Faced with the outrage of the fathers, the assembly pronounces that the women captives are 'free' and may decide their fate.

As a story that openly exhibits sexual violation as both the cause and the cure of social disorder, the *Lévite* can be situated in a tradition of origin stories in which rape serves as a generating moment of the social bond.[11] The biblical narrative from which the *Lévite* takes its subject matter has, in fact, been compared to the classical story of Lucretia whose rape and suicide leads to the founding of the Roman republic.

As Bal suggests:

> The symmetry with the Lucretia tradition is striking: in Rome, the tyranny of the kings had to be replaced by the Republic, whereas in Israel, the internal chaos had to be resolved by instituting monarchy. In both cases, rape, a crime of property, represents the disorder. And that social disorder must be eradicated by a new political structure.
>
> (1991: 83–84)

In Rousseau's story of the social order, the rape the Benjaminites commit is 'authorized'. The paradox of 'authorized rape' (*autorisés ravisses*), as Rousseau calls it in the *Lévite*, epitomizes the strangely repetitive logic that uses rape to cure the damage caused by rape, and murder to repair the losses caused by murder. But what does it mean to 'authorize' rape? That rape is considered a crime, even in this most rudimentary of social orders, is clear: after all, a tribe is nearly extinguished because some of its members rape and murder a young woman. Yet what seems equally clear is that the crime is thoroughly bound up with the law. As Kamuf argues:

> Man's law finds itself condemned to take up again in its own name and on its own account the crimes that it seeks to punish, risking otherwise the loss of the very name by which it is authorised to judge and sanction vengeance ... There is a hole in the whole and no law can heal it over. On the contrary, the law institutes the very separation it also covers over beneath the appearance of retributive justice.
>
> (1988: 90)

In other words, the paradox of the law is that it brings about a traumatic repetition of the event it wants to condemn. In this way, the poison is transformed into a poisonous remedy.[12] Since it is the writing with the raped woman's body that exemplifies this paradoxical logic, it is to that image I now want to turn.

The violence of representation

Recent criticism of the *Lévite* is united on at least one important point: the Levite's dismembering of the dead woman's body is an allegory of the act of writing. 'The Levite, "le barbare", does not so much substitute violence for writing as realize to the fullest and with maximal efficacy the violence that *is* writing' (Jackson 1992: 222); 'Within *Le Lévite d'Ephraim* there is a violent representation of the activity of writing ... It is lethal writing, its matter a corpse, a woman's body divided up by her lover's knife in a horrible parody of the strokes of a pen dividing up the page' (Still 1989: 27).

This lethal or violent allegory of writing has in turn been read as a metaphor for Rousseau's personal relation to writing: 'The central episode in the history of the Levite ... may have taken on the value of a metaphor for Rousseau, a mythic and hyperbolical representation of writing activity, the activity which won him fame and misery, and, continuing on the paths of exile, enabled him to supply, from his own resources, his own compensation' (Starobinski 1979: 163); 'Rousseau's fascination and identification with the figure of the Levite comes at least in part from that character's ability to achieve a perfect act of self-representation' (Kavanagh 1982: 157); 'It seems that by appropriating the biblical tale, Rousseau would have wanted to slip his signature and his demand for justice beneath that of the Levite on the dispersed body (or rather, *in* the intervals of that dispersion)' (Kamuf 1988: 99).

These critics share the view that the Levite's mutilation and dismemberment of the raped woman's body represents the act of writing. Indeed, it is possible to argue the recent interest in the *Lévite* has something to do with its depiction of corporeal violence as writing. In other words, if there is a curiously contemporary feel to this eighteenth-century translation of an Old Testament story, then that contemporaneity has something to do with the way it lends itself to present day theories about the 'violence of representation and the representation of violence' (Bronfen 1992: 3). The above discussions shed light on the 'allegory of writing' in the *Lévite*; what they do not account for, is why the means of allegorical expression is the woman's violated body.[13] For even if we grant the point that the story depicts dismemberment as a superlative form of communication, it is surely necessary to ask: Why does this form of writing take the woman's dead body as its model?[14]

In his discussion of Samuel Richardson's *Clarissa* (1748), another eighteenth-century narrative of rape, Terry Eagleton argues that Richardson's 'little read' novel has become 'readable' for us because of 'certain new ways of reading developed in our own time' (1982: viii). In addition to 'post-structuralist theories of textuality, of vital relevance to an author as obsessed as Richardson was by the act of writing', Eagleton attributes the renewed interest in the novel to feminism: if 'Richardson may once again become readable, it will be in large measure because of the women's movement' (ibid.). Without taking this point too far, it would seem that the present day 'readability' of the *Lévite* also derives, at least in part, from the disturbing familiarity of its narrative of sadistic male violence and female victimization.

In her important study of representations of dead women in Western culture, Elizabeth Bronfen argues that 'representations of feminine death work on the principle of being so excessively obvious that they escape observation. Because they are so familiar, so evident, we are culturally blind to the ubiquity of representations of feminine death' (1992: 3). We can make a similar argument about representations of feminine violation; representations in which rape, if it does not result in biological death, is nonetheless coded as a form of symbolic death. In some criticisms of the *Lévite*, the dismemberment of the raped woman appears to be so banal as to escape comment. Thomas Kavanagh's reading of the *Lévite*, for example, is striking in its failure to discuss the raped woman. He argues:

> In writing this work, Rousseau's identification is with the Levite, the innocent victim ... The Levite's story is a story of faith, of faith in the community, of an unshakeable faith in the collectivity of all as an ultimate instance of judgement capable of righting all the wrongs suffered by an innocent victim who, finally, has only to speak and to die.
>
> (1982: 156)

Remarkably, the 'innocent victim' of Kavanagh's account is not the concubine but the Levite, the man who speaks and then dies. The fact it is the woman, and not the man who gets raped, is ignored; the only victim here is the Levite.

> Rousseau's text...tells the story of an individual who, by reason of his beauty...finds himself the focal point of a criminal and profoundly transgressive desire shared by the men of Gibeah. From their midst, there emerges only one person, himself a foreigner, the Levite's host, who opposes that group. His opposition, however, fails and the crime is committed. The Levite, *in the person of the concubine with whom he will be buried, is its victim.*
>
> (ibid.: 155, my italics)

Kavanagh uncritically repeats the violent substitution that lies at the heart of the story. Thus, the woman is a substitute for the man, but in a way that evacuates the woman's body completely: it is the Levite, 'in the person of the concubine', who is seen to be violated. As the Levite notes upon discovering the concubine's body: 'To me you are more respectable than before *our* misfortune' (1215).

Kavanagh's elision of the raped woman from his commentary brings us to one of the central questions of this chapter: what kind of critical insight can be gained from exploring the blindness towards the *Lévite*? I want to pursue this question by turning to Derrida's reading of Rousseau's *Essay on the Origin of Languages* in *Of Grammatology* (1974). Reading this with the *Lévite* in mind, it is striking just how often Derrida hovers around, but never discusses, Rousseau's version of the story.[15] Given Derrida's interest in, and emphasis on, the violence of writing, it seems important to ask why his reading of Rousseau does not include what, by all accounts, is one of Rousseau's most significant illustrations in the *Essay* – the woman's mutilated body.[16]

As previously noted in my discussion of the *Essay*, Rousseau begins by praising what he calls 'the language of gesture' (1990: 240). According to Rousseau, for proof 'the most vigorous speech is that in which the Sign has said everything before a single word is spoken', one need only look to ancient history.

> What the ancients said most forcefully they expressed not in words, but in signs; they did not say it, they showed it ... Consult ancient history; you will find it filled with such ways of addressing arguments to the eyes, and they never fail to produce a more certain effect than all the discourses that might have been put in their place.
>
> (ibid.: 241)

Rousseau concludes the *Essay* by appearing to argue the opposite:

> In ancient times, when persuasion served in lieu of public force, eloquence
> was necessary. Of what use would it be today, when public force replaces
> persuasion? It requires neither art nor figures of speech to say *such is my
> pleasure* ... Popular languages have become as thoroughly useless as has
> eloquence. Societies have assumed their final forms: nothing can be
> changed in them anymore except by arms and cash, and since there is
> nothing left to say ... to the people but *give money*, it is said with posters
> on street corners.
>
> (ibid.: 294)

As Derrida's reading shows, what is at stake in this apparent paradox is the 'desire
for immediate presence' (1974: 237).

> The mute sign is a sign of liberty when it expresses within immediacy; then,
> what it expresses and he who expresses himself through it are properly
> present ... The mute sign signifies slavery when re-presentative mediacy
> has invaded the entire system of signification: then ... meaning ... is
> carried into an endless movement of signification.
>
> Because it is speech that has opened this endless movement of significa-
> tion – thus constantly risking a loss of signification – it is tempting to
> return to an archeological moment, a first moment of sign without
> speech, when passion, beyond need but short of articulation and difference,
> expresses itself in an unheard of way: an *immediate sign*.
>
> (ibid.: 233–234)

In *Of Grammatology*, the example Derrida refers to in order to explicate the notion
of an 'immediate sign' is love; an example that, I argue, we can read as a substitute
for a discussion of the dismembered female body. On the first page of the *Essay*
Rousseau provides the following discussion of the language of gesture:

> Although the language of gesture and that of voice are equally natural, the
> first is easier and less dependent on conventions. For more objects strike
> our eyes than our ears, and shapes exhibit greater variety than do sounds.
> They are also more expressive and say more in less time. Love, it is said,
> was the inventor of drawing. Love might also have invented speech,
> though less happily. Dissatisfied with speech, love disdains it: it has livelier
> ways of expressing itself. How many things the girl who took such pleas-
> ure in tracing her Lover's shadow was telling him! What sounds could she
> have used to convey this movement of the magic wand!
>
> (Rousseau 1990: 240–241)

For Derrida this is a key passage because it demonstrates how writing is implicated even in the example of a 'first sign before speech' (1974: 234). As he argues:

> The movement of the magic wand that traces with so much pleasure does not fall outside of the body. Unlike the spoken or written sign, it does not cut itself off from the desiring body of the person who traces or from the immediately perceived image of the other … She who traces, holding, handling, now, the wand, is very close to touching what is very close to being the other *itself,* close by a minute difference; that small difference – visibility, spacing, death – is undoubtedly the origin of the sign and the breaking of immediacy; but it is in reducing it as much as possible that one marks the contours of signification.
>
> (ibid.: 234)

This example of the woman who traces her lover's shadow with such pleasure, stands in stark contrast to the Levite's violent writing with the raped woman's body, a writing which appears two pages on in the *Essay* as yet another illustration of how 'the most vigorous speech is that in which the Sign has said everything before a single word is spoken' (Rousseau 1990: 241). But what I find suggestive about Derrida's reading of the 'magic wand' is the way in which it carries, within the terms of its description, the example it would appear to obviate – the Levite's writing with the raped woman. It is possible to discern the example of the dismembered woman's body, that is, within the 'visibility, spacing, death' that Derrida describes as the origin of the sign and the 'breaking of immediacy'. The woman 'who traces is very close to touching what is very close to being the other *itself* … One thinks the sign beginning from its limit. Now this limit – of an impossible sign, of a sign giving the signified, indeed the thing, *in person,* immediately – is necessarily closer to gesture or glance than to speech' (Derrida 1974: 234).

But what does this limit, this 'impossible sign' describe, if not that of the raped woman's mutilated body, the sign that gives the signified, 'indeed the thing, *in person,* immediately'? And does the Levite's writing with the raped woman not reduce that 'small difference' (visibility, spacing, death) in even more dramatic fashion than the example of love? Derrida's decision to focus on love, which is surely the most benign example of the language of gesture in the *Essay,* is striking. For as De Man notes (though does not discuss): 'In the *Essay on the Origin of Languages,* all examples destined to illustrate the "natural" language of man are acts of violence' (1979: 140).

All, that is, except for the example of the magic wand. In this, Derrida finds the structure of supplementarity that, he argues, governs Rousseau's entire discourse. He explains:

> The gesture, that of passion rather than that of need, considered in its purity of origin, guards us against an already alienating speech, a speech carrying in itself death and absence. That is why, when it does not precede the spoken word, it supplements it, corrects its fault and fills its lack.

> The movement of the wand is a substitute for all discourse that, at a
> greater distance, would substitute itself for it.
>
> (Derrida 1974: 235)

Gesture is an 'adjunct of speech'; speech is a supplement for gesture. We see this
structure in the *Lévite*. Prior to the Levite's speech, we have the gesture of the
dismembered body. But once everyone is assembled, speech is required as a supplement to that eloquent gesture. For if, as Derrida notes, 'gesture supposes a distance and a spacing, a milieu of visibility, it ceases being effective when the excess
of distance or mediation interrupts visibility: then speech supplements gesture'
(ibid.: 235).

Derrida considers the series of examples in the *Essay* designed to illustrate the
efficacy of the language of gesture. It is here that we find the clearest elision of
the image of the woman's dismembered body from Derrida's text. In the *Essay*, the
section on the language of gesture, and the substitution of a letter for a sign, is
followed immediately by the example of the Levite, which I will repeat in full:

> When the Levite of Ephraim wanted to avenge the death of his wife he
> did not write to the Tribes of Israel; he divided her body into twelve
> pieces which he sent to them. At this ghastly sight they rushed to arms,
> crying with one voice: *No, never has anything like this happened in Israel, from
> the day when our fathers left Egypt until this day!* And the tribe of Benjamin
> was exterminated.
>
> (Rousseau 1990: 242)

In what is more like a forcible exclusion than an elision, Derrida omits this quo-
tation: 'And after another series of Biblical and Greek examples' (1974: 259).
Immediately, he gives a statement that comes after the example concerning the
Levite in the *Essay*:

> *Thus one speaks more effectively to the eye than to the ear.* There is no one who
> does not feel the truth of Horace's judgement in this regard. Clearly the
> most eloquent speeches are those containing the most imagery; and
> sounds are never more *forceful* than when they produce the effects of
> colours.
>
> (Rousseau, cited in Derrida 1974: 239)

Why, then, does Derrida omit what he refers to only obliquely as a Biblical
'example', when he refers to every one of the neighbouring examples in the *Essay*?

To entertain this question we need to look at what happens when Derrida
is read in terms of Rousseau and his use of the woman's mutilated body as an
exemplary sign. In the *Essay*, the woman's tracing of her lover's shadow is an act
of composition: 'Love, it is said, was the inventor of drawing ... How many things
the girl who took such pleasure in tracing her Lover's shadow was telling him!'

61

(Rousseau 1990: 241). In contrast, the Levite's writing with the raped woman is an act of bodily dismemberment, 'the immediate language of division' (Starobinski 1979: 164). In Rousseau's account, this act of dismemberment is at once more than writing – 'When the Levite of Ephraim wanted to avenge the death of his wife *he did not write* to the Tribes of Israel; he divided her body into twelve pieces' – and the superlative instance of writing – 'another instance of a mute eloquence that has at all times proven effective' (Rousseau 1990: 241). It is important to retain the complexity of the oxymoronic 'mute eloquence'. Complicating any easy division between speech and writing, the raped woman is silently persuasive: the 'ghastly sight' of her divided body parts leads directly to the extermination of a tribe. In the *Essay*, Rousseau compares the Levite's dismemberment of the woman to King Saul who 'returning from the fields, in like fashion dismembered his plow oxen and used a similar sign to rouse Israel to assist the city of Jabesh' (ibid.: 242).

Usage of the raped woman as a dead letter, the dispersion and 'spacing' of her body parts across Israel, appears to at once epitomize and confound Derrida's theorization of textuality and writing. In Derrida's reading, Rousseau is seen to work within the terms of a binary opposition between a fallen and a venerated form of writing:

> On the one hand, *representative*, fallen, secondary, instituted writing, writing in the literal and strict sense, is condemned in *The Essay on the Origin of Languages*...Writing in the common sense is the dead letter, it is the carrier of death...On the other hand...writing in the metaphoric sense, natural, divine, and living writing, is venerated.
>
> (1974: 17)

The Levite's writing with the raped woman troubles any strict opposition between 'bad' and 'good' writing. She exemplifies a notion of writing in the common sense, as a 'carrier of death'. She is the 'dead letter'. But at the same time, the writing with her body is held up as an example of writing in the 'metaphoric sense', a superlative form of communication. In a way that is far more troubling than the metaphoric example of love's inscription, the writing with the raped woman 'exhausts life' (ibid.). As Bronfen notes in another context: 'The "letter killeth" and represents the body textually as well as physically making it present once more, albeit as a dead letter' (1992: 145).

What remains striking is the coincidence between Derrida's occlusion of the Levite example in favour of 'love' and Rousseau's transformation of the Levite of Ephraim into a love story. One way of understanding the curious textual deflection whereby love replaces rape in *Of Grammatology* is that it threatens to expose the sexually differentiated stakes on which Derrida's understanding of 'The Violence of the Letter' (the title to his examination of writing and violence in Claude Lévi-Strauss and Rousseau) rests. Several critics have drawn attention to Derrida's use of gendered terms like 'hymen' and 'double chiasmatic invagination of the borders' (Spivak, in Derrida 1974; Rose 1986; Whitford 1991). Speaking about the way in which 'blanks stand for the spacing of writing' in Mallarmé, Derrida writes: 'Perpetual, the rape has always already taken place and will nevertheless never have been perpetrated. For it will always have been caught in the foldings of some veil, where any and all truth comes undone' (Derrida 1981: 200). This particular quotation from *Dissemination* is but the culminating moment in a detailed discussion which draws upon 'virginity' and 'hymen' as metaphors and tropes for the theorization of textuality and writing. Spivak sees Derrida's use of these terms as a feminist gesture. She argues that his 'hymeneal fable' counters a 'phallocentric fable of meaning' (Spivak, in Derrida 1974: lxvi). And yet there is something troubling about the frequency with which sexually differentiated terms crop up in Derrida's work as tropes that, if 'not reducible to the body of the woman as such', nevertheless are 'anchored in and (take) off from the recognizable historical reference they inevitably invoke' (Rose 1989: 37). As Jacqueline Rose suggests in her gloss on the above quotation from Derrida: 'No rape because the hymen is the point where all truth is undone; but always already rape, because always truth, logos, presence, the violence of the metaphysical act' (ibid.: 36). She asks: 'Couldn't this...be seen as a grotesque recasting of the world (now Western metaphysics) under the sign of a massive violation, if not rape?' (ibid.).

The ambivalence I am identifying in Derrida – whereby the trope of rape is used at the same time that the figure of the raped woman is violently excluded from the terms of discussion – returns us to the contradictory function of feminine violation as depicted in the *Lévite*. The hyper-visibility of the raped woman's body in bits and pieces, the 'ghastly sight' that brings the assembly together, at the same time appears to induce a certain blindness in those who are called upon to 'read' the text of her body. The frantic attempts to repair the damage done to the social order appear to depend on the community's wilful blindness to its compulsive repetition of violence. Even when the community is confronted with the full implications of its violent sacrifice of its daughters, the men of the community will not admit their aggression but will instead attempt to cover it up by recasting rape as marriage.

A daughter's sacrifice

Just as he adds a beginning to the biblical story, transforming the Levite–concubine affair into a pastoral romance, so Rousseau adds an ending in which he introduces a new group of characters. In addition to the Old Man of Lebona, these include Axa, one of the virgin maidens and the daughter of the Old Man, and Elmacin, her betrothed. It is through Axa that Rousseau dramatizes the act of sacrifice that mends the social order. Having decided that the women are free to choose their fate, the Benjaminites plead with the young women to come with them without protest. Enveloped in the arms of her mother, Axa 'glances furtively at young Elmacin, to whom she is betrothed' and 'who at that moment was full of pain as rage coursed through his veins' (1222). At this point, Axa's father, the Old Man of Lebona, steps forward.

Fathers and daughters feature prominently throughout the *Lévite*, and it is through this familial tie that the 'general will' is secured.[17] The Old Man of Lebona is the final, and the most authoritative, father of the prose poem. Though he had chosen Elmacin for his daughter, he is the one who proposes the collective rape to the Benjaminites. Taking Axa's hand, the Old Man urges his daughter to accept her duty to the nation of Israel. He tells her to do her 'duty' and save him from 'shame' among his brothers. Axa mutely agrees and falls 'half-dead, into the arms of the Benjaminite' (1223). This scene of self-sacrifice shadows the earlier episode with the concubine and the Levite. The description of Axa as 'half-dead', *demi-morte*, is a repetition of the phrase used to describe the concubine when she is thrown outside to the rapists: 'They immediately surround the half-dead young girl, seize her, and carry her off without pity' (1214). Ostensibly, what makes this scene different is that Axa 'chooses' to sacrifice herself. Following *The Social Contract*, one might say that she is 'forced to be free' (Rousseau 1968: 64). Inspired by the example set by Axa, all the young women proceed to 'imitate her sacrifice', renounce their first loves, and surrender themselves to the Benjaminites. At this touching sight, a cry of joy rises from the people. The story ends.

Conclusion

The importance of the *Lévite* is that it shows the process by which rape is turned into marriage. Generally, as Pateman argues, 'in the stories of the classic contract theorists the sexual contract is very hard to discern because it is *displaced onto the marriage contract*' (1988: 110). In her discussion of legal debates surrounding the issue of consent, Frances Ferguson has noted how ancient law dealt with the problem of adjudicating rape cases. Rather than get caught up in the tricky business of deciding who to believe (did the man know the woman did not consent to intercourse? Did the woman make her resistance to the act clear enough?), such law simply insisted that the 'parties make the outrage into a way of life' (1987: 92). In this way, the 'legal recompense for rape' was marriage. As Ferguson puts it, 'marriage recasts rape, so that marriage is a misunderstanding corrected or rape rightly understood' (ibid.).

The raped woman, the one who is required to consent to marriage in order to 'recast rape', is the scapegoat by which the civic order reconstitutes itself in the *Lévite*.[19] The boundaries of the social body are once again secure: 'The city's body *proper* thus reconstitutes its unity, closes around the security of its inner courts' (Derrida 1981: 133). For our purposes, what is important is the understanding of the relation between rape and the civic body that the *Lévite* expresses. The new-found civic order, by which brothers agree to share the women among themselves, and where fathers agree to sacrifice their daughters for the greater good, constructs an ideal of the masculine citizen body, an ideal underpinned by sexual aggression. Just as the concubine doubles or ghosts the Levite, the man whose violability ensures her own violation, so the civic order, to protect itself against external (and internal) violation, calls upon the violable feminine body to 'ghost' or shadow the body politic. As Wendy Brown observes: 'Rousseau is quite explicit about a matter that his liberal kinsmen handle more indirectly: it takes two (female and male) to make one (citizen)' (1995: 161). To define the male citizen, it requires that a (raped) woman sacrifice herself, and put her body in place of his.

Not only does the *Lévite* fill in certain silences of Rousseau's pronouncements on sexual difference and the origins of the social contract, but it helps us to historicize the relation between rape and civic space. Rape in the *Lévite* occurs in public space; the rape of the concubine takes place outside of the host's house, her body marks the borderline between 'hospitality and hostility' (Trible 1984: 73). With the collective rape of the virgin daughters at Silo, rape once again occurs outside, in the open space of the festival. One of Rousseau's main concerns in his writing on public life is the demarcation between the sexually differentiated spheres of the private and the public.[18] When woman attempts to usurp the public privileges of man, she is reversing the order of things. As he writes in *Lettre d'Alembert*:

> No longer wishing to tolerate separation, unable to make themselves into men, the women make us into women. This disadvantageous result which degrades man is very important everywhere; but it is especially so in states like ours, whose interest it is to prevent it. Whether a monarch governs men or women ought to be rather indifferent to him, provided that he be obeyed; but in a republic, men are needed.
>
> (Rousseau 1960: 100–101)

With the *Lévite* we see this division between the private and public spheres in the process of being instituted. The rape of women in civic space is used to shore up an image of the invulnerability of the masculine social body – the 'body tightly enclosed within boundaries' as discussed by Pateman (1988: 96). But what I hope to have demonstrated is that this attempt to uphold the civic bond is far from assured. For while the *Lévite* may tell the story of the sexual contract, the 'vehicle through which men transform their ... right over women into the security of civil patriarchal right' (Pateman 1988: 6), it also reveals, with equal clarity, the failure and anxiety that underpin the apparent security of this order. In the process it lays bare what Moira Gatens describes as 'the itinerary of desire that wills or desires that political origins are to be found in an originary penetrative sexual violence' (1996: 87–88). In its uneasy series of repetitions and substitutions, the *Lévite* reveals the anxious nature of the attempt to define and construct the terms of the socio-sexual contract.

Part II

THE SPECTACLE OF RAPE

3

'RAPE IS NOT A SPECTATOR SPORT'

The New Bedford 'Big Dan's' gang rape

The biblical story of rape and dismemberment, as recounted in the previous chapter, bears critical significance to a reading of contemporary rape cases. As Phyllis Trible notes in her reading of the Levite story:

> Violence and vengeance are not just characteristics of a distant, pre-Christian past; they infect the community of the elect to this day. Woman as object is still captured, betrayed, raped, tortured, murdered, dismembered, and scattered. To take to heart this ancient story, then, is to confess to its present reality.
>
> (1984: 87)

Trible illustrates her point by directing the reader to the 1983 New Bedford rape, in which a young woman was gang raped on a pool table in a Massachusetts bar while a group of men watched and cheered, a case I will discuss in close detail in this chapter.

The story of the bar room gang rape is another story of how a community organizes itself around an image of the raped woman's body. As in the *Lévite*, the representation of the city or the body politic is derived from the trope of violated femininity. And, as in the *Lévite*, the rape victim is once more put into the position of the scapegoat, to tragic consequence. That the narrative scenario of rape offered in the *Lévite* is discernible in this contemporary event indicates its force as a fantasy structure in which a variety of cultural anxieties are laid out.

Two years after the four men who gang raped her on a pool table in Big Dan's tavern were sentenced for aggravated rape, the New Bedford rape victim, aged 25, was killed in a car accident in Florida where she had fled after the trial.[1] A close friend told how the traumatic experience of the trial had altered her life: 'She was so scared they would come and kill her, she thought they were following her. When she drove she didn't just look at the rear-view mirror, she stared at it' (cited in Benedict 1992: 141). 'They' were members of the woman's community who blamed her for the adverse publicity of the rape trial. One newspaper editor at the time recalls the woman's treatment by certain individuals in the community: 'People would go to her house...They would throw things at the house and damage it. She became a double–triple victim…There was a real bloodletting in this community. It was the closest I've come to seeing mob hysteria' (ibid: 134).

The woman's fate realized the worst fears of feminists. As a female judge at the time of the trial noted: 'This woman is being subjected to vivisection. She is just being torn apart' (cited in Henry 1984: 64). This idea of the rape trial as a dismemberment of the woman's body returns us to the uneasy liminality of the raped woman as the figure caught 'in-between-two-deaths' (Žižek 1989: 131). As we have seen in the *Lévite*, the woman is 'already dead' from the moment she is pushed outside to a group of rapists. With the New Bedford rape, the woman's literal death is a realization of the civic death that she had already undergone during the rape trial.

In her study of famous sex crime cases of the 1980s, *Virgin or Vamp: How the Press Covers Sex Crimes*, Helen Benedict writes that the victim of the New Bedford gang rape 'should go down in history as one of the worst-treated rape victims of the decade' (1992: 142).[2] For a casual reader of the case this might seem a curious statement to make. One of the first cases to take feminism's arguments about rape on board, the Big Dan's verdicts 'were hailed by the press as a triumph for feminists and proof that "a woman doesn't have to be a saint to get raped"' (ibid.: 141–142). The rapists were convicted and the jury's verdict demonstrated a resolute refusal to entertain the defence's strategy of discrediting the victim for her past sexual history or conduct (Rosen 1985: 207–208).

This chapter tells a different story: about how a woman was rejected by her community and forced into exile. The rape in New Bedford reveals the utter violence of civic identification as it occurs over the violated woman. Picking up on the issue of the relationship between rape and the body politic as discussed in the previous chapter, I want to begin by showing how, in the print coverage of the crime, the story of the woman's gang rape becomes transformed into the story of the violation of a city. Turning to a consideration of the televised trial a year later, I will argue that the spectacle of the rape trial provided another opportunity for collective identification via the witnessing of the woman's 'second rape'. If, as Shoshana Felman has remarked, we live in an 'age of testimony, in which witnessing itself has undergone a major trauma' (1991: 91), I want to argue that the New Bedford rape and subsequent rape trial bring this crisis of witnessing into stark relief.[3]

A story without heroes

In March 1983 reports of a gang rape that took place in a bar room in New Bedford, Massachusetts, appeared in the national media. The following *New York Times* report provides an early account of the crime:

> A 21-year-old woman, recent to the neighbourhood, stopped at Big Dan's tavern for some cigarettes and a drink about 9 P.M. Sunday, March 6. She emerged sometime after midnight, bruised, half naked and screaming for help. Her clothes had been torn from her, she told the police officers who were called by a motorist who had stopped to help her. She said she had

been hoisted to the bar's pool table, tormented and raped beyond count by a group of men who held her there for more than two hours while the rest of the men in the bar stood watching, sometimes taunting her, and cheering. When the police fetched her clothing and took her back inside, two of the men she identified as her assaulters were still there. Big Dan's, which is one large room, had apparently been open for business the whole time. No one had called the police. One unidentified witness was quoted as saying in *The New Bedford Standard-Times*, 'Why should I care?'

(Clendinen 17 March 1983)

It was the cruel indifference of the men who stood watching the rape that attracted national attention and outrage. 'Bar Crowd Cheers as Woman is Raped', 'The Tavern Rape: Cheers and No Help', 'They were cheering like it was a baseball game'. These were among the sensational headlines in early media coverage of the case. Across the nation, news reports and editorials denounced the rape and condemned the male spectators who functioned as 'cheerleaders' to the assault (Starr 12 March 1983). One local resident was quoted as saying: 'I like spectator sports, basketball, football, hockey. But that, that's sick. They should take every one of those guys who were there cheering and fine them $1,000 apiece and put that money in the abused women's program' (Clendinen 17 March 1983).

The title to this chapter, 'Rape is Not a Spectator Sport', is taken from one of the placards carried by protesters during a march that occurred eight days after the gang rape. Organized by local women's groups, an estimated 4,500 men and women marched outside New Bedford city hall, chanting 'No more rape' and 'Rape is hate'. The protest received extensive national coverage and was a feminist milestone. As Benedict suggests, 'It was a reminder to the public that rape had become a politicized crime, that awareness of rape was widespread, and that coalitions had been formed to fight victim-blaming myths' (1992: 100).

Initially, the American public grappled with the question asked by police officer Carol Sacramento: 'How did this happen' (cited in Bumiller 1990: 138)? For some, what was most disturbing about the activity of the spectators was it appeared to be without motive:

> There's no excuse ... not passion, not booze, not an overwhelming desire to brutalize another ... for the gang rape. But there's even less than that for the dozen or so drinkers who watched – and did nothing – while, police say, a woman ... was repeatedly assaulted.
>
> (*Boston Herald* 10 March 1983)

From the start, the category of the 'witness' was in immediate crisis. Journalists expressed bewilderment regarding the men's failure to witness the crime. As one columnist concluded: 'We are talking ... about a deadness, about an inability to feel horror at something and therefore an absolute inability to react to stop it' (*Boston Herald* 26 March 1983).

71

While there was intense speculation as to why the men failed to help the woman, one thing at least seemed certain: all the men present that night at Big Dan's tavern were guilty of a crime. As the victim would later testify: 'I believe everyone that was in there was guilty' (Starr 12 March 1983). But of what kind of crime the men were guilty, and whether they would – or could – be held legally culpable, was another question altogether. The issue of whether the witnesses could be 'brought to justice' was widely debated on television programs and news columns (Blakely 1983: 52). As a *Newsweek* article, 'The Duties of a Bystander', noted:

> Police say that no one came to the victim's aid, not even the man who brushed off her clutching arms as he edged past the attackers. Didn't they at least owe her a phone call to the police? Ethically, most people would say yes. But legally, the answer is no.
>
> (Press 1983: 79)

As the article went on to explain: 'Where strangers are involved, the criminal law does not recognize sins of omission. Witnesses are not required to report crimes, and will not be punished for their silence' (ibid.). In other words, it is no crime to be a spectator, forcing the question of what it means to be a witness. Despite pressure to bring charges against those present in the bar, District Attorney Pina was quoted as saying: 'Mere presence during a crime is not enough to make someone an accessory. You must have participated' (ibid.).

But was looking at a spectacle of violence not a form of participation? What made the rape so disturbing was precisely the way in which it called into question the difference between those who raped and those who watched and cheered. As a *Boston Globe* editorial asked:

> Are the patrons of Big Dan's much different from the rest of us? Probably not. That's the scariest part of this story ... We all like to think we are different, of course. We must believe that we would stand alone in protest ... Still, this grim tale reminds us that failure is always a possibility, and of just how close we are to those who raped and those who watched and cheered.
>
> (cited in Benedict 1992: 94)

Reports of a bar full of men being 'whipped into a lurid, cheering frenzy', however sensational, raised the question of what else we may be doing when we are said to be 'just looking' (ibid.: 93). The men's behaviour gave the lie to a notion of the 'innocent bystander' as one who stands near the scene of violence as an onlooker but who takes no part in the criminal action. In so far as the act of communal spectatorship went beyond 'looking', it disrupted a traditional notion of voyeurism as a surreptitious and guilty looking at a private sexual act or object that should not be seen. As report after report was to emphasize, the incident happened in a public location; rape, a crime historically defined as 'in its nature commonly secret' (Ferguson 1987: 91), was opened onto its collective dimensions as a public event in which the bystanders 'spectated' rather than 'witnessed', the assault. Not only did the men watch the assault, they either didn't know or care that what they were spectating was a crime. When the victim returned to the tavern with the police to identify her assailants, some of the men were still drinking as if nothing had happened. Indeed, the men who were charged for the rape insisted that no rape occurred that night. During the trial, defence attorneys would argue that the victim willingly had sex with the defendants. As one of the accused was quoted as saying: 'At first I thought it was just a free show' (cited in Benedict 1992: 103). This statement, spoken by one of the men in the bar, raises the disturbing possibility that in viewing the rape to which they became spectators, the men were misinterpreting what they saw. What was most troubling about the Big Dan's gang rape, I submit, was the suggestion that the male spectators may have mistaken rape for 'spectacle'. In his summation to the jury, the District Attorney drew attention to the utter indifference of the so-called witnesses to the crime, declaring that 'this was a story without heroes' ('The Crime' 5 March 1984).

In the weeks following the crime, an anxiety about the uncertain distinction between those who raped and those who watched became displaced onto a question about the ethnic identity of the men involved. While early reports left the ethnic identity of the men unmarked, as swarms of newspaper reporters and television crews arrived to report on the crime, stories began to focus on the 'working-class Portuguese community' where the rape took place (Rangel 4 March 1984). As one *New York Times* article reported:

> The young mother of two entered Big Dan's – a seedy bar in the city's predominantly Portuguese North End – to buy cigarettes. Never having been there before, she was apparently unaware of its reputation in the neighbourhood for gambling and brawling.
>
> ('The Tavern Rape' 1983: 25)

What is most striking about this passage, and others like it, is the suggestion that the woman was unfamiliar with the 'neighbourhood'. The fact the woman was born and raised in New Bedford and was herself of Portuguese descent, is tellingly passed over in the media reports of the crime. The woman is described simply as the 'young woman' or the 'young mother of two children'. By contrast, the accused, who initially had only been identified by name, were soon being described as Portuguese immigrants from the Azores.[4]

With the identification of the ethnic identity of those involved, Portuguese-Americans were made to carry the burden of a failed witnessing that earlier reporting suggested was a general social concern. In an opinion piece published in *The National Review*, one columnist argued that the case represented a 'clash between local norms and the wider legal and civic culture' ('Big Dan's' 1984: 20). As he explained, 'in the local Portuguese neighbourhoods, which are highly "traditional", it is the woman *victim* who is widely regarded as guilty' (ibid.). Not only did such a statement ignore the (Anglo-American) defence team's own attempt to paint a picture of the raped woman as 'guilty' for her assault, but it attributed a 'blame the victim' mentality – a mentality endemic to the culture at large – solely to the Portuguese-American community. As John Fiske has noted, 'putting...deep racial–sexual anxieties into the mouths of the criminal or the discredited...serves white America well, for it allows it simultaneously to speak them and disavow them' (1994: xix). The Portuguese-Americans of New Bedford were constructed as 'Other' to white Anglo-America. What was at stake was the issue of national and civic identity.

Media reports told of a 'widespread outpouring of anti-Portuguese feeling, including calls to a local radio station demanding that all Portuguese be sent back to Europe' (Butterfield 5 February 1984). *CBS News* aired the following commentary from a local New Bedford station: 'They contribute nothing to this country. They don't understand our ways, nor do they want to understand that this country is not like Portugal' (cited in Cuklanz 1996: 71). Other callers similarly stressed the 'lawlessness' of the Portuguese: 'They don't try to learn the law of the land. They don't try to become involved in a community' (ibid.). This reference to the 'law of the land' is telling, particularly since it had become common knowledge that the male spectators – those who so outraged the American public – could not be held accountable by the American legal system. 'It's a black-letter rule, as the lawyers say, that people have no duty to rescue strangers ... Strangers need not even call 911', *Newsweek* reported (Press 1983: 79). The 'law of the land', in other words, does nothing to censure those who 'just look'.

In the media accounts of the rape, it was implied that Anglo-America was the guardian of a moral and social code of justice and civic duty. Big Dan's tavern was described as a site of lawlessness and Portuguese-Americans were described as violent drunks, the inhabitants of a locale on the outskirts of society. Big Dan's was a 'loose place' that drew a 'rough crowd ... There was late drinking on the street, and men and women pulling at each other's clothing, and "big fights"' (Clendinen 16 March 1983). The close relationship between citizenship, nationality and rape was made explicit in the cited comments from certain members of the Portuguese community in New Bedford. 'I believe in women's liberation, but what I'm doing is defending the right of an immigrant to live in this country without being judged guilty', declared one woman (Butterfield 5 February 1984). Newspapers reported on the outraged reactions of Portuguese residents to the publicity surrounding the rape trial. 'We've been badly harmed by this whole thing. It tore our community apart,' one resident said (Rangel 4 March 1984). Another report concluded: 'Portuguese immigrants are worried that the gains they have made, particularly over the past decade, have been obscured or negated by the reported rape of a young mother of two children in a bar' (Rangel 16 March 1984).

Since it was the accused men who were routinely identified as 'the Portuguese', the community began to identify their own alleged victimization with the situation of the defendants. Aldo Melo, spokeswoman for the Committee for Justice, a group formed to monitor the trial for ethnic prejudice, told the *New York Times* that 'she and others were afraid the (women) coalition's tactics and the public outcry over the incident had resulted in a "lynch-mob" attitude toward the Portuguese population' (Rangel 8 March 1984). This reference to a 'lynch-mob attitude' put the controversy in the context of 'the major ethnic divide presented by Western society, "black" and "white"' (Dyer 1988: 45). Within the context of American race relations, the lynching of black men wrongly accused of raping white women is a powerful symbol of racial persecution. By drawing upon the lynching metaphor, the Committee for Justice was implicitly invoking historical cases of lynching that have wide cultural currency in America as 'hallmarks of racial injustice', among them the Emmett Till and the Scottsboro Nine cases (Crenshaw 1993: 417). By casting the Portuguese community of New Bedford in the role of the unjustly accused black man, the Committee for Justice was endorsing the defence's claim that a rape did not occur that night in Big Dan's tavern. It was also openly declaring its hostility towards the raped woman who, despite her identity as a Portuguese woman, was implicitly cast in the role of the lying (white) woman.[5]

In lieu of a narrative about the raped woman as a Portuguese woman, we are provided with stories of Portuguese women defending and justifying the right of Portuguese men to rape.[6] In the media representation of the Big Dan's gang rape, it was the Portuguese women who were most often quoted offering their support for the defendants. 'I don't believe her story one bit, and I don't feel sorry for her either', said one woman. Another said: 'The fact is a decent woman would not go into any bar to buy cigarettes. Or if she did go into a bar to buy cigarettes, she would go right out' (Minsky 1 March 1984).[7] In the media reports the Portuguese women are, in effect, represented as the 'cheering squad' for the rapists.

Although lynching may have been the privileged metaphor in the rhetoric surrounding the Portuguese community's struggle for 'justice', it was an image of rape that was implicitly employed to demonstrate their persecution. Remarkably, as sociologist Lynn Chancer suggests, 'the Portuguese community began to feel that it, not the woman, had been raped, and as if the woman, not the Portuguese, were the rapist' (1987: 248–249). As the media turned its attention to the pain and anguish of the city of New Bedford, the rape was re-cast as a metaphor for the violation of civic space. As Susan Jeffords has observed, as rape becomes metaphorized to 'stand for a threat to the community at large', there is little room for the discussion of the actual violation of women (1991: 212). Indeed, the subject of the media accounts was no longer the rape or the raped woman, but the city of New Bedford itself.

New Bedford's glory days had long since passed. John Bullard, a leader of the restoration of New Bedford's waterfront, said:

> This city has had hard times since the textile strike of 1928. It's been economically depressed for two generations. Expectations have been lowered. People have become sincerely negative about themselves, about this city. It [the rape] hurts us more than it would a lot of other cities. It's one more

nail. It's, "Oh, my God, we really are a terrible place". Then we just have to try that much harder to get back up to zero.

(Clendinen 16 March 1983)

Reporters provided detailed descriptions of New Bedford, virtually personifying the city as a principal player in the drama. One of the first national stories to go into detail about the city of New Bedford, 'Barroom Rape Shames Town of Proud Heritage', began:

> While the story will remain inexplicable at least until the four men who have been charged go to trial, it has caused great pain in a city that has been economically and psychologically depressed for two generations. The search for an explanation has stirred speculation about the character of the woman, the character of the bar and the character of the Portuguese community.
>
> (Clendinen 16 March 1983)

What is most remarkable about this passage is the way the pain of the raped woman is transmuted into the pain of a city. In headlines such as 'A City and Its Agony', 'The Crime That Tarnished a Town', 'City Agonises over "Why?" in Pool Table Gang Rape', the raped woman's body is conflated into the 'body' of the city. As with the *Lévite* in the previous chapter, there is a definite resonance between the imaging of the violability of the female body and the violability of the body politic. An article written at the height of the trial, 'Portuguese Immigrants Fear Rape Case May Set Back Gains', provides a list of the civic 'accomplishments of the immigrants from Portugal and the Azores', and recounts the community's worries that these achievements will now be overlooked because of the rape trial: 'This is a solid working-class town that's made progress in education and the economy' (Rangel 16 March 1984).

On 17 March 1984, one year after the rape, four of the defendants were found guilty of aggravated rape. The verdicts caused widespread outrage in the Portuguese community. One local was quoted as saying: 'Why don't they bring that girl out in handcuffs! Get her too!' (cited in Benedict 1992: 130). However, the two men charged with 'joint enterprise' were acquitted. The *Boston Herald* reported:

> A hero's welcome greeted Jose and Virgilio Medeiros as the two vindicated Big Dan's defendants bounded out of a Fall River courthouse as free men ... Outside, cheers and applause erupted from the crowd as the innocent men ran to a waiting car with scores of reporters and cameramen behind them.
>
> ('Tears' 23 March 1984)

76

Suddenly, and disturbingly, the Big Dan's case became a story with heroes. Shortly after the conviction of the remaining defendants, a reported 3,000 Portuguese residents participated in a candlelight vigil and march. In stark contrast to the protest by feminist groups one year earlier, this march was in support of the rapists; people carried signs proclaiming, 'Where is Justice?', 'Was She Willing?', 'Remember Justice Crucified, March 17, 1984'. One resident was quoted as saying: 'I don't care if these people were guilty or innocent, what hurts is what this case has done to my people' (Beck 1984: 39). New Bedford residents complained bitterly about the ethnic prejudice that surfaced during the case but the most hostility was reserved for the raped woman who herself was seen to bring the harm onto New Bedford (Chancer 1987: 252–253).

In so far as it played upon underlying public anxieties regarding the relationship between class, ethnicity and sexuality, the media representation of the rape set a paradigm for highly publicized cases in its wake. As Valerie Smith among others has noted, the contemporary American rape case operates as a 'site where ideologies of racial and gender difference come into tension with and interrogate each other' (1990: 273). The Big Dan's gang rape was the first in a series of media spectacles involving rape that gripped the attention of the American public throughout the 1980s into the early 1990s. These include: the 1986 sex-related killing of Jennifer Levin by Robert Chambers in New York; the 1988 Tawana Brawley case in New York; the use of the Willie Horton case in the 1988 George Bush presidential campaign; the 1989 gang rape and beating of the Central Park Jogger in New York; and the 1991 William Kennedy Smith and 1992 Mike Tyson 'celebrity' rape trials.

Feminist commentators from a wide number of disciplines have discussed the importance of the Big Dan's rape case as a crime that 'evoked some profound and unarticulated social questions about the conflicting claims of class, ethnicity, and gender in our society' (Rosen 1985: 207).[8] But a consideration of its representational significance is missing from the feminist discussion of the case to date. For although rape cases and trials have long been sensationalist fodder in America, the incident in New Bedford has a unique status in the representational history of sexual violence. Most obviously, of course, there is the fact that it is the only American rape case ever to become the subject of a major Hollywood movie. Five years after the gang rape, the image of a raped woman running out of a bar screaming for help was immortalized in *The Accused*. In the film's re-enactment of the event, discussed in the next chapter, a young woman (played by Jodie Foster) is gang raped on a pinball machine while a bar full of men cheer the rapists on. But there is a less well-known way in which the rape in New Bedford makes representational history: it is the first criminal trial ever to be nationally televised by CNN – a fact that has never, to my knowledge, been considered in any detail.[9] Recent accounts of the history of CNN neglect to mention the Big Dan's gang rape, even though the live coverage of the trial in 1984 was seen to 'redefine' the face of journalism (Henry 1984: 64).[10] As William Henry, reporting on the trial for *Newsweek* proclaimed, such a public airing of the private details of a rape trial made instant media history:

> The words that came into millions of American households last week told a story as tawdry as any soap opera, in language sometimes more explicit than any prime-time series... But the speech was testimony, not dialogue, and the courtroom melodrama could claim the legitimacy of a news story.
>
> (ibid.)

However, instead of a discussion of this 'courtroom melodrama', commentators refer to 1984 as the year when CNN first began to earn 'widespread recognition and praise for its around the clock coverage of the Democratic and Republican conventions' (Gomery 1997: 271). Interestingly enough, it seems as if CNN has itself perpetuated the critical neglect of the rape trial: as sociologist Lisa Cuklanz has discovered, 'taped copies of CNN coverage are "unavailable" from CNN because the trial was so long ago' (1996: 10).[11]

But despite, or perhaps because, of this curious elision of the trial from recent accounts of the history of CNN, it seems necessary to ask: what does it mean that the first nationally televised trial in American history is a rape trial? What is the relationship between the rise of CNN and rape? CNN is renowned for its so-called 'real time' coverage (Dahlgren 1995: 56). CNN's instantaneous, 24-hour coverage of news events reached its pinnacle with the Gulf War in 1991, during which it reported 'everything that the military permitted – from the first bombing of Baghdad to the tank blitz that ended the conflict' (Gomery 1997: 271). CNN, and the televisual aesthetic of 'live and instantaneous coverage' it is seen to embody, purports to provide a form of representation that depicts real life as it occurs. Although such an aesthetic may be epitomized by CNN, it is by no means exclusive to it. The wildly popular 'true-life' genre of television has proliferated extensively in the past two decades, 'changing the established forms of journalism' (Bondebjerg 1996: 28). Among the most spectacular of these recent 'true-life' media events are the representations of the Gulf War, the Anita Hill/Clarence Thomas hearings, the Rodney King beating, and more recently, the OJ Simpson trial.

But in 1984 Courtroom Television, a cable network broadcasting trials, did not yet exist, and the levels of publicity accorded the Big Dan's rape case were unprecedented. What I want to suggest is that it is possible to read the Big Dan's rape trial as the inaugural moment for the establishment of a new representational mode.[12] 'Reality programming' and 'television verité' are the names ascribed to this new genre of televisual viewing, which proclaims to show the American public hitherto private 'realities' (Bondebjerg 1996: 33). In so far as it was the first trial of its kind to be televised, the Big Dan's rape trial inevitably raised questions regarding the role that such 'reality programming' plays in American culture. What happens when 'real-life human tragedy' is viewed as fictional entertainment? Are the televisual viewers of reality TV concerned 'witnesses' or voyeuristic 'spectators'?

To this list of questions we can add another: what is the relationship between the crisis of witnessing at Big Dan's tavern and the spectatorship of the televised rape trial? I want to consider how a case that initiated widespread anxiety about the relationship between looking and raping is transformed into a televised trial, which, in turn, raised serious questions about the act of spectatorship. There is something suggestive about the way debates surrounding the ethics of televising the trial (debates that, as we will see in the next chapter, anticipate and resemble those surrounding the ethics of filming rape in *The Accused*), repeat and play upon the crisis of spectatorship that marked the trauma in the first place.

Looking and raping

Does viewing pornography lead men to rape?[13] For anti-pornography feminists the answer has been a resounding 'yes'. Best captured by Robin Morgan's slogan, 'Pornography is the theory, rape is the practice', the claim that there is a causal link between representations of rape and the act of rape is one of the most highly disputed issues within the feminist debate on representation and sexuality.[14] Feminist activist and writer Andrea Dworkin and civil rights lawyer Catharine MacKinnon are the most famous proponents of the argument that pornography causes men to commit rape. In 1983 they formulated a Minneapolis city ordinance that would allow 'those who are represented by pornography as victims, to challenge those who profit financially from such representations' (*Pornography* 1988: 3). Though in the end it was vetoed, the ordinance publicized MacKinnon's and Dworkin's stance on pornography.[15] The publication of the ordinance by Everywoman, *Pornography and Sexual Violence: Evidence of the Links* (1988), characterizes pornography as a 'blueprint of the state of women's conditions in society'; 'a diagram with instructions on how to degrade a woman'; the 'permission and direction and rehearsal for sexual violence' (ibid.: 99, 107).

One of the examples drawn on here as 'evidence of the links' is the New Bedford rape case. As Barbara Chester, director of a rape and sexual assault centre, is quoted as saying in the official transcript of the hearings:

> Many of us reacted with shock and horror to the gang rape of a woman on a pool table in a bar in New Bedford in March of 1983, while bystanders cheered and applauded. Yet in the January issue of *Hustler* a layout appeared of this exact scenario, a woman spread-eagled on a pool table being gang raped. I wonder if any of the participants in New Bedford two months later were readers of *Hustler*.
>
> (ibid.: 107)

The possibility that there could be a causal link between a photograph and a crime has troubled critics of the anti-pornography movement. For against the view that representations lead directly to actions, a number of feminists have argued that it is difficult, and indeed futile, to attempt to prove a causal connection between watching (or reading) pornography and committing acts of violence against women. Laura Kipnis argues that pornography's violations are 'symbolic', taking issue with any account that would treat 'images of staged sex and violence as equivalent to real sex and violence' (1992: 388). Particularly absurd, according to Kipnis, is the suggestion that there is 'a direct line from sexual imagery to rape – as if merely looking at images of sex magically brainwashes any man into becoming a robotic sexual plunderer' (1996: 147, 157).

While such arguments have undoubtedly played an important role in curbing some of the excesses of the anti-pornography position (the dubious use of statistics, the reliance on crude behavioural notions), I am nevertheless concerned with the way the 'anti-censorship' faction ultimately seems to discount the possibility of a connection between looking and raping. For although it is necessary to question any account that would assert a direct causal line between images and acts, it seems that an important question about the relationship between acts of rape and representations of rape has gone missing.

Consider Sara Diamond's critique of the anti-porn position in 'Pornography: Image and Reality'.[16] Against behaviourist psychology, 'according to which the human male runs the treadmill of sexual violence for gratification in the same way a caged rat will run for cheese', Diamond argues that 'there is no direct relationship between what an image shows and what its viewer acts out' (1985: 47). 'In fact one of the attractions of pornography is that it shows illicit acts that are safer, both legally and emotionally, when kept in the realm of fantasy' (ibid.: 48). Where Diamond accuses anti-pornography feminists of collapsing the boundary between fantasy and reality, she wants to re-establish a distinction between those realms. While not going so far as to view pornography as a 'healthy release for men', she nevertheless argues that 'there is a wide gulf between the fantasy, no matter how grotesque, and the reality' (ibid.).[17]

Critics have begun to question a defence of pornography that rests on a distinction between the symbolic and the 'real', the representational and the actual. As Mark Seltzer argues in *Serial Killers*:

> There is something magical in the understanding of the imagined or symbolic simply as the opposite of "real" sex. (As if there were not always a symbolic and fantasmatic component in "real" sex.) And there is something incoherent in the simple antinomy of "merely looking" at images and robotic or automatistic acts of sexual violence. (Is looking merely the opposite of doing? Is there not always an element of the mechanical or automatistic in "real" sex?)
>
> (1998: 188)

In other words: is there ever really such a clear-cut distinction between a fantasy and an act, a representation and an event? In relation to his account of serial killing, Seltzer concludes by noting that:

> Neither generalized anti- or generalized fan accounts of pornographic sexual violence will do, on two fundamental counts. The simple equation of images of violence and acts of violence must of course be resisted: the thought or representation of murder is of course not equivalent to the act

of murder. *But the thought or representation of murder is by no means separate or apart from the act of murder: it is part of it.*

(ibid.: 188, my italics)

This point can also be argued in relation to rape. Representations of rape are by no means separate or apart from the act of rape: they are part of it. As Seltzer argues, it is necessary to understand 'fantasy or intention not as the *cause* of an act but as *part of* an act' (ibid.: 187). The debate over the connections between pornography and rape maintains the distinction between reality and representation, even as it worries about their breakdown. Rather than attempting to prove or refute a view of representation as the cause of 'real rape', we need to think about how representation is a part of rape. For to acknowledge that there is not a simple causal relation between watching a representation of rape and committing one, is not to say that there is not any relation at all. This point is implicitly acknowledged by those feminists who argue there is 'no direct relationship between what an image shows and what its viewer acts out' (Diamond 1985: 47). To say there is 'no direct relationship' presumably allows for the idea that there is an indirect connection.

Rape as representation

If you go past the horror show at the beginning, there are a number of valuable and resonating criticisms of MacKinnon's obsession with pornography and her willingness to outlaw expression so broadly defined by her that it could well include sections of the Old Testament (Chapter 19 of the *Book of Judges*, for example).

(Nat Hentoff)[18]

The driving motivation behind MacKinnon's career as a lawyer, an anti-pornography campaigner, and as an intellectual, is the attempt to prove that pornography hurts women.[19] At the heart of her book *Only Words* is the argument that pornography is an act. Drawing on speech–act theory, MacKinnon argues that pornography is performative because it not only represents or reflects sexual inequality but also constitutes it: 'Social inequality is substantially created and enforced – that is, *done* – through words and images' (1994: 9).[20]

Critics of *Only Words* allege that MacKinnon confuses the realms of reality and representation.[21] By way of example, they direct readers to statements like the following: 'In terms of what the men are doing sexually, an audience watching a real gang rape in a movie is no different from an audience watching a gang rape that is re-enacting a gang rape from a movie, or an audience watching any real gang rape' (MacKinnon 1994: 20). This statement has been taken up as an outrageous example of the wilful denial of the realm of representation. As Parveen Adams and Mark Cousins have argued in their commentary on the above quotation: 'A function of sadism is to deny difference. In this example of gang rape, there are obviously socially and legally recognised differences between an audience at a film, witnesses at a crime, and rapists' (1995: 101).

On one level, this criticism of MacKinnon is valid. I wonder, though, whether such a statement does not gloss over the extent to which it is precisely the 'obvious' nature of the differences between 'an audience at a film, witnesses at a crime, and rapists', that is increasingly being called into question in public debates on violence and representation. MacKinnon struggles to answer the question posed in the media discussion of the Big Dan's rape case, 'how great a distance it is from the reader to the voyeur to the cheering squad' (cited in Benedict 1992: 109). In the following passage MacKinnon considers the argument that pornography is a 'representation':

> The most elite denial of the harm is the one that holds that pornography is 'representation', when a representation is a nonreality. Actual rape arranges reality; ritual torture frames and presents it. Does that make them 'representations', and so not rape and torture? Is a rape a representation of a rape if someone is watching it? When is the rapist *not* watching it? Taking photographs is part of the ritual of some abusive sex...So is watching while doing it and watching the pictures later. The photos are trophies; looking at photos is fetishism.
>
> (1994:19)

This passage returns us to the proposition that representations of rape are by no means separate from the act of rape – they are part of it. As MacKinnon puts it: 'Representation *is* reality' and 'pornography is no less an act than the rape and torture it represents' (ibid.: 20). This is a criticism of pornography and the violence of representation that cannot simply be written off as a reductive 'causal' argument. In her important essay, 'Pornography: The Theory' Frances Ferguson argues that the 'fundamental insight' of MacKinnon's argument 'is the claim that pornography is only significant insofar as it involves acts – as it puts representations to use' (1995: 673). 'Far from being naive about representation or unable to tell the difference between an act and the representation of that act the strength of MacKinnon's position is precisely its focus on the representation as act...MacKinnon is concerned with what action a representation might be used to perform' (ibid.: 682). Moreover, Ferguson argues, 'a simplistic claim that pornography directly causes readily predictable instances of extreme violence' is not central to that position (ibid.: 673). By focusing on the coerced performance of women in pornography, MacKinnon forces us to confront the possibility that 'the production of a representation of a rape could sometimes itself be a rape' (ibid.: 682). In doing so, Ferguson argues, she puts her finger on the paradox of pornography:

> The camera continually captures actions but, paradoxically, nullifies the possibility of their being witnessed by the very act of displaying them as representations. Acts are treated as fictitious representations merely

because of their being watched by a camera and, subsequently, by an audience.

(ibid.: 685)

This idea of representation as nullifying the possibility of a real action being 'witnessed' is crucial to MacKinnon's theorization of pornography. In the dramatic opening pages of *Only Words* MacKinnon provides an origin story of women's subordination:

Imagine that for hundreds of years your most formative traumas, your daily suffering and pain, the abuse you live through, the terror you live with, are unspeakable – not the basis of literature. You grow up with your father holding you down and covering your mouth so another man can make a horrible searing pain between your legs...

The camera is invented and pictures are made of you while these things are being done... You always know that the pictures are out there somewhere, sold or traded or shown around or just kept in a drawer. In them, what was done to you is immortal.

(1994: 3)

This sexually explicit passage has been read as a prime example of how MacKinnon 'practises what she preaches against' (Morgenstern 1997: 50). Significantly though, it sets out what I see as one of the most interesting aspects of MacKinnon's work: her persistent questioning of how technologies of vision not only replay and repeat woman's original trauma, but produce a new dimension of pain: 'What he felt as he watched you as he used you is always being done again and lived again and felt again through the pictures... Watching you was how he got off doing it; with the pictures he can watch you and get off anytime' (ibid.: 3). What MacKinnon is exposing, through her focus on the technology of the camera, is the anxiety regarding visual technologies in relation to rape.[22]

In her discussion of the relationship between rape and technology in the war in the former Yugoslavia, MacKinnon notes that male soldiers filmed as they raped: 'As they do it, they watch, laugh, encourage each other, and spew ethnic curses and epithets' (1994: 75). MacKinnon quotes one rape survivor: 'These soldiers would invite their friends to come watch the rapes. It was like in the movie theater' (ibid.: 78). Noting the ubiquity of pornography during the war, MacKinnon concludes: 'When pornography is this common and this accepted, the lines dividing it from news, entertainment, and the rest of life are so blurred that women may know no word for it' (ibid.). Though it is at times occluded by an idea of pornography as an 'instruction manual' for violence, MacKinnon's questioning of how rape troubles the boundaries between news, entertainment, and the 'rest of life', is central to a consideration of the unsettling relation between rape, spectatorship and spectacle.

Before I return to a discussion of the rape in New Bedford I want to briefly consider the preface to the British edition of *Only Words*. MacKinnon opens with an account of a crime reported in *The New York Times* on 17 August 1992 in which a woman was stabbed to death while a group of people chanted 'Kill her! Kill her!'. The police were seeking to charge those who participated in the crime by cheering it on, for aiding and abetting a murder (1994: ix). Though MacKinnon does not make the comparison between this case and the rape in New Bedford,[23] she does ask what might happen if we substitute the act of rape for the act of murder:

> Suppose, instead of a murder, the bystanders were watching a rape. Would chanting "Rape her! Rape her!" not be participation? Suppose pictures were taken of the rape, and sold to people, some of whom chanted "Rape her! Rape her!" as they watched. The onlookers in Oakland just happened on a murder already in progress. Suppose they had paid to watch and chant during an arranged one? Imagine that a whole industry creates and sells pictures of women and children sexually violated and sometimes killed. Isn't this also participation? And those millions who create the market for those films, who watch them and chant "Rape her! Rape her!" and "Kill her! Kill her!" – do they not also participate?
>
> (ibid.)

This passage foregrounds what Seltzer calls ' "spectacular violence": that is, a violence inseparable from its reproduction as spectacle' (1998: 186). This idea of spectacular violence is central to the story of the gang rape of a woman in a bar room, filled to capacity with cheering spectators. When the New Bedford case went to trial one year later, the worry about what it meant to watch rape as a representation surfaced again, this time in relation to the public spectatorship of the nationally televised trial.

Live and in colour on CNN

While the communal spectatorship of rape trials is not a new phenomenon, television has stepped up the implications of such public spectatorship. To watch a trial one no longer has to attend the courthouse. Drawn out over the course of several weeks, and months, and shown on a daily basis, the live televised trial has the episodic structure of soap operas and deals 'with similar issues such as sex, disease, crime, drug addiction' – and, we can add, rape (Bruzzi 1994: 174).

The New Bedford rape trial was carried on several local cable and radio outlets and was also televised nationally. From the beginning television played a major role in determining how the trial was covered. The decision of newspapers to print graphic trial testimony, for example, was framed by the fact that it was already being relayed through television, 'in language sometimes more explicit than any prime-time series' (Henry 1984: 64). Newspapers carried still photographs of scenes from the courtroom. Since the victim was not allowed to be filmed or photographed, and since there was no visual record of the rape itself, the photographs showed people spectating the events as they unfolded in the courtroom. One photograph, displayed in the *New York Times*, featured the following caption: 'Part of the crowd of spectators attending the rape trial last week in Fall River, Mass.' In the photo, a crowd of spectators are all looking in the same direction, their eyes raised to a scene beyond the frame of the picture; one woman's head is slightly tilted towards her companion, as if they are having a whispered exchange about the proceedings. Without the caption, the spectators could easily be mistaken for a crowd of people at a baseball game or a tennis match. But the accompanying article drew another kind of analogy; as New Bedford housewife Cheryl Machado was quoted as saying: 'It's like a soap opera' (Rangel 4 March 1984).

On 24 April 1984, District Attorney Pina, and several others caught up in the Big Dan's rape trial — broadcasters, newspaper editors and rape crisis representatives — submitted testimony on the 'rape publicity issue' to a Senate Hearing Committee. The hearing centred on two questions: what kind of effect do these trials have on the rape victim, and what is the right of the press to have access to such proceedings?[24] An inquiry into the impact of the Big Dan's rape trial, the hearing was also an inquiry into what it meant to have the American judicial system exposed 'live and in color' on CNN. As the chairman to the committee declared:

> Recent events surrounding the notorious incident at Big Dan's Tavern in New Bedford, MA, exemplify the growing impact of the media on criminal trials. The media coverage of that trial not only had a profound impact on the local community — as demonstrated by the angry crowds in the streets — it also had a dramatic effect on the entire Nation.
>
> (2)

What is most striking about the hearing, for the purposes of this book, is the way the attempt to establish guidelines for what it is acceptable to show in this new genre of television, is clearly drawn from, and played out over, an image of the raped woman's body.

For those in favour of allowing television cameras in the courtroom, the public viewing of the Big Dan's rape trial was seen as an important enactment of basic democratic rights. As James Ragsdale, editor of the *New Bedford Standard-Times*, argued:

> In a case as notorious as Big Dan's, the community shares a vital concern to see that justice is done. What better way to be assured than to enlarge the number of spectators far beyond a courtroom's seating capacity... The physical size of courtrooms need no longer restrict the number of citizens who are allowed to view important court proceedings.
>
> (34, 35)

In other words, a case that received extensive publicity because it exposed a communal failure to witness a woman's rape, inaugurates a form of representation premised on the idea that communal looking serves the ends of civic justice. It was an irony lost or ignored by those who spoke out in favour of televised trials.

To justify having television cameras in the courtroom, it was necessary to prove that the visual representation of the rape case fulfilled one of the founding rules of the American justice system: 'Justice cannot survive behind walls of silence' (2–3). Thus Ragsdale argued: 'There is no better way to build public confidence in the courts than to open them up to this kind of coverage' (25). And he insisted: 'This is ... the most publicized rape case in the history of the country. Publicity about this case has brought about many long-range benefits for the public at large' (24). The trial increased 'awareness, from coast to coast, about the crime of rape ... There are benefits from this heightened awareness. Such benefits as rape crisis centres that are now going to be receiving greater attention, greater support' (24). Not only that, he argued, but the case would also educate – and possibly deter – potential rapists (24). On this view, the televised rape trial serves an important civic function from which everyone benefits: as future rape victims, women can be assured of better treatment by the authorities, while men, as future rapists, might actually think twice before sexually assaulting a woman in light of the heavy prison sentence they now know they might receive.

Significantly, a feminist argument about the necessity for publicizing the effects of rape in order to create greater public awareness of the crime was used to some advantage by the proponents of televised trials. The panel of Radio–Television News Directors, for instance, had clearly done its homework: 'We agree with author Susan Brownmiller, whose book "Against Our Will" is a well researched and eloquent indictment of the way society treats the crime of rape, that it was not a mistake to televise the New Bedford rape trial' (80). The same group of (male) broadcasters then proceeded to provide the following quotation from Brownmiller:

> Historically the time was right in America to take one case and to examine it thoroughly, and the Big Dan's gang rape on the pool table case became a morality play, a public morality play for the Nation. I think this case served to enlighten a Nation as to what actually happens in a rape and what actually happens in a courtroom.
>
> (Brownmiller cited in Senate Hearing 1984: 80)

It should be stressed this is the panel's interpretation of Brownmiller's comments, taken from a television interview she gave during the rape trial. My point in including these comments is to demonstrate the way the figure of Brownmiller circulates in public discourse on rape. Conveniently, the broadcasters used this view of the case to argue that the media exposes, and does not create, the 'societal problem' of rape:

> We hope the day will come and come soon when society treats them [the victims of rape] just like the other victims of crimes, and the news media can do the same without setting off a fire storm of criticism. We believe that if there is a fault, it lies within the courts and the society they reflect, not in the media which merely exposes what already exists.
>
> (81)

As Katha Pollitt has noted, the argument 'Rape is like other crimes and should be treated like other crimes. Isn't that what you feminists are always saying?' is fraught with difficulties. For one thing, 'rape isn't treated like other crimes. There is no other crime in which the character, behaviour and past of the complainant are seen as central elements in determining whether a crime has occurred' (Pollitt 1991: 850). But the real difficulty with the above argument, I think, is the idea that the broadcasting of the Big Dan's rape case was merely exposing what already exists. As noted earlier in this chapter, what makes CNN notable, is the way in which it is seen to present real life *as it happens*. Television viewers, subsequently, are not merely 'spectating' events, they are participating in them. With the rise of CNN, Brent MacGregor notes, 'television is no longer a spectator…as you observe a phenomenon with television, instantaneously you modify it somewhat' (1997: 12). As we have seen, the story of a group of men cheering, laughing and goading on a woman's gang rape threw the category of the witness into crisis. The act of viewing a spectacle of violence was revealed as participation in that violence, muddying a distinction between those who raped and those who watched. Having the rape trial aired on national television raised a troubling question about the complicity between the television audience and the spectators at Big Dan's.

Those against the idea of televising rape trials were clearly anxious about the connection between looking and raping. As District Attorney Pina testified:

> I think one of the scariest things is that on March 26, 1984, this year, I had just finished sentencing the four individuals who were found guilty, and on that same day, in Rhode Island, a 12-year-old boy had watched the trial on television and reportedly threw a ten-year-old girl onto a pool table in his home and sexually assaulted her as other children watched.
>
> (4)

The 'Russian doll effect' of representation at work here – from the story of a group of men who mistook rape for 'spectacle', to the story of a young boy who watched the spectacle of the rape trial on television and committed rape for 'real' – speaks to an anxiety about copycat violence. The figure of the 12-year-old-spectator-turned-rapist is a key emblem of this anxiety. In the Senate hearing transcript, the impressionable and immature young boy is cast as the prototypical spectator of the rape trial. When Pina later discusses the accessibility of the broadcast, he refers again to the 'chilling effects' it might have on a young boy, who comes home from school and is able to watch the trial 'live and in color' (5). What might happen when a *female* child watches a rape trial is not discussed, presumably because it is thought there is no need to: her fate is already sealed in the disturbing story of the young boy who threw a girl on a pool table and tried to rape her.

Ragsdale ultimately dismisses the complaint that 'televising rape trials amounts to "oral pornography"', but a worry that the raped woman's testimony comes dangerously close to porn lies at the centre of a debate over how to, or whether to, show the raped woman (34). One of the things being decided in this hearing is what is at stake in the communal and televisual 'look' at the raped woman.[25] Although the rape is obviously told, rather than shown, during the course of a rape trial, several theorists argue that the re-telling of a rape in the courtroom always conjures up a visual image of the rape. In *Feminism and the Power of the Law*, Carol Smart argues that the woman's testimony of her violation in court 'becomes a pornographic vignette'. Smart explains:

> Bits of female anatomy are heavily encoded with sexual messages and women are aware, whether consciously or not, of the sexual meanings of their bodies...In a rape trial she knows that she must name parts of her body, parts which in the very naming overtly reveal their sexual content.
>
> (1989: 38)

According to Smart, 'it is not just that (women) must repeat the violation in words, nor that they may be judged to be lying, but that the woman's story *gives pleasure* in the way that pornography gives pleasure' (ibid.: 39). But unlike pornographic photographs the 'woman in the dock is there in the flesh to feel her humiliation. The judge, the lawyers, the jury, and the public can gaze on her body and re-enact her violation in their imaginations' (ibid.).

This brings me to the crux of the matter: the raped woman's representation of her trauma. Several feminists have noted the way in which rape, like other traumatic events, precipitates a crisis of representation. To quote one rape survivor: 'I couldn't scream. I couldn't move. I was paralysed...like a rag doll' (cited in Herman 1992: 42). This crisis of representation is carried over into the courtroom, where the rape victim is required to put her experience into discursive form, and therefore make the 'unrepresentable' representable. The status of the raped woman's testimony brings into critical focus the question at the heart of the Big Dan's rape trial: who can witness a rape? Trauma is, as Cathy Caruth notes, the 'literal return of the event against the will of the one it inhabits' (1995: 5). According to Caruth, one dominant feature of all traumatic experience is 'the inability fully to witness the event as it occurs' (ibid.: 7). The idea that the traumatic re-experiencing of the event contains the 'collapse of witnessing...that first constituted it', has a special relevancy to the New Bedford rape, a crime which, as we have seen, occurred without any 'witness' (ibid.: 10).

Because the raped woman is forced to re-live her trauma when she testifies, more often than not in front of the man (or men) who attacked her, feminist activists and rape counsellors refer to rape trials as a 'second rape'. It is the raped woman's experience of the rape trial as a second rape that dramatically exposes the identification between the television audience and the spectators at Big Dan's. As rape victim Jennifer Barr told the Senate Hearing Committee on the New Bedford case, the courtroom experience is a repetition of the original trauma:

> I was forced to relive the rape in front of strangers and my assailant...I was aware that the court proceedings were open to the public and it

threatened me. If I had had to face TV cameras in that courtroom, being exposed to anyone in the community at the flick of a dial, I can say for certain I would not have testified.

(57)

In the Big Dan's rape trial, the woman had to deal with a courtroom packed with spectators, television cameras and news reporters. She had to testify for over three days, for over fifteen hours in total. If the woman's recounting of the event on the witness stand 'is as much of a crisis as the actual rape itself', then the role of the spectators, both inside and outside of the courtroom, has potentially scandalous implications (cited in Herman 1989: 34–35). To watch a rape trial is to participate in, and to be an integral part of, the raped woman's ordeal. Lynn Comerford has suggested that 'twentieth-century American rape-trial television audiences might be regarded as similar to seventeenth-century French audiences who gathered around the public scaffold to witness public torture and execution' (1997: 241).[26] She explains:

> In a Foucauldian sense, patriarchy *needs* the public ceremony of televised rape trials to demonstrate women's subordination ... What better way for modern patriarchy to silence rape victims than to threaten them with a televised replay of their assault?
>
> (ibid.: 241, 233)

This is Brownmiller's argument about rape extended to television: patriarchal culture needs televised rape in order to renew the force of male domination.

Seltzer argues that today people take part in 'public violence' from a distance that nevertheless has a 'heightened immediacy' (1998: 183). As he writes: 'A phantom public ... gathered around collective bodily violence leaves its body behind: information and representation replace bodies' (1998: 183). Though some might see this distance from the event as 'despicable' (Canetti 1984: 52), Seltzer argues that there is something more at stake in 'the uncertain distance between viewer and event and between information and body' (1998: 183).

> If there is "a special thrill" in this mass-media witnessing, if there is a "pleasure" in this way of assembling around collective killing, this may be in part because such phantom events hold the places of the public sphere, albeit a public that meets in pathology. One discovers here an identification with others *by way of* the witnessing of public violence and its simulations.
>
> (ibid.: 184)

With the televised rape trial we might say we have arrived at another way of understanding how rape operates as a generating moment of the civic bond. The 'mass-media witnessing' of the rape trial, in which the 'phantom public' gather around the spectacularization of reality, becomes another way of locating what

I have been calling the socio-sexual contract; a contract that is made, and then violently reproduced, over an image of the raped woman's body. While CNN executives argue the televised trial has a civilizing influence on American culture, educating those who watch the channel, critical observers of the first trial ever to be televised by CNN know better. As correspondent Betsy Aaron puts it: 'These trials have become spectator sport' (cited in Henry 1984: 64).

Conclusion

One of my aims in this chapter has been to shed some light on the Big Dan's gang rape case and the critical role it played in the development of the electronic news medium. It is an event that deserves to be included in, and is too often strangely left out of, a list of the great televised media events of the twentieth century. As Frank Tomasulo notes, 'contemporary history in the era of global media capitalism is increasingly being "written" on film and videotape' (1996: 71).

Technology played a critical role in constructing the 'reality' of the Big Dan's rape trial. At the same time, I argue that rape played a pivotal role in establishing the technology of a new genre of reality programming. But if the Big Dan's rape case demands to be recognized as the founding event for a new representational style epitomized by CNN, it must also be recognised that it throws into crisis the very representational form it is called upon to secure. That is, at the very moment that it was being used as a vehicle for the expression of a new representational form predicated on the idea of communal participation in the 'experience itself', the Big Dan's rape case exposed the limits of this notion of participative spectatorship (Donovan and Scherer 1992: xi). It gave the lie to a notion of a benign or innocent form of spectatorship in which distance from the event is seen to distance the viewer from participation in violence. That we may be participating in a rape by 'just looking', be it in Big Dan's tavern or in the comfort of our living rooms, is the underlying anxiety – and ultimately, perhaps, the appeal – of the rape trial as contemporary American spectacle.

4

'THEY DID WORSE THAN NOTHING'

Rape and spectatorship in
The Accused

Hollywood's first feature-length film on rape was released in 1988, four years after the televised trial of the Big Dan's rape case.[1] In its dramatization of gang rape on a pinball machine, Jonathan Kaplan's *The Accused* invokes the popular memory of the pool table rape in New Bedford.[2] As Richard Corliss, reviewing the film for *Time*, writes: 'The film carries echoes of a generation of violence and apathy, from the Kitty Genovese case in 1964 to the New Bedford, Mass., rape in 1983' (1988: 127). In the actual event, the cheering spectators were never brought to trial and the two men charged with 'joint enterprise' (for aiding and abetting the rapists) were acquitted. In a major break from its real-life referent, *The Accused* re-writes the verdict to examine what happens when spectatorship is made literally criminal through the legal indictment and conviction of a group of men who watch a gang rape 'as though it were a live sex show'. Scriptwriter Tom Topor acknowledged it was a conviction that 'would probably be thrown out in real life' (cited in Corliss 1988: 127). But according to Topor: 'We were just raising it as one possible inter-pretation and using it to make a point. And the law says that anyone who encour-ages a crime is culpable. We all depend on each other to act when we get into trouble. If you and I abdicate, the bad guys win' (ibid.: 127).

In its re-writing of legal precedent, *The Accused* seems to respond to a desire for justice and civic reparation generated by the actual case. If one of the central ques-tions raised by the Big Dan's case was whether or not the spectators to the rape could be brought to justice, then *The Accused* reassures its audience that 'looking' can be bound to the law. Where the rape in New Bedford revealed that 'strangers need not even call 911', the film not only begins with a stranger making that call to the police, but it concludes with the spectators being tried and convicted (Press 1983: 79).

There is another significant way in which *The Accused* engages in historical revisionism, which has gone conspicuously unnoticed by the majority of critics. In the version of events offered in *The Accused*, the ethnic tensions that character-ized the rape in New Bedford are omitted.[3] Instead, an Anglo-American cast is used to tell a 'universal' story about 'human nature, individual moral conscience, and a judicial process that treats the victim like a criminal'.[4] In the film, the central framing issue is class: the victim, Sarah Tobias, is a young woman from a 'white trash' background with a history of drug and alcohol abuse.

The film has two major Hollywood actresses in the title roles: Jodie Foster as the rape victim and Kelly McGillis as the assistant District Attorney who prosecutes her case. But it was not, or at least not only, the star appeal that drew mass audiences to the film. What attracted the American public, earning the film $18 million in its first twenty-four days of release, was its harrowing depiction of Foster being gang raped on a pinball machine. As one female cinema-goer recalls, the intense publicity surrounding the film's 'controversial rape scene' invited viewers to go and have a look for themselves: 'There's this rape scene in it. Everybody's got to go and see it' (cited in Schlesinger *et al.* 1992: 136).

With *The Accused* the question raised by the New Bedford rape comes full circle: what does it mean for an audience to 'spectate' a gang rape on film? Susan Faludi's report that young men watching *The Accused* 'hooted and cheered the film's rape scene' brings out the dramatic implications of the coincidence between the looking in Big Dan's tavern and the looking at *The Accused* (Faludi 1992: 170). The debate triggered by the film's representation of rape is a repetition of the debate on the ethics of televising the Big Dan's rape trial. What happens when rape is turned into sensational public entertainment? What is at stake in the communal 'look' at a re-presentation of rape?

The explosive debate over the gang rape scene remains part of the mythology surrounding the film. In the 1996 anthology *Screen Violence*, for example, the rape sequence from *The Accused* has a prominent place in the list of famous violent scenes and images in films. Taking its place alongside *Straw Dogs* (Peckinpah 1971) and *A Clockwork Orange* (Kubrick 1971), *The Accused* is here defined as a 'classic' by virtue of its relationship to a wider, well-established cinematic tradition of sex, violence and brutality (French 1996: 3). But another strand of argument holds that *The Accused* is a classic precisely because it stands apart from Hollywood's typical portrayal of sex and violence. Thus, in a *Sunday Times* article, 'Rape: The Dangerous Trend Stalking Hollywood', we find *The Accused* taken up as a test-case against which a diverse range of filmic representations of rape from the 1990s are to be judged: from *Leaving Las Vegas* to *Dead Man Walking*, *Rob Roy*, *Kids*, *Strange Days* and *Showgirls*. 'Unlike *The Accused*, this new crop of films is not *about* rape. Though they depict it, they do not in any way confront the subject' (Goodwin 1996: 4). *The Accused*, then, is a film that confronts, and fights back against, sexual violence.

While this reading of the film as exemplary side steps the much debated issue of whether the film itself employs an image of rape as a 'sensational device', it is nevertheless indicative of the way *The Accused* tends to get treated as a special case. In its representativeness (as part of a long-standing tradition of screen violence) or in its distinctiveness (as the first serious Hollywood depiction of rape), *The Accused* marks a turning point in the history of Hollywood's representation of sex and violence. *The Accused* constitutes the border-line between the unreflective, pre-feminist depiction of rape found in *Straw Dogs*, a film in which the woman is portrayed as enjoying her violation, and the self-reflexive 'post-feminist' portrayal of rape found in Kathryn Bigelow's *Strange Days* (1995), a film in which the scene of a woman's rape and murder becomes the means for a metatextual commentary on cinematic identification and voyeurism.

It is possible to complicate this 'before and after' schematic. As Clover has argued, the story line of *The Accused* is hardly original: it has its antecedents in the low-budget rape-revenge films of the late 1970s and the early 1980s. Long before the release of *The Accused*, 'exploitation' flicks like *I Spit on Your Grave* (Zarchi 1978) and *Ms. 45* (Ferrara 1980) were dealing with the issue of rape 'in terms more or less explicitly feminist' (1992: 16). For Clover the mainstream success of *The Accused* is due to its 'civilised', stream-lined version of a story that has been told many times before, by films 'that said it all, and in flatter terms, and on a shoestring' (ibid.: 18).

Without disputing that the mainstream status of *The Accused* grants it a certain legitimacy denied to exploitation films like *I Spit on Your Grave* and *Ms. 45*, I think what is most interesting and problematic about *The Accused* is precisely the question of its popularity with the mainstream public. It is available on home video and is shown on terrestrial and satellite television in both the US and Great Britain (Schlesinger *et al.* 1992: 129). To put it simply, *The Accused* contains one of the most watched rapes in cinematic history. It is therefore striking to note the dearth of critical material on the film. When *The Accused* is raised in the context of discussions about violence, representation and cinema, it is usually only to cite it as an example of the dilemma regarding the ethics of filming a rape scene. This critical oversight is even more odd when we consider the importance of the film for feminism. As one of mainstream culture's most explicit representations of rape, *The Accused* is a key, if problematic, film for feminists: it clearly owes a debt to feminist consciousness-raising on rape; but its explicit depiction of gang rape belongs to a cinematic tradition in which the victimized female body becomes the body of cinema (Lebeau 1995: 139). On the one hand, critics like Cindy Fuchs argue that the film's attempt to implicate the cinematic audience in the act of on-screen voyeurism provides an effective commentary 'on the way this culture looks at women's bodies' (1989: 28). On the other hand, some see the film as submitting to the structures of voyeurism it professes to subvert. As Pam Cook notes, 'it is debatable whether the explicit portrayal of Sarah's painful humiliation (which is most likely to disturb those who either have been or might be raped) is necessary' (1989: 36).

The Accused constitutes an especially charged example of the pitfalls inherent to any film that attempts to uncover the penetrating nature of what Laura Mulvey (1975) famously theorized as the masculine 'look'. One way of accounting for the lack of detailed analysis of the film is to argue, paradoxically, that *The Accused* – or at least its rape scene – is abundantly explained. This is to say it is almost as if the difficulties presented by the film are in some way too obvious: in drawing a correlation between the violence of rape and the violence of spectatorship, *The Accused* is merely exposing and compounding a violence already in place.

While the existing commentary on the film gives voice to the debate over whether the rape scene is a 'good' or 'bad' image – often through the most cursory of references to the real-life case – the full implications of the connections between the filmic representation and the actual event remain untouched. Reading

The Accused in light of the rape in New Bedford, I want to expose the blind spots of the white feminist acclaim of the film. As I will show, the attempt to classify *The Accused* as 'feminist' is contingent on a wishful misreading of key scenes. By passing over the film's problematic depiction of masculinity, and by failing to consider how the film represents not just the rape of a woman but the rape of a white woman, these wishful readings perpetuate, rather than explore, the film's 'constitutive omissions'.[5] Looking at what happens when the issue of race is factored into a reading of the film, I reveal the exclusionary violence underlying its 'universal' narrative of rape.

James Snead has argued that 'although films are not necessarily myths ... certain films have managed to remain repeatedly compelling and thus to assume a permanent, quasi-mythic status in a society's consciousness' (1991: 53). What Snead says of films in general can also be applied to particular scenes and images from films. The bar room rape scene from *The Accused* is one such filmic image that has assumed a quasi-mythic status in the popular imaginary. As Ruby Rich notes: 'By now the scene of gang rape on a bar-room pinball machine has been described over and over, until it has gathered a totemic significance equal to that of the original rape perpetrated in an actual bar in New Bedford, Massachusetts, in 1983' (1993: 56). My concern is to consider how *The Accused* relates to the public fascination with real-life stories of rape, whereby the event of a white woman's sexual violation comes to represent a constitutive working through of fantasies about civic accountability. Considering the links between *The Accused* and two more recent depictions of rape by female directors, Kathryn Bigelow's *Strange Days* (1995) and Kimberley Peirce's *Boys Don't Cry* (1999), I explore how all three films present rape in the form of a flashback, raising questions about spectatorship and complicity, memory and trauma.

As the filmic memorialization of the rape in New Bedford, *The Accused* is a powerful preservation of a historical event. Significantly, it is also a preservation of the crisis of witnessing that marked both the original trauma and the subsequent trial. For it is at once entirely fitting and deeply problematic that the rape should be turned into cinema, 'the art *par excellence* which calls upon witnessing by seeing' (Felman 1991: 90).

Dramatizing reality

The Accused opens with a shot of a roadside tavern called The Mill – the film's equivalent to Big Dan's Tavern. As the film's menacing soundtrack plays, and day passes imperceptibly into night, the camera stays fixed on the quiet entrance to the bar. The stillness of this opening credit sequence is broken by a shot of the raped woman running out of the bar, screaming for help. As the camera moves in for a close-up, we see a woman, barefoot and clutching her torn shirt to her chest, running out into the road and flagging down a passing truck-driver. At this point the camera shifts to a telephone booth at the side of the road. A young man is phoning for help. The film's first words belong to him: 'There's a girl in trouble ... There

was a rape...I don't know, three or four guys...There was a whole crowd...
I don't know...Send somebody!'

As the first half of the film goes to some lengths to show, the prosecution's
attempt to 'make a rape case' has little to do with questions of guilt and innocence.
Although Katheryn Murphy, the assistant DA, tells her boss she believes Sarah was
gang raped, she also concedes that she does not have much of a case. 'If I take it to
trial they'll destroy her. She walked in there alone. She got drunk. She got stoned.
She came on to them. She's got a prior for possession. She's a sitting duck.' The
strategy of the defence team is simple: there was no rape. Given that the 'eye-
witnesses' either 'didn't see anything or didn't think they were seeing anything
special', Katheryn is encouraged by her male superiors to plea-bargain the
'unwinnable' case down to a charge of 'reckless endangerment' (incidentally, the
film's original title). The rapists are put away, but the crime of rape is elided and
Sarah is denied the opportunity to testify. Sarah confronts Katheryn and demands
to know why she was not given a chance to tell her story. However, it is only when
Sarah is wounded in a run-in with one of the men from The Mill that Katheryn
feels guilty and decides to re-open the case by prosecuting the men who cheered
on the rape. Listening to a tape of the anonymous phone call made to the police,
Katheryn tracks down Kenneth Joyce, the bystander who made the call. As he takes
the stand to testify, the film finally shows what 'really happened' that night in The
Mill. The prosecution wins its case and the jury finds the men who spectated the
rape guilty of criminal solicitation.

As the first Hollywood feature-length film to deal directly with the trauma of
rape, *The Accused* attempts to provide popular culture with an authoritative depiction of the 'reality' of rape. To this end, the postscript that appears on-screen at the
film's conclusion is intended to provide documentary backup of its claims: 'In the
US, a woman is raped every six minutes. One out of every four rape victims is
attacked by two or more assailants.' This asserts the historical truth of the story that
has just been depicted but more than that, it presents the film as a kind of memorial to all rape victims. It is perhaps for this reason that the film does not want to
associate itself too closely with the events in New Bedford: going far beyond any
one story, *The Accused* wants to tell *the* story of rape.

Reviewers routinely acknowledged that *The Accused* was based on, or inspired
by, a 'true story', though more attention was paid to the general social reality the
film was seen to reflect. As Suzanne Moore writes in a review for the *New
Statesman*: 'Statistics show a quarter of all reported rapes in America involve two
or more men, and the central dynamic of gang rape appears to have as much to
with men's relationship to each other as with their relationship to women' (1989:
16). This idea of rape as a crime between men is indeed central to the film's vision
of masculinity; I will return to this idea of the 'dynamic of gang rape' in my
discussion of the film's use of the flashback.

In *Women Viewing Violence*, an audience reception study that calls 'upon women
of diverse backgrounds to respond to a variety of television programmes in which
women are beaten, raped and/or murdered', the section on *The Accused* is preceded

by a chapter on *Crimewatch UK*, a popular BBC reality TV programme 'that aims to mobilise the television audience in order to assist the police in catching criminals' (Schlesinger *et al.* 1992: 43).[6] Though the study does not pursue the connection, I would suggest the link between *The Accused* and *Crimewatch UK*, a programme that regularly features rape as one of the crimes that needs solving, bears examination. As John Sears puts it, *Crimewatch UK* seeks to 'perform a social function by helping to solve crime, drawing on the collective responsibilities, experiences and knowledge of the viewing audience in order to do so' (Sears 1995: 52).[7] One of the organizing images of the programme is of hands dialling telephones; representing the active citizens who will report crimes that they have witnessed to the police (ibid.: 52). Interestingly enough, *The Accused* organizes its narrative structure around these two images: it begins with a young man, the 'active citizen', dialling a telephone to tell the police of a rape he has witnessed, and it concludes, over an hour and a half later, with a dramatic re-enactment of the rape.

What I find particularly intriguing about the relationship between *The Accused* and *Crimewatch UK* is the stress that both place – albeit differently – upon participative spectatorship. As the introduction to *Crimewatch* runs: 'Welcome to the programme where once a month instead of just hearing about crimes you can perhaps actually do something about them' (cited in Schlesinger 1992: 46). *The Accused* too is based on the premise that it serves a civic function. Its indictment of the on-screen looking of the male spectators at the rape serves as a framing device for its larger commitment to what Rich has elsewhere labelled 'conversion cinema': films that attempt to horrify or shock the spectator into ethics (Rich 1983: 58).[8] Accordingly, the film's decision to depict the aftermath of the rape first, before showing the traumatic event itself, is accounted for by a language of social concern that issues itself as a challenge to the cinematic spectator. 'We wanted to lull the audience and then turn things around', script writer Topor explained. 'We were saying, "As a spectator, you're part of the problem. What would you have done?"' (cited in Corliss 1988: 127). If the real-life case raised the question of what it means to spectate a rape as though it were a 'representation', *The Accused* raises the question of what it means to spectate a representation of a rape as though it were 'real'. Shock aesthetics to be sure, but not, as the producers were careful to qualify, in the tradition of 'shock for shock's sake'. As producer Sherry Lansing was quoted as saying: 'We're hoping that no one seeing *The Accused* will ever again believe that rape is sexy or that any woman asks for it' (ibid.: 127). She adds: 'If anyone thinks this movie is anti-feminist, I give up. Once you see this movie, I doubt that you will ever, ever think of rape the same way again. Those images will stick in your mind, and you will be more sympathetic the next time you hear of somebody being raped ... Until I saw this film, I didn't even know how horrible [rape] is' (cited in Faludi 1992: 170).[9]

On this view the invitation to look at the scene of a woman's rape serves a wholly curative function: the film is forcing us to see the worst so that we may be educated and transformed. The earnest tone struck by Lansing calls to mind a tradition of documentary filmmaking that emphasizes the civic role of cinema as a site for social consciousness. In its professed concern to effect a change in social attitudes towards rape and the rape victim, *The Accused* draws upon a key tenet of this tradition: the assumption that 'films about social problems help solve these problems' (Jones 1989: 76). But how can *The Accused*, which invites its audience to look at the scene of a gang rape, hope to cure the 'problem' raised by the real event, in which a group of men 'spectated' rather than 'witnessed' a woman's rape? This paradox – how can looking cure the damage caused by looking – recalls the strange dynamic that characterizes the *Lévite* as discussed in Chapter 2, in which rape is used to repair the damage caused by rape. With *The Accused* we find the same apparent need to repeat the trauma in order to cure the trauma. But can the film make the difference? Does it heal or perpetuate the original trauma?[10]

This is the challenge the film wants to lay at the doorstep of the cinematic audience. For critics like Cook, this is a violation of the cinema–spectator contract: 'To conflate the audience for the film with witnesses to a real crime, and to condemn them for the impulse which brought them to the cinema in the first place, smacks of wanting to have it too many ways' (1989: 36). In other words, the film makers want to have their cake and eat it by punishing the audience for spectating a visual spectacle they have invited them to look at. Something of the ambivalence of the film's project is captured in Lansing's statement: 'we're hoping that no one seeing *The Accused* will ever again believe that rape is sexy or that any woman asks for it' (cited in Corliss 1988: 127). Such a statement begs the question of why, and by whom, rape is ever considered 'sexy' in the first place? Catharine MacKinnon would have a ready answer to this question: men. If rape is, in fact, considered by some men to be sexy, then how is the rape scene in *The Accused*, a rape scene that deliberately portrays its female character as a 'slut' (Lansing's description) going to change minds?

In fact, the publicity surrounding the film suggests its intended audience is women. If this is the case, then it may be a matter of preaching to the converted. As one reviewer suggested at the time: 'The film provokes no emotion other than disgust over the crime, an easy accomplishment under the circumstances. In a sense, the picture is preaching to the converted, since no one is going to side with the rapists, and the outrage that is justifiably aroused by the way the justice system can treat crime victims is assuaged by story's end' ('The Accused' 1988: 14). Indeed, while the film's rhetoric insists 'seeing is believing', a closer look at the feminist reception of the film suggests that it is more a case of seeing what is already believed.

A women's picture

With its focus on two independent female protagonists and their struggle to battle the legal system, *The Accused* can be described as a 'women's picture'. But while *The Accused* may be a women's film, is it a feminist film? Patrice Fleck suggests the film can be considered feminist because it 'focuses on a brutal rape, condemning it in a variety of ways, primarily through "good guy" (strong female protagonists) and "bad guy" (monstrous rapists and rape solicitors) cinematic codes' (Fleck 1990: 49).

But approaching the film through the real event one might say *The Accused* is a feminist film because it fulfils the wish expressed by several women's groups at the time of the rape in New Bedford: it brings male looking to accountability through the legal indictment of the onlookers whose cheering encouraged the sexual assault. *The Accused* can be seen to answer the question asked by Mary Kay Blakely, writing for *Ms.* at the time of the Big Dan's gang rape: 'Can the "witnesses" – for it is really they who have enraged the American public – be brought to justice' (1983: 52)?

Given the reaction of several Portuguese women in New Bedford, it is important to specify that if the film is feminist, it is an Anglo-American feminist work. In this train of thought it is possible to read the film's elision of the ethnic tensions that characterized the real event as another form of Anglo-American feminist wish-fulfilment. During the height of the media controversy over the Big Dan's gang rape, feminist activists repeatedly argued rape was endemic to all American culture and therefore was not a crime specific to New Bedford's Portuguese population. As Elizabeth Bennett told reporters: 'Rape is something that happens at all times, in all cultures, in all races' (Beck 1984: 39). By deliberately excluding the ethnic tensions that caused such furore, *The Accused* is forcing a white audience to confront their involvement in the film's critique of violence and spectatorship.

The class dimension of the film significantly problematizes such an argument. For the moment, however, I want to continue to consider what it means to read *The Accused* as feminist wish-fulfilment. For although there is a tendency to think of it as a deeply problematic film for its female – and in particular its feminist – spectators, it is important to stress that, in feminist publications like *Ms.* and *Spare Rib*, it was cast in no uncertain terms as a breakthrough film for women. In her recent discussion of the critical reception of *The Accused* Jacinda Read has remarked on the 'absence of debate about the film's status as a feminist text' in popular reviews (2000: 105–106). Indeed, I would suggest that, in feminist reviews of *The Accused*, the film's feminist status is readily assumed.

One of the main contentions of the film's favourable reviews is that it stands out from the usual cinematic treatment of rape. According to Penny Ashbrook, *The Accused* is 'different' to other films that have attempted to depict rape, because the ending of the film 'offers up the possibility of change' (1989: 38). This idea of the film as effecting a change in social attitudes about rape links up with my earlier discussion of *Crimewatch UK*, and the idea of television and cinema as the site for political and civic engagement. Praising the film for 'indicting *all* men in complicity for rape and insisting that they share the guilt', Ashbrook goes so far as to suggest *The Accused* comes 'remarkably close to a conceptualisation of Susan Brownmiller's famous assertion that "Rape is a conscious process of intimidation by which *all* men keep *all* women in a state of fear"' (ibid.: 39). Ashbrook concludes by confirming the particular value of the film for its female spectators: 'A rare chance to see our experiences as women validated and endorsed on the big screen in a powerful and yes, entertaining movie about a subject that matters profoundly to us' (ibid.). Moore similarly remarks on the film's 'difference':

> Serious issues can make good cinema, but we also know from the tabloids that rape, child abuse, and all kinds of sexual violence, sell well. *The Accused*, though, is *different*, a far more difficult and provocative film around a very *old* issue. It makes public what is part of every woman's hidden agenda – the threat of rape – and it makes the smugness of the "post" in post-feminism, look decidedly questionable, if not downright stupid.
>
> (1989: 16)

For Moore, the film's difference lies in its willingness to make 'sexuality itself a problem': 'The bravest thing about *The Accused* is that it makes it clear that Sarah, who is gang-raped on a Slam Dunk pinball machine, is a sexy young woman who drinks, smokes and flirts. She is in no way the "ideal" rape victim' (ibid.: 17).

Those seeking to herald *The Accused* as a feminist film must necessarily contend with the argument that the rape scene is titillating. Not surprisingly, then, all the favourable reviews argue that *The Accused* destroys the potential visual pleasure to be derived from the depiction of rape on screen. Cindy Fuchs, reviewing the film in *Cineaste*, reads its depiction of rape in terms of Mulvey's influential argument about the classically voyeuristic and fetishistic economy of looking in the cinema: 'the "gaze" is male, the object is female' (1989: 26). According to Fuchs, one of the most remarkable achievements of *The Accused* is that it 'undermines the opposition of watching and being watched by turning the look around' and forcing 'us to see what Sarah (the alleged object of our gaze) sees' (ibid.). On this reading, the final visualization of the rape is the film's 'most potent accusation' against the act of spectatorship:

> This is an ugly scene. Yet what would seem unwatchable – Sarah's body laid out on the pinball machine – is stunning to watch, precisely because we see not only the body but the act of watching which accuses us. Offering no voyeuristic "visual pleasure", *The Accused* turns a disturbing mirror on the way this culture looks at women's bodies.
>
> (ibid.: 28)

This oxymoronic notion of the film as 'unwatchable' and 'stunning to watch' seeks to defend the film from the charge of sensationalism.

It is important to note that those seeking to defend the film from its detractors do not discard the idea of 'pleasure'. Beatrix Campbell, reviewing the film in *Marxism Today*, argues that its graphic representation of women's victimization and suffering is essential to the female spectator's 'pleasure' in the film.[11] For Campbell, the female spectator's pleasure is not only derived from the film's storyline, its 'metamorphosis of the classic portrayal of women as victims . . . into women as survivors, and more than that, as protagonists' (1989: 42). Even more important, argues Campbell, is the spectatorial pleasure to be had from an identification with the 'positive' images of women offered by Foster and McGillis, actresses who have 'expressed not only pride in their performances, but in the politics of the whole project' (ibid.). Central to this identification is publicity regarding the actresses' 'real-life experiences' of 'sexual terrorism' (ibid.).

I have already talked about how *The Accused* can be read as fulfilling the wish expressed by women's activists at the time of the Big Dan's gang rape: that the male spectators be held legally accountable for their look *in extremis* at the raped woman. In fact, one need look no further than the reviews themselves to see how the film works as feminist wish-fulfilment. For what becomes especially fascinating when studying the favourable feminist response to the film, is the wishful thinking that characterizes the attempt to positivize the film's depiction of rape.

In certain reviews, the attempt to see the film in the best possible light is contingent upon a misreading of key scenes. For instance there is the question of when, precisely, the film depicts the flashback of the rape. Though the film does not show the rape until Ken, the bystander, takes the witness stand, it is this significant plot detail that seems to go missing in the wishful readings of the film's rape scene. Moore, for example, in her contribution to the debate about whether the rape scene is exploitative, describes the film's plot as follows: 'In court, Sarah finally gets to tell her version of events. The film then depicts the controversial rape scene' (1989: 17). Cuklanz provides an even more blatant misreading of the sequence of events in the film: 'In *The Accused*, the trial serves as the place where Tobias finally gets to tell her version of what happened, and it is during her testimony that the film finally depicts the rape, as if to contend that the reality of it did not exist outside of her telling of it' (1996: 106).[12] Campbell, who describes *The Accused* as the 'most important movie of the decade', rewrites the film's conclusion into a triumphant vindication of women's 'historic subordination in film':

> Two words haunt the trial of the bystanders. Sarah is asked what she said when she was being raped. Did she cry for help, her interrogator asked. No, says Sarah, but what she did say, over and over again was "NO". Was 'No' not enough? These are key words, they challenge women's historic subordination in film – the heroine's salvation is traditionally supposed to lie in her proper dependence on a solitary hero, who in avenging her also avenges his own insulted masculinity. Here, Sarah's integrity is restored by her own demand that her word was enough.
>
> (1989: 43)

These readings fail to account for the role Ken the bystander plays in confirming the 'reality' of the rape because to do so would be to undermine the view of the film as a woman's story. For as those critical of the film have pointed out, Ken's privileged point of view as the 'hero' of the narrative is deeply problematic. As Clover argues:

> Although *The Accused* seems to bring male gazing to account … the authority for that conviction … rests finally and solely on the authority of

> a male spectator: Ken, the college boy who witnessed the event … Seldom
> has a set of male eyes been more privileged; without their witness, there
> would be no case – there would in fact, as the defence attorney notes, be
> no rape.
>
> (1992: 150)

Here we find a clear example of how the ability to witness and to represent
amounts to making rape 'real'. By producing the category of the witness, *The
Accused* is attempting to resolve the judicial crisis regarding the issue of who can
witness rape. But for Clover and a number of other critics, the problem with *The
Accused* is its final message: a woman's word is simply not good enough.

So far I have given the impression that feminist reviews ignore the figure of Ken.
This is not the case. Though they may downplay the pivotal and problematic role
he plays, most of the positive reviews read Ken as the film's attempt to rehabilitate
masculinity. Here we find another important link to the feminist response to the
Big Dan's gang rape. 'Gang Rape: Who Were the Men?' is the title to Blakely's
aforementioned 1984 *Ms.* article. Setting out to answer the question 'How could
this happen?', Blakely's article is an attempt to come to terms with the 'chance that
(her) sons could one day be among the anonymous bystanders at Big Dan's' (1983:
51). After reviewing the alarming details of the Big Dan's gang rape, Blakely makes
the following request of her female readers: 'I am asking you to hand this section
of the magazine to the man you love' (ibid.). Blakely addresses the rest of the article
to a 'man I can depend on to feel the tragedy of rape … one of the 34 per cent of
men who are repulsed by the sexual violence of men against women' (ibid.). With
the figure of Ken, the one 'good man' who will testify to the gang rape, *The Accused*
appears to produce the kind of reformed masculinity Blakely demands of her
hypothetical male reader:

> I want you to feel fear. I want you to understand that every two-and-a-
> half minutes, another woman in this country is raped, that one third of all
> rapes are committed by two or more "offenders". I want you to imagine
> that you have only 20 seconds to think what to do. And, if you don't want
> to be among the anonymous bystanders in Big Dan's, if you are horrified
> that more than a dozen men could actually cheer for a rape in progress,
> then imagine that you have only another two minutes to act. I want this
> fear to give you the courage to take risks, to object, to do something.
>
> (ibid.: 101)

The figure conjured up in the above passage is Ken, the man who admits to Sarah
that he too is 'afraid', and who finally objects to the rape that is occurring before
his eyes. Like Biff in Marilyn French's *The Women's Room*, discussed in the first
chapter of this book, Ken is the 'non-participant', the 'gang member who refuses
to participate' (Amir 1971: 192). But is this right? Does Ken not participate? The
difficulty is how to account for the fact that Ken looks at a rape in progress. After

all, his decision to take a risk, to object, to do something, comes only after three men have raped Sarah. The film deals with this difficulty by attempting to distinguish between the spectator and the participant. When her boss expresses angry disbelief at her attempt to 'prosecute a bunch of spectators for clapping and cheering', Katheryn retorts: 'They're not spectators. They solicited the rape. Not just clapping and cheering, but pushing and goading'. The distinction the film makes between 'just looking' at a rape and actually making one happen is key to its attempt to rehabilitate Ken's and the audience's 'look' at the woman's body. In her summation to the jury Katheryn justifies Ken's look at the rape:

> Kenneth Joyce testified to watching a rape. He told you that everyone in that bar behaved badly and he's right. But no matter how amoral it may be it is not the crime of criminal solicitation to walk away from rape. It is not the crime of criminal solicitation to silently watch a rape. What *is* the crime of criminal solicitation is to induce or entreat or encourage or persuade another person to commit a rape.

As Katheryn later tells the jury, the spectators 'did worse than nothing. They made sure Sarah Tobias was raped and raped and raped'. It is this distinction between silently watching a rape, and inducing, entreating and encouraging one, that allows the film to keep to the terms of its contract with the cinematic audience: enabling them to watch a woman's gang rape without recrimination.

The look of redemption

I now want to return to a question raised earlier in my discussion of the feminist response to *The Accused*: by deliberately excluding the ethnic tensions that characterized the real-life case, is the film forcing an Anglo-American audience to recognize their complicity in the film's critique of violence and spectatorship? Strikingly absent from the feminist reading of the film is any consideration of the whiteness of the film's characters. Indeed, *The Accused* gives further proof that the women's film is 'more accurately described as the white woman's film' (Doane 1987: 232).

Difference in *The Accused* is organized along class lines. Sarah, while never explicitly named as such within the film, is heavily coded as 'white trash'. She is an uneducated waitress who lives in a trailer park. Katheryn, on the other hand, is clearly coded upper-middle-class and is shown to view Sarah's ways with some distaste. But if 'white trash', as several theorists have recently argued, is not just a classist slur but a 'racial epithet that marks out certain whites as a breed apart', then Katheryn and Sarah could be said to be polarized along racial lines as well (Newitz and Wray 1997: 2). By considering the role class plays in the narrative, we can begin to discern the film's hidden racial plot and consider why, in the shift from the real event to cinema, the ethnic aspect of the story goes missing.

Clover argues the 'displacement of ethnic otherness onto a class of whites' is 'far and away the most significant "ethnic" development in popular culture of the last decade' (1992: 135). In *White Trash*, Annalee Newitz similarly argues that 'white trash, by occupying the position of "bad" Other, offer a perspective from which "good" whites can see themselves as a racial and classed group' (1997: 136). Newitz's argument is that whites 'use images and acts of victimization to reimagine themselves as civilized and just' (ibid.). This process often involves 'the look of redemption', a 'gesture of concern' that gives the appearance of 'white racial redemption' (ibid.: 139). The 'look of redemption' is 'achieved in a number of movies which do not, on the surface, appear to be explicitly addressing questions of racial identity' (ibid.). *The Accused*, of course, is one such film that does not explicitly address questions of race. With its focus on a 'universal' story of victimisation and redemption, it rewrites the story about the 'Portuguese working class' into a story about the disreputable working class. But although it is ostensibly a story about class, the film contains a covert storyline about racial difference.

As almost every reviewer of the film has noted, *The Accused* portrays masculinity as monstrous. Though we know very little of the men present in The Mill, they all fit a stereotype of lower-class males who drink and engage in criminal behaviour: they are noisy, violent drunks as in the media's representation of the rape in New Bedford. As 'college boy', Bob is linked to the working-class men in the bar by dint of his participation in a violent masculinity. Of all the male characters, one figure stands out as especially monstrous – Cliff 'Scorpion' Albrecht, the ringleader of the group of cheering men. The only male spectator – apart from Ken – that the film shows in scenes outside of the barroom and the courtroom, Cliff is marked out from the other men present at The Mill by dint of a large tattoo of a scorpion on his arm.

As Fleck observes, Cliff 'emerges out of a dark corner of the bar; himself of *swarthy complexion*, he is surrounded by a dark red glow and decorative scorpion emblems as he begins to cheer on the rapists' (1990: 54, my italics). What Fleck does not remark on is the way Cliff's class difference also functions as a racialized difference. His dark skin and hair are held in deliberate contrast to the 'blond and cherubic Kenneth Joyce' (ibid.). In fact, the character of Cliff could easily be taken for Portuguese-American. Perhaps this is what Cuklanz has in mind when she makes special reference to his 'dark hair and eyes' (1996: 104). What this racialized class difference brings into relief, I suggest, is a representation of a lower-class whiteness that is 'savage and more primitive than other kinds of whiteness' (Newitz 1997: 138).

Cuklanz, one of the few commentators to focus on the relationship between the real event and the film, speculates how *The Accused* could have depicted the 'difficult yet important question under discussion during the actual trial: would the Big Dan's defendants have been treated differently ... had they not been members of an ethnic minority who did not speak English?' (1996: 103) According to Cuklanz, 'by depicting a mixed-race group of rapists and a black man as the one who repents and testifies, the film could have given this complex topic the attention it deserves' (ibid.: 103–104). While Cuklanz is the only critic I have come across to remark on the film's erasure of ethnic tensions, she remains ambivalent as to the positive or negative valence this carries.[13] At the very least, she concludes, the film is 'certainly not to be condemned because it does not include minority rapists' (ibid.: 103). That is, while the film perhaps should have tackled the difficult questions raised by the real-life case, it is ultimately not to be faulted for its failure to do so. The question that remains is why the film's occlusion of ethnic tensions is considered significant in the first place.

In this respect, the most curious aspect of Cuklanz's reading of the film and her attempt to people *The Accused* with the missing ethnic component is the absence that grounds the imaginary narratives of racial presence that she offers. For nowhere does she imagine a woman from an ethnic minority in the role of the rape victim.[14] Here, as in the media reports, the term that undergoes erasure is the non-white woman. It thus seems important to ask: what happens if we attempt to substitute a woman of colour for the white woman? In *Women Viewing Violence*, the audience reception study referred to earlier in this chapter, the question of the raped woman's ethnicity emerges as a key issue. Whilst the study does not mention the real-life case, the ethnic dimension of the film appears to have been a central issue for the film's black female spectators. English Afro-Caribbean women with an experience of violence were reported to have challenged the film with the following question: 'What if the rape victim had been black?' (cited in Schlesinger *et al.* 1992: 141) It is worth quoting one of the female participants at some length:

> I found myself saying that in the film ... if I change that woman into a black woman, it would be even more painful for me. Because I know that the whole line of the story would've changed ... and I know that the verdict could have been different. And I know that the support ... the sympathy would've been very different ... It is a very painful film.
>
> (ibid.: 141, 143)

With regard to the real event, this spectator's affective response to the film is uncannily accurate. As we have seen, the verdict in the Big Dan's rape case was indeed different, as was the level of sympathy accorded the raped woman by the community. In this passage, the substitution of black for white shows up the active suppression of race in the white feminist acclaim of the film. If, in the actual case, the white media's sympathy for the victim seemed to hinge on the concealment of her ethnic identity, *The Accused* makes this whitewashing explicit with Sarah taking on the role of the 'quintessential Woman as Victim' (Dowd Hall 1983: 335).

A myth of substitution, in which one body is made to stand in for another, is an integral part of public fantasies of white social justice. This process of substitution emerges clearly in another Hollywood rape–revenge movie, Joel Schumacher's 1996 *A Time to Kill* (based on the novel by John Grisham). The movie revolves around the story of Carl Lee Hailey (Samuel L. Jackson) whose ten-year-old daughter is raped by two drunken rednecks. Realizing justice would never be served, Hailey takes the law into his own hands and murders the two rapists. The rest of the film traces the attempt of a white lawyer, Jake Brigance (Matthew

McConaughey), to ensure his client is not convicted. Despite the film's liberal overtones it is caught up in a series of highly ambivalent substitutions, continually showing the image of a young blond girl, Jake's daughter, in place of a visual image of the young black girl. This is meant to solicit Jake's (and by extension the white audience's) identification with Hailey's killing of the two rapists. This visual strategy of substitution culminates in the lawyer's final summation to the all-white jury. Asking them to shut their eyes and listen to a story, Jake tells in graphic detail the story of a young girl who is beaten, urinated on, raped and eventually thrown into a river, by two drunken men. After detailing outrage upon outrage, he concludes: 'Now imagine she is white.' In so explicitly tying the black girl's gang rape to the symbolic violation of white womanhood, Jake secures freedom for Hailey.

The emphasis in Jake's summation is on the act of 'seeing'. 'Picture this', 'see' the scene of this violation and torture in your mind's eye, he urges the jury. The film unashamedly exploits and reveals the way in which, as Judith Butler notes, 'racism pervades white perception, structuring what can and cannot appear within the horizon of white perception' (1993: 15–16). Butler concludes that 'the visual field is not neutral to the question of race; it is itself a racial formation, an episteme, hegemonic and forceful' (ibid.: 17). In *The Accused*, the racially coded 'field of visibility' may be covert but it is no less forceful for that: within the scene of a white woman being raped we witness a hyperbolic attempt to reassert the primacy of white legal and civic culture.

Rape and flashback

As a film about a vicious gang rape, *The Accused* can be classed as what Janet Walker has termed 'trauma cinema' – cinema about traumatic events from the past (2001: 214).[15] One of the characteristics of trauma cinema is its tendency to portray the traumatic past through flashbacks. Portraying rape via flashback demonstrates how trauma returns and imposes itself upon the subject, but also self-consciously positions the cinema audience, calling attention to their role as spectators. What is interesting is thus not only the content of the rape scene but the way it is presented; and what that presentation suggests about the relationship between film and audience, and reality and representation.

In the final section of this chapter then, I want to examine the filmic representation of rape through flashback in *The Accused*. To do this, I want to look at two more recent films that extend, and further complicate, the depiction of rape onscreen, Kathryn Bigelow's *Strange Days* (1995) and Kimberley Peirce's *Boys Don't Cry* (1999). It is interesting to note that women directed both.

Directly invoking the video images of the Rodney King beating at the hands of the Los Angeles Police Department (LAPD) in 1991, Kathryn Bigelow's 1995 *Strange Days*, a film that depicts the 'first virtual reality rape', confronts a question about violence, spectatorship and replay (Lyttle 1996).[16] Described as a 'techno noir thriller' and a 'millennial fantasy', *Strange Days* takes place in Los Angeles (LA) during the last two days of the twentieth century. 'An extreme taste of reality' is how the film poster advertises *Strange Days* to its potential audience. Lenny Nero (Ralph Fiennes), the anti-hero of the film and a peddler in underground virtual reality clips of real-life experiences, describes his wares in similar terms: 'This is not – like TV only better – this is life. This is a piece of somebody's life. Pure and uncut, straight from the cerebral cortex. You're there. You're doing it, seeing it, hearing it … feeling it'.

Since its inception this is what cinema has always promised its viewers – a form of representation so real that it is as if you are there living it. *Strange Days* makes good on this promise through its representation of virtual reality technology as 'Cinemascope for the mind', as Dave Gardetta calls it (1995). Likened by Bigelow to a 'kind of director-to-producer of heightened reality documentaries' (cited in Fuller 1995), Lenny roams the streets of LA in search of people who are willing to record their experiences on the device called SQUID – Superconducting Quantum Interference Device. His job is to sell these recorded experiences as 'playback' to clients who want to feel, taste and live the reality of another individual's experience.

According to Bigelow, 'One of the things the film is about is watching, the consequences of watching, the political consequences of experiencing someone else's life vicariously' ('Kathryn Bigelow' 1995). In *Strange Days*, the virtual reality rape of the significantly named Iris, Lenny's prostitute friend, is the pivotal event that pushes the film's exploration of the relationship between spectator and participant, audience and film to its limits. Here we find another instance in which rape, to refer once again to Frances Ferguson's influential notion, serves as the foundational moment for a new representational mode: in this case, virtual reality.[17] In contrast to classical notions of cinema and television spectatorship, which as Anne Friedberg notes, 'relied on the relative immobility of the viewer', virtual reality technology switches the 'viewer from a passive position to a more interactive one, *from an observer separate from the apparatus to a participant*' (1993: 144). By drawing a correlation between SQUID and cinema, *Strange Days* calls into question the idea of looking as passive.

The film appeared at both the New York and London film festivals. In both cases, several members of the audience were reported to have walked out, disgusted by a scene in which a young woman is raped and murdered while hooked up to a 'playback' machine. One reviewer, Alison Mayes, assured her readers that she would have been one of those people walking out of the cinema had she not been called upon to review the film, declaring herself 'appalled by the sick scene which is filmed from the exact point of view of the rapist-murderer' (cited in Portman 1995). But for defenders of the film, such critics are missing the point. As Lizzie Francke suggests, the question of cinematic voyeurism and the limits of mass entertainment is something that *Strange Days* sets out deliberately to explore (1997: 12). According to this reading of the film, stories of outraged spectators leaving the cinema in droves only add to the allure of *Strange Days* as a confrontational film that forces cinematic spectators to recognize their culpability in on-screen violence. Either way, the film, which cost over $40 million to make, was a box-office failure and jeopardized Bigelow's Hollywood career.

Does the film sensationalize sexual violence? This question was also raised in regard to other films featuring graphic rape scenes made in the same year as *Strange Days*, films such as Mike Figgis' *Leaving Las Vegas* (1995) and Paul Verhoeven's *Showgirls* (1995). One of the things that sets *Strange Days* apart from these other films, of course, is that a woman directs it. For many, this was to add insult to injury. According to Karla Peterson: 'That this harrowing scene ended up in a mainstream film is creepy enough, but the fact that a *woman* helped orchestrate it makes the nightmare even harder to shake ... As a woman, Bigelow shouldn't have pulled the rape card out for one more play' (1995).

True, the rape and murder of a female prostitute in *Strange Days* is deeply disturbing. As Bigelow repeatedly tells her detractors, it is meant to horrify. She is openly using the rape scene to comment on the role of the spectator in cinema and to raise the question of viewer culpability. According to Bigelow: 'The intention was to break the fourth wall. Not only are you having this intense voyeuristic experience, you are participating at the same time. You cross into another dimension' (cited in Nathan 1996).

In a homage to Michael Powell's 1960 shock classic *Peeping Tom*, *Strange Days* opens with an extreme close-up of a human eye, followed by a dramatic opening sequence in which we are thrust into the point of view of an armed robber as he falls to his death.[18] The screen goes black, and we are presented with a disgusted Lenny Nero who has just experienced this scene vicariously through the SQUID device. It is only then that we realize that what we have just seen is cinematic entertainment. Furiously, Lenny tells the man who supplied the clip of the robbery: 'You know I don't deal in blackjack! It's policy. I got ethics here!' The response of Lenny's supplier is that of the film producer: 'Oh yeah, when did that start? Come on! It's what people want to see, and you know it ... You're always saying, "Bring me real life. Bring me street life."' This exchange between the angry spectator, who asserts the limits of what he is willing to watch, and the supplier/film producer who points out that he is only supplying what the audience demands to see, rehearses the two dominant, polarized positions in the argument over screen violence. *Strange Days* reproduces this debate as a key part of its self-reflexive exploration of virtual reality technology. The discussion between Lenny and his supplier also bears more than a passing resemblance to recent discussions about the rise of voyeuristic reality TV and the worry that this popular genre of televisual viewing will ultimately lead to a demand for ever more excessive and extreme material (see my discussion of televised public rape in Chapter 6).

With *Strange Days* we find the crisis of witnessing exemplified by the rape in New Bedford, as discussed in Chapter 3, pushed to its furthest extremes. Like the other playbacks, the rape clip is shown to us from the point of view of the wearer of the SQUID equipment, in this case the rapist/murderer. The film's screenplay draws attention to our intimate involvement in the scene through use of the collective 'we':

> Our hands unbuckle the ... pack ... Pull out something ... a set of playback trodes. Our hands place them on her head. She stares uncomprehending. What?

What's he doing? He's jacked her into his own output, Lenny says, *She's seeing what he's seeing. She's seeing herself.*

Iris can now see herself as the Wearer sees her... wide-eyed with terror, white-lipped, weeping. Helpless. And she can feel what he feels. The Wearer's hand goes back into the pack and pulls out something else... We slip it over her head, down over her eyes. A blindfold. Now she can only see what the wearer sees...

Iris is feeling and seeing what he sees and feels... She feels what the attacker feels as he slides inside her, her pain and humiliation swirling with the killer's exhilaration.

ON LENNY, sweating and barely able to breath. Mace stops the tape... concerned by Lenny's reaction. He opens his eyes... Mace sees the fear there, of what the tape may reveal... But he shakes his head. He has to know. He pushes her hand away and punches PLAY.

(Cameron 1996: 98–99)

This 'snuff' clip upset some critics who argued that the attempt to make us see things from the point of view of the rapist/murderer was especially unpleasant.[19] However, it is vital to point out that we do not see the scene solely from the rapist/murderer's point of view. The scene is inter-cut with shots of Lenny's horrified reaction to what he is seeing and feeling. Whereas in the opening scene of the film we are directly involved in the action as a participant, Bigelow handles the rape scene differently: 'You see it through the eyes, attitudes and emotional reactions of the main character Lenny Nero (who is wearing the headgear). It is he who emotionalizes the piece for you, as opposed to the opening sequence where it is without a kind of interlocutor' (cited in 'Virtual Vision' 1996). Lenny's reaction to the rape/murder, like Ken's in *The Accused*, is therefore a central part of the scene. Unlike *The Accused*, however, the male character does not just watch the scene of rape, he lives it. Not only does he feel the terror of the victim, he is also experiencing the exhilaration of the rapist. He does not have the safety of voyeuristic distance, nor can he rely on any easy distinction between silently watching a rape and participating in one. He does not, in other words, have the 'get-out' clause provided for Ken in *The Accused*.

Well versed in cinematic critical theory, Bigelow's depiction of rape and murder is designed to reveal what Mulvey defined in her 1975 essay, 'Visual Pleasure and Narrative Cinema', as the sadistic pleasures of the male gaze. The film's interrogation of the violence and sexual voyeurism of cinema is openly revealed in the final image of the rape/murder scene, in which the rapist opens the dead victim's eyes and frames her face as though he was a film 'director lining up a close-up' (Cameron 1996: 100). In this account of the sadistic nature of cinema, Iris represents the historical position afforded the female spectator in Hollywood cinema – the victimized woman.

Bigelow is quoted as saying that with the rape/murder scene she wanted to 'match the shock effect of Hitchcock's shower scene' in *Psycho* (1960) (cited in

Tasker 1999: 14). But while *Psycho* and *Peeping Tom* are obvious influences, I would suggest that *The Accused* is another important, if unacknowledged, inter-text. It is instructive to inquire into the very different reception accorded these two films. As we have seen, there was a certain amount of controversy surrounding the rape in *The Accused* but it was nevertheless an establishment film whose representation of rape received widespread legitimization, often by feminists, as an important interrogation of cinematic voyeurism and violence. By contrast, the rape scene in *Strange Days* was vilified as a sadistic act on the part of the director.[20]

What is at issue in criticism of the film's Peeping Tom motif, I contend, is its depiction of a kind of grotesque sympathy, an enforced perversity of identification with both the victim and the aggressor. The depiction of sympathy and identification in *Strange Days* reinflects the 'positive' reading of *The Accused* as a film that forces its audience to identify with the victim. Recall producer Sherry Lansing's account of the film: 'Once you see this movie, I doubt...you will ever think of rape the same way again. Those images will stick in your mind, and you will be more sympathetic the next time you hear of somebody being raped' (cited in Faludi 1992: 170). What is so disturbing about *Strange Days*, I think, is that it calls into question a *benign* view of identification, demonstrating how sympathy, 'the capacity to feel the sentiments of someone else...the experience of transporting oneself to the place and person of someone else', opens up the possibility of experiencing their violence (Marshall 1988: 3).

Until this scene, Lenny has been a firm advocate of the pleasures of playback. The rape is the moment when Lenny, and by extension the cinema audience, is forced to confront the violent reality of the playback clips. The screenplay says that Lenny looks as if he has been 'gut-punched'; the film shows him doubling over and vomiting. What makes Bigelow's depiction of the rape scene so challenging is that it literalizes what other filmic representations of rape only imply: namely the spectator's participation in the scene. It is not that the technology leads to rape, but that the technology and the structures of looking which are built into it are a part of the rape. The rape and murder scene is the moment, Bigelow says, when the 'spectacle is no longer just spectacle' (cited in Gardetta 1995). In this scene, Lenny is captive to the image. Like the cinema audience, he is 'caught in the moral ambiguity of looking', to borrow Mulvey's phrase (1999: 842). Where *The Accused* binds looking to the law, and provides us with a male character who phones the police in an attempt to get help for the raped woman, *Strange Days* refuses the illusion of any such agency. Though Lenny tells Mace, the black heroine, to drive to the hotel to save Iris when he realizes what is happening, it is too late to do anything about it because the event has already happened. It is a recording.

Regardless, Lenny is complicit in the scene of violence he watches. He goes into the scene with excitement, assuming that it is going to provide some light entertainment. Mace is there to remind us of the troubling links between the scene of murder and sexual violence that follows and the other scenes Lenny has watched and produced. Speculating on why the killer sent the recording of his kill to Lenny, Mace says: 'Maybe he just figures Lenny will appreciate what he's created. It's the dark end of the street, Lenny. How do you like it now?' Previously, Lenny's clients are shown to be nervous, furtive men looking for a quick sexual fix; Mace calls them 'techno-perv jerk offs'. The rape clip counters these images of sexually pleasurable male playback experiences and cautions viewers about the implications of participatory viewing. Like *The Accused*, however, one could argue that Bigelow is preaching to the converted. As Gabe Elias suggests, Bigelow's 'overt work to render the gaze explicit appear to be employed not for the benefit of the informed female spectator, but rather for the uninformed male and female spectators who gain pleasure from these structures' (2002).

It is important to note that there is a second rape scene in *Strange Days*, one that did not receive much attention in the midst of the storm over the 'snuff clip'. This second rape scene is a repetition of the first: Lenny receives a black jack tape, puts on the SQUID and watches, horrified, as Faith, his beloved former girlfriend, is blindfolded, jacked up to the SQUID and viciously sexually assaulted. The difference is that this second rape scene turns out not to be a rape after all. As the SQUID is removed and she is untied from the bedposts, Faith smiles and tells her assailant she loves him. Faith is a woman who identifies too deeply with the patriarchal structures of looking that the film attempts to critique.[21] She likes to be watched, as she tells Lenny and Max. I would also suggest that this second 'rape' is designed to unnerve the cinematic spectator. The scene plays on an anxiety regarding our trouble with interpreting the cinematic distinction between sexual consent and violation. Like Lenny, we initially believe what we are watching is a real rape. The scene trips us up, and puts us in the position of the child of the Freudian primal scene who at first sees the act of parental intercourse as a rape, and is bewildered when the mother expresses signs of pleasure.[22]

Does Bigelow's disturbing representation of rape succeed in calling cinema to account for itself? It is a difficult question and one that I'm not sure Bigelow has been entirely successful in answering in interviews, despite her valiant efforts to do so through sophisticated readings of Barthes and Freud. When pushed by those who criticize the scene for what Peterson refers to as 'its sacrifice of another woman to Hollywood's thrill machine', it is telling to observe that Bigelow ends up making statements not unlike those offered by Lenny in his defence of playback (1995). As she tells one interviewer: 'I think the film has held a mirror up to society. And you can't fault the mirror, it's just a mirror (cited in 'Kathryn Bigelow' 1995). This response – 'I don't shape reality, I just reflect the world as it is' – is not nearly as provocative or complex as *Strange Days'* exploration of the ways in which structures of looking and representation are implicated in violence. Stepping up the exploration of violence and spectatorship in *The Accused, Strange Days* exposes how rape is bound up with anxieties regarding the limits, as well as the possibilities, of new media technologies.

In its use of rape as a means of commenting on the nature of spectatorship, both inside and outside cinema, *The Accused* deals with similar issues to *Strange Days*. One interesting point of comparison between the two films is they both present their 'controversial rape scenes' in the form of a visual memory. As we have just seen, in *Strange Days*, the rape is shown via playback; when we see the clip of Iris's rape and murder through Lenny's point of view, 'the act of violence is happening now, before our eyes, but it has also already happened. It is a memory' (Rascoroli 1997: 236). Similarly, in *The Accused*, when the rape scene is finally shown, it is presented as flashback, as Ken's personal memory of the event. However, once the film begins to show the bar room scene, the point of view dramatically opens up beyond anything Ken himself could have seen from his vantage point in the bar (Riggs and Willoquet 1989: 218). Such a broadening of visual perspective is consistent with the film's attempt to portray not just any one 'reality', but rather *the* historical reality of rape. As Maureen Turim suggests in *Flashbacks in Film*: 'If flashbacks give us images of memory, the personal archives of the past, they also give us images of history, the shared and recorded past' (1989: 2). In so far as it merges the 'two levels of remembering the past, giving large-scale social and political history the subjective mode of a single, fictional individual's remembered experience', *The Accused* is following an established cinematic tradition of the flashback (ibid.).

Before discussing the rape flashback in *The Accused* in further detail, it is productive to compare it to that found in *Boys Don't Cry* (1999), a film that includes a rape scene *The New York Post* described as the 'most sickeningly graphic' since *The Accused* (Foreman 2002). Like *The Accused*, *Boys Don't Cry* is based on a true story that grabbed national headlines; the gang rape and murder of a transgender individual, Brandon Teena, in Falls City, Nebraska in 1993. Also like *The Accused*, the film received great acclaim from Hollywood for its sensitive depiction of sexual violence earning its lead star (Hilary Swank) a Best Actress Academy Award.[23] But while there are certain similarities to *The Accused* on the level of both content and form, including its exploration of the legal system's appalling treatment of the rape victim, its portrayal of poor white people, and its decision to visually represent the trauma of rape, *Boys* presents its flashback of the crime in much more personal, subjective terms.[24]

Boys Don't Cry tells the story of how Brandon Teena managed to 'pass' as a man in small town America. The people of Falls City are poor and white and profoundly distrustful of any kind of sexual or social difference. When Brandon is revealed as a biological woman, he is punished for his transgression by two of the men in the group he befriends, John and Tom, who rape and eventually murder him. Where *Boys* significantly differs from both *The Accused* and *Strange Days* is in its depiction of rape from the viewpoint of the victim. In *The Accused*, as already noted, the film distances itself from the real-life victim's narrative in order to tell a universal story. By contrast *Boys* presents itself much more directly as a memorial for the victim as explicitly indicated by the epitaph with which the film ends: 'Brandon Teena 1972–1993'. This mourning for the victim contrasts with the impersonal documentary statistics regarding the frequency of rape in America with which *The Accused* concludes.

In *Boys* the rape scene is revealed as a memory, a flashback, when Brandon is being brutally interrogated by the sheriff. The interrogation is based on an actual taped recording in which the real-life Brandon is tormented into telling a male authority figure about the rape.[25] Where *The Accused* shows the rape scene only when Ken, the one 'good' spectator who will say what he has seen, takes the stand, *Boys* gives the silenced Brandon Teena the opportunity to tell his story through powerful cinematic images. As the sheriff asks unconscionable questions that belie his identity and further violate him, the film interpolates images of the gang rape.

Boys Don't Cry realizes the 'wish' of the feminists who praised *The Accused*, however mistakenly, for portraying the rape from the victim's point of view via flashback. In *Boys* it is only when Brandon is interrogated that we are provided with visual images of the rape, visual images that are presented to us as the truth of his memory and the only reality that matters. In this respect, Cuklanz's reading of *The Accused* could be said to apply more accurately to *Boys*: 'it is during [the woman's] testimony that the film finally depicts the rape, as if to contend that the reality of it did not exist outside of her telling of it' (1996: 106). *The Accused* begins its flashback of the rape with Ken's testimony ('Would you please recount for us what happened') and throughout the depiction of the rape it returns to that testimony – and the image of Ken in the witness box – four times.

The rape flashback in *Boys* is similarly set in a legal milieu, which gives emphasis to narration, story telling and testimony. Peirce theorizes her use of the rape flashback in terms that directly call attention to the film's address to the cinematic spectator: 'The story was supposed to be reflected in the film-making – for instance in the rape scene there are four frame flashes viscerally knocking into you, like memory knocking on consciousness' (cited in Leigh 2000: 20). The presentation of rape through flashback is thus meant to echo the trauma of rape itself. We move from images of Brandon's face in the police station to images of the rape, cued by the distant echoes of Brandon's screams and protests and the grunts and cheers of the men. The final flashback ends with the blinding white headlight of a car and Brandon lying bloodied on the ground.

The film explicitly makes the point that the police interrogation is a second rape of Brandon, an ordeal in which, as already discussed in regard to the televised New Bedford rape trial in Chapter 3, the rape victim is forced to 'name parts of her body, parts which in the very naming overtly reveal their sexual content' (Smart 1989: 38). In the case of Brandon Teena, a transgender individual desperate to conceal his biological gender, the fact that he, like other rape victims, is made to 'talk in public of her breasts, her vagina, her anus and, of course, what the accused did to these parts of her sexualised body' (ibid.) is especially traumatic. *Boys* directly quotes from the actual transcript of the police interrogation in its fictionalized depiction of the scene, with the Sheriff asking Brandon: 'What did they try to poke it in first at?' and a softly spoken, weeping Brandon responding 'My vagina'. The interrogation, like the rape, is designed to reinforce sexual difference through violability by making Brandon name female parts of his body and reveal himself as a woman.

As the film makes clear, Tom and John rape Brandon because their own masculinity is threatened by his gender transgression. It is only by positioning him as a rapeable object that the men can reassert dominant lines of sexual difference.

As Rachel Swan notes, 'If we assume, for a moment, the cruel logic of Tom and John and break down the categories of man and woman to their functions in sexual intercourse, then the rape repositions everyone according to their "god-given" gender' (2001: 50). What is perhaps all the more interesting then, is that the confusion and uncertainty of these lines of difference nonetheless remain even in the midst of the rape. When Tom pulls Brandon out of the car he punches him (as he would a man). He then immediately grabs his face and tries to kiss him passionately (as he would a woman). After the rape, both men immediately try to return to the terms of their previous relationship with Brandon by calling him 'little buddy', the expression they have always used to refer to the slight and 'pretty' Brandon. In effect, they urge him to 'take it like a man' (the original title of the film).

In both *Boys Don't Cry* and *The Accused* rape is a group affair designed to reaffirm masculine bonds. In *The Accused* the men egg each other on to commit the rape. They taunt one man with shouts of 'faggot', deriding his masculinity and suggesting that it is only through participating in the rape that he can prove his manhood. In *Boys*, as Tom rapes Brandon, John watches, swigs his beer and cheers and hoots his friend on. When they have both raped Brandon, they embrace each other triumphantly. Similarly, hugs and embraces and enthusiastic cheering and clapping among the men accompany the homoerotic ritual of rape as presented in *The Accused*.

As noted earlier in this book, one of the key insights of feminist legal theorists is the recognition that rape cases are decided in interpretative arenas. As Ellen Rooney writes: 'For [Catharine] MacKinnon what is at stake in a rape case is a hermeneutic, a question of meaning, and a question of the power of certain readers – "under the conditions of sexual inequality" – to make their point of view coextensive with the real, to universalize their particularity' (1991: 89). The feminist discussion of rape as a 'hermeneutic, a question of meaning' has direct relevance for a consideration of the flashback which, as Turim notes, is 'hermeneutically determined' (1989: 11). The flashback, a 'hermeneutic code, or code of enigmas', is one 'way in which narrative organizes the exposition of events so as to keep interest invested in a posed question, the answer to which is delayed' (ibid.).

Though *The Accused* leaves little or no doubt that a rape has occurred, it nonetheless offers us conflicting stories or testimonies about what 'really happened'. First of all, there is Ken's call to the police: 'There was a rape … I don't know, three or four guys.' Then there is the 'evidence' of Sarah's battered and bruised body, along with her account that she was gang raped. The rapists (and their defence attorneys) offer yet another version of the event: there was no rape. Indeed, the film suggests that one powerful form of social identification rests on a denial of rape. As Bob, pressuring Ken to recognize the bonds of male friendship, asks: 'Did you see me rape her, Ken? You didn't, did you?' Cliff 'Scorpion' Albrecht offers another kind of denial of the crime: 'Raped? Are you kidding me! That woman was doing the show of her life – she loved every minute of it!'. This attempt to pass the rape off as a spectacle echoes the much publicized comment of one of the accused in the New Bedford gang rape: 'At first I thought it was just a free show'.

The film's visual disclosure of the rape scene seeks to resolve these conflicting, multiple narratives. The rape scene is what Turim calls the 'final flashback of narration', in which the solution to the enigma posed by the film is provided (ibid.: 13). Of trial testimony flashbacks Turim writes that they:

> Represent the imaginary fulfilment of the "dream" of trial lawyers and the dread of trial justice, to have verbal accounts transformed into images so vivid that they efface the verbal and subjective aspects of testimony. If film has so readily been appropriated for this type of fictional legal spectacle, it is due to both the mythic charge of the eyewitness, the one who saw the truth that the fictional film can represent, and the taboo on taking photographs or filming inside the courtroom (only recently lifted), a taboo that the fiction film can transgress.
>
> (1989: 45)

By deploying the device of flashback during the courtroom scenes, *The Accused* – the fictional re-enactment of the first criminal case ever to be televised in America – is capitalizing on cinema's ability to represent verbal accounts as images. To this end the film's failure to include the issue of cameras in the courtroom is revealing: by ignoring the question of what happens when a rape trial becomes 'spectator sport' *The Accused* is condemned to repeat the violence it sets out to critique.

In the best tradition of the liberal trial film, the good guys win the case, 'with back-slappings, embraces, and sanctimony all around' (Bruzzi 1999: 40). But, I wonder, does the film's final, hyperbolic image of the law not betray the anxiety underlying its fantasy of civic justice? For what *The Accused* reveals with some clarity is the ambivalence of rape and the double role it plays in securing and undermining an image of culture. As most critics of the film note, a culture of male violence comes in for sharp criticism in *The Accused*. Drawing heavily on an analogy between rape and participation in male sport, the film underlines the homoeroticism of rape as crime 'between men'.[26] But despite this criticism of rape as male bonding, some critics worry about the implications of the film's image of rape as the model of collective identification. As Adam Mars-Jones argues, 'the issue that the film really wants to address is the extent of a citizen's responsibility, and it is certainly interesting that other legal codes than America's make much stronger attempts if not to enforce Samaritan behaviour, then at least to penalise the Levite option (of passing by on the other side)... Applauding a rape is one of the few social activities that the film seems to recognise, and if that is the truth about America the situation is beyond legal remedy' (16 February 1989). That 'applauding a rape' is a social activity is indeed one of the film's underlying messages. For what *The Accused* offers us, finally, is a grotesque and masculinized image of the civic bond premised on a look at the raped woman; a look that is finally, and unequivocally, bound to the very law it threatens to expose. Taking full advantage

114

of the reparative power of its visual medium, two moments in *The Accused* are only possible in cinema: the replay of the bar-room rape as eyewitness testimony and the final aerial shot of the courthouse. What fascinates me most about the film is how it reveals, once more, the way in which sexual violence needs to be brought back into the fold of the law. More than that, that rape needs to be repeated by – and on behalf of – the law. By revealing the rape via flashback the film is demonstrating how 'the legal order necessarily finds its origins in the sort of violence that compromise its very legitimacy'.[27] It is only by taking up the rape on its own terms that the law can work its power effectively.

Conclusion

I began this chapter by classifying *The Accused* as a film that contains one of the most watched rape scenes in cinematic history. One of the underlying questions of my inquiry has been: what is at stake in the spectatorship of the rape scene over a decade after the film's release? In *Women Viewing Violence*, the female spectators expressed concern about the damaging effects such a re-presentation of the scene might have on a victim of rape. In the course of a group discussion about the decision to show the film on television, anxious questions were also raised about how the film might be viewed by other spectators. As one woman suggested: 'There's a lot of people who would actually watch the film and would not see it the way we're seeing it at the moment and would think, "Oh, a bit of fun" or take it the wrong way, and it could lead to rape' (cited in Schlesinger *et al.* 1992: 155). This worry relates to a debate within media studies about the role of the audience in producing meaning. The idea that the text is open to interpretation by its spectators and cannot be limited to a single meaning is seen to have dangerous implications when it comes to images of rape. My point in entertaining a question about the relationship between violence and spectatorship has not been to prove that watching *The Accused* 'could lead to rape', but to demonstrate the ways in which rape renders the complexity of spectatorship.

As a film that continues to serve as a benchmark for more recent cinematic representations of rape, it is important to renew critical discussion of *The Accused*. Moving away from a generalized consideration of the film's depiction of rape as either 'positive' or 'negative', I have examined how its representation of sexual violence, as well as the commentaries on it, bring to light cultural unease regarding gender, race and ethnicity. The representation of rape continues to be one of the most highly charged issues in contemporary cinema. And while popular images of rape will undoubtedly continue to be decried for sensationalism and exploitation, what needs to be explored further is how these images open up wider questions about changing viewpoints on the relationship between audience and film.

Part III

REWRITING RAPE

5

'MORE INTIMATE THAN VIOLENCE'

Sarah Dunant's *Transgressions*

So far I have considered how an image of the raped woman serves as the means for securing individual and collective identity, even as it throws that identity into crisis. In this chapter I shift my attention to feminist literary representations of rape, addressing the relationship between rape, fiction and feminism. If previously I have explored gang rape as a site for collective masculine identification, this chapter approaches the question of rape from a different angle. Exploring its recurring presence in feminist crime writing, I want to consider how feminist writers employ images of rape to articulate women's identification with other women. This chapter returns to the question raised in the opening chapter of this book: how does an image of rape as primal scene work to secure feminism's foundations?

The following *Daily Mail* headline captures the crux of the controversy surrounding Sarah Dunant's 1997 thriller *Transgressions*: 'How can an intelligent, famous feminist write a book in which a rape victim is sexually aroused by her brutal ordeal' (cited in Dunant 1 June 1997)? As the outraged reviewer warned potential readers, the unspeakable had occurred. Dunant, a self-identified feminist, had written a novel including one of the oldest pornographic scenarios in the world: a rape scene in which a woman ends up enjoying the experience. According to the reviewer, *Transgressions* was nothing more than 'panting prose pornography', written by Dunant as part of a 'cynical ploy to reposition herself in the public eye' (Gordon, cited in Porlock 15 June 1997). Though few reviewers joined the *Mail* in its denouncement of *Transgressions* 'as explicitly erotic and exploitative of women as strip joints, sex shops, and the worst hard-core porn', a taboo did, in fact, appear to have been broken (cited in Neustatter 27 May 1997). As *Guardian* reviewer Angela Neustatter asked: 'Is accusing *Transgressions* of being exploitative pornography missing the point, or has the writer got it right this time in suggesting that Dunant, 46, has abandoned her feminist principles and gone sleazy' (27 May 1997)?

Dunant is a rather unlikely candidate for a literary sex scandal. Best known in Britain as the red-spectacled former presenter on the BBC arts programme, 'The Late Show', Dunant has since become recognized for a series of well-received feminist detective novels. It was the apparently scandalous incongruity between the alleged pornographic subject matter of the novel, and the second-wave feminist politics of its author, that turned *Transgressions* into a media sensation before it hit the shelves. As one commentator summed up the controversy: 'Nothing gives quite the same pleasure as a story about a feminist stepping out of line' (Porlock 15 June 1997).

In an interview with *The Guardian*, Dunant dismissed the charge of pornography: 'It genuinely never occurred to me that anyone would call me exploitative. I was so clear that this was a major fictional attempt to take exploitation by the scruff of the neck and shake it' (cited in Neustatter 27 May 1997). For Dunant, reviewers were reading something into her novel that simply was not there. Nowhere, she insisted, did she depict a woman who enjoys getting raped. 'For a second when she is seducing the man, she recognises that she has actually got control and she experiences a *frisson* of power', Dunant explains. 'We know there is a connection between power and arousal, and I think that is the point, rather than that she actually gets turned on' (ibid.). Leaving aside for the moment the distinction Dunant makes here between sexual arousal and sexual pleasure, it is worth pointing out that, despite the media pronouncement to the contrary, it is by no means certain that *Transgressions* does depict female sexual pleasure in male sexual violence.

At the centre of the debate over the feminist status of *Transgressions* lies a question about the contract between the feminist writer and her female readers. After considering Dunant's argument that her novel challenges fictional stereotypes of women as passive victims, Neustatter asked: 'This is all very well, but couldn't it be deeply upsetting to a woman who has been raped and felt paralysed with fear, unable to do anything but exist, to see fiction suggesting she could have done better if she had been up to a quick seduction?' By introducing this figure of the raped woman as potential reader of the text, Neustatter is articulating the demand that feminism – in literature, as in life – must not risk upsetting a victimized woman. The underlying concern is that female readers who come to the novel expecting a feminist representation of rape may be sorely disappointed – even deeply traumatized – by what they find. Though what a feminist representation of rape might look like is certainly open to debate, the assumption here is that it is one that is inextricably connected to the 'real' of women's lives. Neustatter's complaint is that, in depicting 'something like a moment of pleasure in a situation that holds, for most women, the worst of terrors' (ibid.), Dunant is refusing the 'feminist literary imperative to "tell it like it is" – to be authentic, confessional, and realistic' (Munt 1994: 201).

But is there, as the dispute over *Transgressions* implies, such a thing as a 'feminist representation' of rape, a specific image we can readily identify? If we turn to the favourable reviews of the novel, we find critics insisting that *Transgressions* and its representation of rape is 'feminist', though what that means exactly remains unclear. Acknowledging that the novel 'provoked fierce debate about female response – physical and psychological – during a sexual attack', Joan Smith dismisses the charge of pornography on the following grounds: 'I do not think many women readers will be in much doubt about the legitimacy of the course of action Elizabeth embarks on to save her life, nor the label the act deserves' (Smith 'A Woman's Right' 8 June 1997). Putting to one side the ambiguity of this statement (what label, one wonders, *does* the act deserve?) it begs the question: if female readers will not be in much doubt about the legitimacy of Elizabeth's course of action, is the implication then, that male readers will be? And if so, what does this tell us about the classification of *Transgressions* as feminist?

By raising these questions, I do not mean to suggest that it is important, or even possible, to come up with a definitive feminist representation of rape. What is most interesting about this dispute is not the question of whether *Transgressions* is pornographic (indeed, as several commentators noted, the novel hardly qualifies as the 'worst hard-core porn'), but, rather, the claim that is being made for literature in the scandal surrounding the novel's fictionalizing of sexual violence. For, what is being argued over in the debate about the novel's so-called 'rape scene', is the more general question of how we should think about the relationship between fiction and sexual violence. Is it possible to fictionalize rape? Do feminists want to preserve literature as a space where something can happen that does not usually happen?

In its explicit engagement with these questions, *Transgressions*, along with the responses it provoked, invites us to examine the role that rape plays in the establishment of feminist fiction. Situating *Transgressions* in the wider context of feminist detective/thriller fiction, I want to consider the ubiquity of images of sexual violence in the work of contemporary women writers such as Barbara Wilson, Elisabeth Bowers, Barbara Neely, Jenny Diski and Susanna Moore. My contention is that scenes of sexual violence are central to the female crime writer's attempt to refigure the terms of the male crime novel.

In her introduction to a collection of stories on the art of seduction, Jenny Newman suggests that 'if there is any relationship at all between literature and life, the history of fictional seduction is bound to throw the nature of our sexual politics into sharp relief' (1988: ix). This observation is followed by another: 'Women writers have always been slower than men to look on the bright side of seduction, perhaps because as members of the second sex they are more aware of its dangers' (ibid.: xviii). It is in terms of a question about how to negotiate this dangerous space between 'courtship and rape' and between 'pleasure and danger', that we can read *Transgressions* and its representation of seduction. What Dunant is doing with male sexuality in *Trangressions* is at least as interesting – and perhaps as scandalous – as what she is doing with female sexuality. That the issue of male sexuality is the blind spot in the dispute over the novel attests to the continuing reluctance to read for anything other than male brutality and female victimization – what Carol Clover refers to as 'our ultimate gender story' (*Men* 1992: 227).

Rape, fiction and feminism

At the extreme end of the attempt to characterize *Transgressions* as a feminist text is the argument that it serves an educative purpose for its readership. As one reader,

Henry MacGregor, suggested, in a letter to the *Sunday Times*:

> Dunant has tried to envisage how a woman might gain some control back
> in her life when such a horrific event takes place. The unfair treatment
> that Dunant has met at the hands of some critics, who have accused her
> of making her female character enjoy a rape scene, misunderstands what
> she is trying to do. There is a huge difference between taking control
> when your life is at risk and seeking enjoyment from such frightening
> sexual attacks. This is an instance of fiction helping us to come to terms
> with fearful situations in real life.
>
> (15 June 1997)

There is something almost desperate about the attempt to characterize *Transgressions*
in this way. It is as if the only way to answer the charge that Dunant makes her
female character enjoy being raped is to cast the novel as a user's manual for coping
with real-life rape. Where the novel's critics worry that actual female victims might
not be able to live up to the seductive ways of Dunant's fictional heroine, the novel's
proponents argue that, in fact, the rape scene might help women to cope with real-
life trauma. Both views posit a notion of fiction 'predicated on the idea that stories
are supposed to function as instruction manuals' (Gaitskill 1994: 43).

The question of what it means to fictionalize rape has emerged as a major bone
of contention in discussions of feminist literature. This debate has perhaps found
its sharpest expression with regard to a text many consider to be the definitive
feminist representation of rape, and which I will pause briefly to discuss – Andrea
Dworkin's *Mercy* (1990). The novel's heroine is called 'Andrea', although Dworkin
insists that she is a fictional character. The publishers describe *Mercy* as a 'stark,
uncompromising and extremely moving novel', in which Dworkin 'uses the experience of a young woman raped many times – as many women are – to explore
the cultural, spiritual and political implications of the act of rape in our society.
The result is a monumental work of fiction'.

In many respects, *Mercy* is the fictional equivalent to *Intercourse* (1987), Dworkin's
non-fiction polemic. *Intercourse*, in its attempt to show the oppressive and male
dominated nature of heterosexual intercourse, focuses on fiction written by male
authors as diverse as Leo Tolstoy, Tennessee Williams and Gustave Flaubert.
Similar to one of feminist criticism's founding works, Kate Millett's 1970 *Sexual
Politics, Intercourse* uses fiction as a means to critique rape as the paradigmatic experience of women under patriarchy. But as Mandy Merck notes in her discussion
of *Intercourse*: 'There is a huge array of contradictions in Dworkin's presentation of
these fictions – beginning with her reluctance to read them as fictions at all'
(1993: 200). As Merck observes, Dworkin ignores questions of form, style, narrative structure and point of view, 'to elide these stories into various non-fiction
commentaries on intercourse, some written by the authors in question, some
not' (ibid.). Given the way Dworkin reads fiction, or rather refuses to read it, the

question is: what role does fiction play in her literature? Do we, in fact, read it as fiction at all?[1]

On the one hand, those who read *Mercy* as an important feminist representation of rape, argue that the novel reveals the terrible 'truth' about sexual violence. Mary Smeeth and Susanne Kappeler argue: 'We live in a rape culture. And *Mercy* reminds us exactly what that means' (1990: 27). Smeeth and Kappeler define *Mercy* as a feminist depiction of rape by stating what it is not: 'This isn't the sort of rape we are used to seeing in pornography. Nor is it an account of a particular, singular experience of rape by the victim-survivor. It is about rape as a condition of women's existence which is all-pervasive and continuous' (ibid.: 27). Something other to the rape that appears in mainstream pornography, and something more than an individual account of a survivor, *Mercy* is the story of Everywoman in patriarchy. In a statement that harks back to Susan Brownmiller's conceptualization of sexual violence, Smeeth and Kappeler suggest that it is the awareness of rape as the 'condition of women's existence' – the means through which 'men of every kind' forge the social bond – that makes *Mercy* a paradigm for the ultimate feminist representation of rape (ibid.).

But the novel's opponents have faulted Dworkin for treating the 'facts' of sexual abuse in literary and fantastical ways. Roz Kaveney, for example, takes Dworkin to task for the 'contemptuous way she endeavours to manipulate her women readers with rhetorical trickery' (1991: 85). Kaveney is referring to the novel's use of magic realist techniques, in which 'kisses open up infected wounds', and 'unhealed wounds bleed the green of rot and corrosion' (ibid.). In light of these peculiar descriptions of the wounded female body, Kaveney wonders what we are thus to make of the 'claim that fellatio has denatured the narrator's voice – is this a realist claim about physical injury, or a metaphysical claim about the loss of personal integrity and authenticity' (ibid.: 83)? Dworkin cannot have it both ways: 'an author who is playing Prophet cannot also play Trickster' (ibid.).

For all Dworkin's claims concerning her attempt to articulate the 'simple-minded' proposition that '*bad things are bad*', her writing goes far beyond the bounds of realism in its excessive depiction of violence and suffering (Dworkin 1990: 334, her italics). What Parveen Adams and Mark Cousins note of Catharine MacKinnon's work can equally be applied to Dworkin's writing: 'The world of MacKinnon's text requires *the indestructibility of the woman's body* ... The body is always ready to be abused again' (1995: 99). In Dworkin's fiction, the woman's body must be ever ready for more and greater violation: 'I am a moving mountain of pain ... I am marked and scarred and black-and-blue inside and out, I got torn muscles in my throat and blood that dried there that won't ever dislodge and rips in my vagina the size of fists and fissures in my anus like rivers and holes in my heart' (1990: 318). Though she remains reticent on the issue, the reason Dworkin turns to fiction, I would argue, is because it enables her to provide a fantasy of the raped woman as a figure caught in between two deaths. Ironically, in this Dworkin is conforming to a vision of violence not unlike that offered by the Marquis de Sade. Slavoj Žižek describes the terms of the Sadeian fantasy:

> His victim is, in a certain sense, indestructible: she can be endlessly tortured
> and can survive it; she can endure any torment and still retain her beauty.
> It is as though, above and beyond her natural body (a part of the cycle of
> generation and corruption), and thus above and beyond her natural death,
> she possessed another body, a body composed of some other substance,
> one excepted from the vital cycle – a sublime body. Today we can find this
> same fantasy at work in various products of 'mass culture', for example in
> animated cartoons.

(1989: 134)

Žižek refers to Tom and Jerry: 'the cat is stabbed...he is run over by a steamroller
and his body is flattened into a ribbon, and so forth; but in the next scene he appears
with his normal body and the game begins again – it is as though he possessed
another indestructible body' (ibid.: 134–135). This is reminiscent of Marilyn French's
discussion of representations of rape in *The Women's Room*, discussed in Chapter 1, in
which traditional fictional descriptions of sexual violence are likened to cartoons 'in
which the cat or bear or whatever gets smashed over and over, but always rises from
its own ashes' (1997: 30). In contrast to *The Women's Room*, which implies that feminist writers should portray the reality of rape, Dworkin's representation of the violated female body is more in keeping with the cartoon fantasies described above.
Andrea, the protagonist of *Mercy*, is raped, forced to perform fellatio, ripped open by
her doctors, tied up, burned, beaten and tortured. At the end of this exhausting catalogue of violation and abuse, a battered but miraculously still alive, Andrea, now
accompanied by an 'army of raped ghosts', rises to take vengeance (Dworkin 1990:
318). This place 'between the two deaths', as Žižek, following Lacan, calls it, is, in a
very real and intractable sense for Dworkin, the raped woman's position in culture
(1989: 131). In Dworkin's narrative world, the gap between life and death is filled in
with the sublime body of the raped woman. This representation of the raped woman
as a liminal figure, sitting on the boundary between life and death, between fiction
and real life, points to the purchase of rape for feminist literature.

While Dworkin does not explicitly address the role that fiction plays in her
literature,[2] Dunant appears to have a clear idea of its significance. In her defence of
Transgressions, Dunant suggests that she uses fiction to empower her female heroine:
'I wanted to see what it felt like to give a woman a fair chance in a sexually aggressive
encounter – one not of her own making, but one in which she triumphs, albeit briefly.
She decides she will do whatever it takes not to be a victim' (Dunant 'Rape' 1 June
1997). If, as I have suggested, part of the scandal of *Transgressions* is that it is seen to be
inadequate to the demands of the 'real', this response asks us to remember that we are
dealing with fiction, not real life. As Elizabeth Cowie argues, it is precisely because rape
represents the extreme of women's disempowerment in the 'real world' that it can be
used – in fiction – to represent a fantasy of women's empowerment (1992: 142).

Nevertheless, in contrast to someone like Kathryn Bigelow who responds to
criticisms of her erotically charged images of sex and violence by contending that

'fantasies of power are universal, filmmaking is not gender specific' (cited in Gristwood 25 February 1996), Dunant does not dispute the demand that images produced by women should adhere to the category of 'feminism'. On the contrary, I would suggest that Dunant has a very clear idea of what a feminist representation of rape should look like, a conviction that is largely based on her understanding of feminism as that which is defined through its active differentiation from pornographic masculine discourse. Without actually defining pornography, Dunant knows it when she sees it, and can claim in good conscience that her novel is its emphatic opposite. It is against the extreme negativity of images in which women are 'silenced, literally, in most cases, because they are dead' that Dunant endeavours to provide a 'positive' image of a woman who saves herself from a life-threatening situation ('Rape' 1 June 1997). As she declares:

> I refuse to be rendered terrified or sexless by fear. And if the popular culture around me is only interested in exploiting my fear by repeatedly showing what happens when we get in the way of male violence (and here the women can be as guilty as the men, as anyone who has seen Kathryn Bigelow's viciously voyeuristic *Strange Days* can testify), then my response is to write myself some alternatives. And if they are transgressive, then so be it.
>
> (ibid.)

The striking tautology of the statement, 'I refuse to be rendered terrified … by fear', betrays something similar to the desperation of the attempt to defend *Transgressions* on the grounds that 'there is a huge difference between taking control when your life is at risk and seeking enjoyment from such frightening sexual attacks' (MacGregor 15 June 1997). As I will suggest in the reading of the novel to follow, this passage repeats the fantasy of omnipotence found in *Transgressions* itself.

Rape and the origins of feminist crime writing

Stripped to its essentials, the plot of *Transgressions* can be summarized as follows: a woman finds herself in a life-threatening situation. Refusing to become a victim she manages to empower herself within a sexually violent scenario. In the aftermath of the event, she must cope with the 'physical, emotional and sexual ramifications of violence' (Dunant 'Rewriting the Detectives' 28). Ultimately, she emerges bruised but triumphant. With certain variations, this narrative scenario occurs repeatedly in feminist crime thrillers. More than simply a backdrop to women's crime narratives, scenes of rape and sexual victimization articulate a fundamental conflict between the role of the female heroine as an investigator and as a victim of crime. As a text in which sexual violence is closely bound up with the attempt to refigure the meanings of the thriller, *Transgressions* is an exemplar of this significant genre of women's writing, in which the primary concern is to find a way out of what Ruby Rich has called one of the great feminist debates – 'women-as-agent versus women-as-victim' (1986: 556).

As the novel begins, Elizabeth Skvorecky, a self-described 'single white female', has just received instructions to translate a hard-boiled Czech thriller into English.[3] The narrative of *Transgressions* is interrupted by several extracts from this thriller, which forms a separate, but related text: a thriller within a thriller. The first person narrative tells the story of Elizabeth's life as she attempts to recover from the end of a long relationship; the thriller, told in the second person, narrates the adventures of American cop, Jake Biderman, on assignment in Prague to break a drugs ring when his ex-wife, Mirka, is kidnapped by drug barons. The novel is structured so that the two different worlds – Elizabeth's and the pulp thriller novel – run alongside each other, often without any warning or introduction from the main narrative. As the narrative progresses, the two different worlds become more and more intertwined; steadily bleeding into one another to such an extent that it is at times difficult to tell which 'text' the reader is in.

Elizabeth's running commentary on the conventions of the thriller represents *Transgressions'* attempt to use fiction as a means of critiquing the cultural fixation with images of sexual violence. From the start, it is clear that Elizabeth does not approve of the story she is translating:

> As a story the whole thing was shot through with a careless misogyny. All acceptable within the genre, but none the less distasteful for that. How will I feel, she had thought when she decided to take it on, sitting at night in an empty house translating scenes of women being threatened and abused by men who enjoy their pain rather than their sexuality? Rape, fear, torture – it was so common nowadays that it was almost a form of punctuation for a certain kind of novel.
>
> (26)

This passage casts rape as a syntax of culture. As Dunant argues elsewhere:

> Crime thrillers – particularly American ones – are as much about graphic violence as they are about plot and within this landscape women have become easy targets. Terrorised, battered, sexually assaulted, mutilated, even dismembered, [women's] bodies have become part of the grammar of the form.
>
> ('Rewriting' 1993: 28)

As the prototypical feminist reader who criticizes the misogyny of male-authored texts, Elizabeth fits the description of what Judith Fetterley first defined in 'the resisting reader': a woman who challenges a tradition of male writing that excludes and objectifies her (Fetterley 1978). Elizabeth deals with the 'careless misogyny' of the genre by taking advantage of her role as a translator to make subtle changes to the text. She reads the text back to herself, dissecting words and imagery for the gender bias they are invariably seen to yield up.

There is a very suggestive comparison to be made between the role of the female translator and the job of the female crime writer. In *Murder by the Book? Feminism and the Crime Novel*, Sally Munt argues that the parodic character of detective fiction is willingly appropriated by feminist writers seeking to attack 'dominant myths of gender and sexuality' (1994: 206). This idea of parody as undermining dominant gender codes, turning established representations of sexuality into something less familiar, links up with a definition of translation: to be transformed or converted. By including excerpts from a male thriller and by having her female heroine comment on, and dissect, its workings, Dunant is inflecting the rewriting of convention that is an integral part of the genre of feminist detective/thriller writing.

What role does rape play in the feminist attempt to rewrite the conventions of the crime novel? Despite a widespread acknowledgement of rape as one of the central themes of women's crime writing, it remains curiously under theorized in the by now extensive literature on feminist crime fiction. While this may reflect the schematic format that the survey literature on feminist detective fiction tends to take, it may be, too, that there is a tendency to treat rape as a transparent issue. In her discussion of women's crime writing, Barbara Wilson suggests that:

> The appeal of the investigator novel to women writers and readers would seem obvious. For to be a woman is ... to have been the victim or bystander of many nameless and hidden crimes: battery, rape, sexual abuse, harassment. To take the role of investigator means to open the doors upon silence, to name the crimes, to force the confessions, to call for justice and see justice done. And even, sometimes, to take justice into one's own hands.
>
> (1994: 222)

Beyond an obvious understanding of the significance of rape for feminist crime novels, it is possible to argue that the story of rape is inseparable from the establishment of the contemporary feminist crime thriller. It is not, or not only, that the inception of feminist work on rape in the late 1970s and early 1980s coincides with the genesis of feminist detective fiction, but that the political and representational issues surrounding rape are in some way inextricably connected to the form of the thriller itself. In particular, that subgenre of the thriller Tzetan Todorov has deemed 'the story of the vulnerable detective' (1988: 164). As Todorov defines it, 'its chief feature is that the detective loses his immunity, gets beaten up, gets badly hurt, constantly risks his life, in short he is integrated into the universe of the other characters, instead of being an independent observer as the reader is' (ibid.).

In feminist crime novels, rape is the privileged means of turning the female detective back into a female like any other character/reader. Wilson's *Sisters of the Road*, for example, one of the most important feminist crime novels from the 1980s, concludes with the rape of female sleuth Pam Nilsen.

> He raped me. With a punishing violence that had nothing to do with sex and everything to do with rage and hatred. My vagina was as dry as my mouth and every pounding blow stabbed through my body like a sword dipped in fire ... I almost blanked out; my whole being reduced to a tiny pinprick that cried out *no*.
>
> (Wilson 1986: 194)

127

The rape is the point of identification between Pam and her female client, a young prostitute Trish, herself a victim of rape. As Trish tells Pam: 'When I heard you struggling and moaning... it was like I felt it was happening to me. And it hurt me in a new way. Like it was the first time I really felt it' (ibid.: 199). This depiction of rape as a moment of identification between women provides an important counterimage to the vision of rape as the site of civic identification between men, discussed in the previous two chapters of this book. The idea of rape as a means of sympathy and identification between women also returns us to Brownmiller's origin story of how she became a feminist: her recognition that rape could happen to any woman, regardless of her 'combative, wary and verbally aggressive' nature (1991: 8). While the traumatic aftermath of the rape in *Sisters of the Road* is described in graphic terms, ('Rape is something you recover from, but at first you don't believe you ever will... I had back pains and pains that shot down my legs. The entrance to my vagina was torn and my face was battered black and blue') [1986: 195], the recovery is nonetheless cast as a new beginning for Pam. In narrative terms, the rape is the image through which Wilson secures her vision of an investigator 'not immune from injustice and stigma, nor invulnerable to violence against women' (Wilson 1994a: 224). As Wilson suggests, 'the incident at the end of *Sisters of the Road* did not shock because it is uncommon, but because it goes against what we expect in crime novels. Investigators may be threatened, drugged, beaten up, tortured and left for dead, but their sexual boundaries are never disturbed' (ibid.). However, in the genre inaugurated by novels like *Sisters of the Road* rape scenes may be precisely what we have come to expect. In these novels, sexual violence is a way of establishing the female heroine's vulnerability, but also, significantly, her determination and resistance.[4] In Elisabeth Bowers' *Ladies Night* the work that rape is used to perform in the feminist thriller is made explicit:

> Once I was a suburban housewife, washing diapers and chasing the neighbours' dog out of my azalea bed, reading murder stories with my ears plugged so I wouldn't hear my kids screaming at each other. I had a model husband, a week's worth of casseroles in the freezer – and one evening as I was pushing a cart full of groceries across a supermarket parking lot, I got yanked into a car and raped at knifepoint.
>
> (1990: 62)

As Bowers writes, this 'rape marked a turning point', the point of origin of her heroine's change of lifestyle and her new career as a private investigator: 'First I joined a judo club; a year later I switched to Aikido ... Women are taught the world is dangerous, that to fear it is only common sense ... Therefore, as I became better able to defend myself physically, I changed psychologically; I became braver, more outward looking' (ibid.: 63). Rape, then, is the event that provokes or initiates woman's entry into feminism. In Leah Stewart's debut novel, *Body of a Girl* (2001), we find a similar use of rape as an origin story – as the crime that initiates the woman's turn to detective work. The female journalist heroine is all too aware of the fact that girls like her are raped every day. Her job as a crime reporter comes about when she attempts to write a story about rape and realizes that:

> There was no statistic for rape, as though the terrible things that happen to women are either too shameful or too commonplace to report. Flushed with indignation, I went to the managing editor and asked him why we never ran rape stories. An hour later he was having a heated conversation with the news editor. This is how I ended up on the police beat.
>
> (2001: 44–45)

Rape is shown to epitomize the difficulty of representation, of turning violence into a palatable 'story' for public consumption.

In feminist crime writing, rape is also a way of linking the personal with the political, the private with the public. In Barbara Neely's feminist detective series, featuring black heroine Blanche White, the motif of rape is used to comment on – and expose – the racism and classism of American society. Rape is the back story for Neely's first three novels, but the subject is fully explored in her fourth novel, *Blanche Passes Go* (2000), when Blanche finally has the opportunity to confront the white man – the son of her employer – who sexually assaulted her at knifepoint eight years ago. In exploring the public fantasies that circulate around rape, in which the figure of the black male rapist looms large in the white imagination and the black woman is all too often the invisible victim of white male violence, Neely reveals rape as a crime 'by which some white men keep some black women and even some black men in a state of fear' (Barnett 1998: 84). In the African American community, the word rape has immediate racial connotations as here noted by Neely: 'The memories of innocent black men dragged from their beds and lynched or otherwise murdered for being black were as fresh in people's minds as yesterday's newspaper' (2000: 58). The black woman's personal trauma cannot be separated from the stories that are woven around rape in the public domain, stories that assume all black men are guilty of harbouring base desires to defile white womanhood and that therefore ensure the silence of the black female who is raped. As Neely observes, 'their rapes and mistreatments at the hands of powerful white men could...cost them the black men who loved them' (ibid.: 23).

It is interesting to note that the novel concludes with a radical feminist statement very similar to that found in Marilyn French's *The Women's Room*, when Val declares that 'it was males against females and the war was to the death' (1997: 469). *Blanche Passes Go* concludes with the assertion that:

> They were all the same, those raping, kicking, punching, killing motherfuckers. This was what they wanted: a woman cringing in a corner, a woman begging him to be careful with that knife, that gun, that rope around her neck, that threat to destroy her face, hurt her kids, or whatever else the rotten shit used to scare her out of herself, to keep her from running.
>
> (2000: 316)

Always uneasy of a potential alliance with the white woman on the basis of their shared sexual victimization, Blanche, 'the vulnerable detective', eventually comes to recognize the importance of women standing up for other women: 'All this woman-hurting shit had to stop' (ibid.). The recognition of her vulnerability in the face of male violence is what connects her to all women, black and white. As in other feminist crime novels, the challenge is for the woman to 'find a way to fight back' (ibid.: 32). It is in the wider context of feminist crime writing, in which rape serves as a founding event for woman's newfound feminist independence, that we can read *Transgressions* and its representation of seduction.

Fighting fantasy with fantasy

Disgusted by the sadistic treatment of female victims in the male-authored thriller, Elizabeth complains that the least the author could have done was 'to fight fantasy with fantasy' (105). In the fantasy Elizabeth imagines, the female victim of a psychopath would be turned into 'a kind of avenging angel for women in trouble, swooping down on violent men and snapping their bodies between their dog-like teeth' (105). This notion of fighting fantasy with fantasy comes up again in the text, when Elizabeth imagines how she would exact her 'own revenge like the avenging angels' of her fantasies (153). It is in the next chapter that fantasy becomes 'reality' when Elizabeth awakes to find that this time 'the nightmare was real' (156).

Awaking to find a male intruder sitting on the edge of her bed, Elizabeth's first thought is that she is going to die. Her second thought is to wonder how she can survive the attack. Dismissing the advice typically given to rape victims – 'If you can't fight it, lie back and let it happen' – as 'bullshit', Elizabeth also dispenses with the idea of physical resistance: 'If she resisted he would hit her. He could do it now if he wanted; smash in the side of her head with his hammer, then fuck her in a pool of blood' (162). As minutes pass, and the intruder makes no move to hurt her, Elizabeth 'instinctively' realizes that his death threat ('You move any more, you touch anything, you do anything funny and I'll kill you d'you hear?') is really an expression of his underlying fear and longing (159). With its connotations of mindlessness and brute natural impulse, 'instinct', I would argue, is one of the primary means by which the text attempts to qualify Elizabeth's seduction: 'She was working on instinct now, moving to a place where reason couldn't reach. Survival versus fear' (163).

Considering the fuss surrounding the scene that follows, the casual observer of the controversy might be forgiven for expecting – if not necessarily the 'worst hard core porn' – then, at the very least, a titillating read. Suffice it to say, the reader will be sorely disappointed. As Vicky Hutchings notes:

> Awash with bodily secretions of one kind or another, the seduction is not a pretty read. He has a soft, sibilant voice, damp palms, a pasty skin, thin lips, stubbornly limp penis and bad teeth. Trembling and clammy under his layer of clothes, he wears frayed underpants and a vest.
>
> (1997: 9)

As the novel describes it: 'The taste of him repulsed her, the saliva and the smell making her want to puke. She punched away the thought and sucked his tongue back into her' (166). Overcoming her urge to vomit, Elizabeth carries on with the grim business of seduction, disarming her assailant of his weapon and gradually 'teasing' his penis into erection.

One of the most striking, and strangely unremarked, aspects of this scene is its depiction of masculinity. For if, following Dunant's own commentary, we read this scene as a fictional attempt to show a woman as something other than a victim to the event of male violence, the question becomes: what has to happen to male sexuality in order to turn rape into seduction? What's interesting is that in order to effect this transformation the text has to produce an utterly emasculated version of male sexuality. On the feminization of the stalker, the text could not be more blatant:

> She took a breath, then with her forefinger she pulled down his bottom lip, feeling the moistness, exposing the fleshy bit inside…The flesh was alive with muscle, rough and quivering, almost like the feel of her own vagina. It sent a shudder through her and she had to steel herself not to pull out. No time for the faint-hearted now.
>
> (164)

And then: 'She took his hand in hers, entwining their fingers, using her thumb to play with the inside of his palm. The skin was surprisingly soft, almost like a girl's, soft and wet with sweat. She felt a sudden shaft of power' (166). It is as if the categories of masculinity and femininity are being redistributed here: as the stalker becomes like a 'girl', Elizabeth gains the potency of masculinity with her 'shaft of power'.

During the seduction, Elizabeth finds a certain 'pleasure in her own control' (166). But along with this pleasure comes the controversial sexual arousal of the media reports: 'She was about to help him further when his fingers found her nipples, swollen from the cold and the fear and a sudden, muddied, confused kind of desire' (167). Again, this 'sudden, muddied, confused kind of desire' is presented as an instinctual, indeed involuntary, reaction. What follows next is the text's most direct depiction of the woman's sexual arousal: 'To her amazement she realised she was wet. The discovery sent its own shock wave through the pit of her stomach' (168). Sexual arousal, certainly, but sexual pleasure? It is telling that in the reviews of the novel the sexual arousal described in the above passage is simply conflated with the 'pleasure' of a few pages before. To refer to Dunant's commentary on the scene: 'We know there is a connection between power and arousal, and I think that is the point, rather than that she actually gets turned on' (cited in Neustatter 27 May 1997). This idea of desire without pleasure, arousal without enjoyment, is central to Dunant's vision of women's agency in scenes of sexual danger.

The seduction scene ends with the stalker's (though notably not Elizabeth's) climax. Determined to get on with the rest of her life, Elizabeth makes the decision not to phone the police, knowing that 'in some unfathomable way what had passed between them was more intimate than violence, and she would never be able to tell it' (172). Something more, and something different than, the scene of male violence and female sexual subordination, 'more intimate than violence' represents the novel's attempt to complicate a well-known narrative of male sadism and female victimization. But does it work? Is *Transgressions* transgressive?

Susan Suleiman has noted how 'the experience of transgression is indissociable from the consciousness of the constraint or prohibition it violates; indeed, it is precisely by and through its transgression that the force of a prohibition becomes fully realized' (1986: 75). By this account, transgression is about exceeding the bounds of 'rational, everyday behaviour', the accepted modes of being. 'The characteristic feeling accompanying transgression,' Suleiman writes, 'is one of intense pleasure (at the exceeding of boundaries) *and* of intense anguish (at the full realization of the force of those boundaries)' (ibid.). In *Transgressions*, the fleeting pleasure Dunant's heroine experiences as a result of her 'transgression' is followed by remorse and anguish. More interesting, perhaps, is the question of how Dunant copes with her transgression as a feminist author. For while the novel's critics may accuse Dunant of betraying her feminist principles in writing *Transgressions*, I would argue that Dunant is in fact nowhere more aware of those principles than in her depiction of seduction. To put this in Suleiman's terms, Dunant's depiction of seduction is indissociable from the consciousness of the constraint or prohibition it violates: namely the feminist taboo on female rape fantasy. In Chapter 1, I discussed John Forrester's observation that 'many feminists have written as if the very *existence* of rape fantasies were an embarrassment, a collective shame of women' (1986: 63). As we have seen, in classic second-wave feminist work such as Brownmiller's, rape fantasy is attributed to masculine culture and placed squarely on the 'outside'. It is noteworthy that in the latter half of *Transgressions* there is an anxious attempt to put violence back on the 'outside'. The irony is that *Transgressions* ends up reasserting the very series of oppositions it has been attempting to undermine: between rape and seduction, between woman as victim and man as aggressor. The text veers between wanting to complicate the implications of the seduction scene and wanting to contain them. On the one hand, any equivocation or ambivalence the seduction scene may have suggested, is tempered by the retrospective rewriting of the seduction as a 'rape'. Evoking the memory of her dead mother, Elizabeth tells herself: 'Maybe what she really needed was a pair of arms to hold her and let her cry it out. Forget it, Elizabeth. She's dead and you're raped' (177). But at other moments the novel returns to the implications of the woman's sexual arousal, entertaining the possibility that a woman might find pleasure *in* danger: 'Sex. Everyone's dark secret...She could do what she liked. With whom she liked. So what was it she wanted to do? Was this about the power of powerlessness?' (261). Yet the novel does not really pursue the idea of a sadomasochistic sexuality. Instead, in passages that portray Elizabeth attempting to understand the 'pain' beneath the violence of her stalker/rapist, the novel comes dangerously close to endorsing what Robin Morgan referred to in 1980 as 'the Pity the Poor Rapist approach', a fiction that 'tells us we must be sorry for our attacker. He is sick, he cannot help himself, he needs help'

(1980: 135). The text seems to need this fiction of the 'Poor Rapist' in order to account for woman's complicity in the scene of sexual violence.

There is another fiction the text seems to require as well. As if aware of the implausibility of Elizabeth's dark identification with the stalker, the second half of the novel transforms this image of the Poor Rapist into a more unremittingly violent masculinity: the serial rapist/sex murderer, 'a figure darker than the darkness... no character, no feeling, just a cold madness intent on violence' (88). In *Transgressions*, the woman's bid for empowerment requires – indeed demands – these two forms of violent masculinity be played off against each other.

Far from being exclusive to *Transgressions*, this plot device of the 'two rapists' is commonplace in the emerging genre of feminist sex thrillers. It is the central plot twist, for example, in Susanna Moore's 1995 novel, *In The Cut*. By the story's end, the heroine's inability to tell the difference between the good cop and the bad cop (the sadist and the serial killer) results in her gruesome death. It is also the central premise of Jenny Diski's *Nothing Natural*, published in 1986. Described as 'an honest and startling look at the angry face of sex', *Nothing Natural* centres on a sadomasochistic relationship between Rachel, a thirtysomething woman who lives alone with her young daughter, and Joshua – the sadist to Rachel's masochist. At the opening of the novel, Rachel is reading the newspaper when she comes across an artist's impression of a man wanted by the police. Realising the man in the drawing resembles Joshua, her lover for the past three years, Rachel becomes further concerned when she reads about the nature of the crime: 'COUPLE SOUGHT IN SEX ATTACK ... A girl aged sixteen had been lured by the couple into their car... and raped. Afterwards she had been forced to take part in other sexual acts with the couple' (1990: 8).

The organizing dilemma set out by this opening chapter is whether Joshua, who was on holiday in Scotland at the time of the crime, is the man in the drawing. But *Nothing Natural* is not a crime novel – at least not in any conventional way – and the point of the book is not to determine whether or not Joshua 'really' committed the crime. Beyond its significance as a framing device, the crime itself has little or nothing to do with the story. Rather, its significance depends on how Rachel's desire is able to move between these two different conceptions of male sexuality – the sadist and the rapist.

> The point was that she knew him to be capable of exactly that sort of thing... She had come to understand that, given the chance, people could live out their fantasies, and that, given their head, the fantasies could grow and seep into real life until sometimes it was hard to tell the difference.
>
> (ibid.: 10)

Acknowledging the fact that, in spite of their intimacy, Joshua remains a mystery to her, Rachel wonders: 'What if this cipher turned out to be a rapist, a real force of destruction out there in the world, what did that mean for her, about her' (ibid.: 13)?

Like *Transgressions*, *Nothing Natural's* exploration of female sexuality deals with an underlying tension between women's fantasies of rape and violation and the impact of feminist consciousness-raising about women's victimization under patriarchy. As Rachel puts it:

> A woman in her thirties at the end of two decades of the women's movement, who assumed equality and lived equally with men, was not supposed to admit to rape fantasies and submit herself to the power play of perverted male sexuality, let alone like it. That was it: she was appalled at how much she had enjoyed being ordered about, assaulted, and degraded.
>
> (ibid.: 34)

The novel's final sequence brings the reader full circle: Rachel is again contemplating the newspaper report. 'Now ... with the newspaper cutting in front of her, she was not exactly surprised at the possibility that Joshua was a rapist. Disturbed, distressed, but not surprised' (ibid.: 219). Rachel casts Joshua's actions as a dissolution of the boundary between fantasy and reality:

> One was always reading about men going out into the world assaulting, raping, killing – doing what they must for years have only fantasised ... Joshua had gone a step further than fantasy with her and probably others; did that make him safer or more likely to act out there in the real world finally? She had no idea. She didn't feel that *she* could ever really blur the boundary between fantasy and the real.
>
> (ibid.: 220)

This worry about fantasy seeping into 'real life until sometimes it was hard to tell the difference' captures an anxiety concerning a lack of distinction between the real and the fake, the actual and the represented, in relation to sexual violence (ibid.: 10). In his discussion of serial killers, Mark Seltzer notes how, in recent accounts of the relation between sadistic fantasy and sadistic violence, 'there is a basic inability to find a distinction between ... "statistically normal individuals" and pathological ones' (1998: 142). The question is, why is it that some men act out their fantasies, 'going out into the world, assaulting, raping, killing', while others seem content to let fantasy remain fantasy (Diski 1990: 220)? One way of dealing with this problem is to level the distinctions between normal and pathological male fantasies entirely: to assert that 'sadistic violence is a permanent and transhistorical component of the male psyche' (Seltzer 1998: 143).

Nothing Natural offers another way of dealing with the problem. Realizing that she might never know 'whether her suspicions were real or not', Rachel begins to think that she wants Joshua to be guilty: 'Vindictive bitch. You love the idea of him suddenly in a panic, on the defence, no longer in control, having to put himself outside of the safety of fantasy' (ibid.: 223). In order to assert her own power in the relationship, and thus find a way of playing out the sadomasochistic relationship without the 'paradox of the willing victim', Rachel decides to write out a fantasy on paper and send it to Joshua: 'A rape. That was it, she would invite him to a rape.

Let him steal what he had been getting for nothing for the past three years' (ibid.: 228). She then finds herself going to the police station to report a 'stalker'. In the novel's final scene, Joshua arrives at Rachel's flat, prepared to act out the 'rape fantasy'. He ties her up, whips her with a leather strap and anally rapes her. At that moment, two policemen enter the house and arrest Joshua: 'This is a misunderstanding... this isn't what it seems,' he pleads. Rachel turns to look at Joshua and says: 'This *is* what it seems, this is real life' (ibid.: 239).

Like Rachel in *Nothing Natural*, Elizabeth decides to entrap her stalker by providing more fodder for his fantasies; she writes a final sex scene for the thriller and sends it to him. Her plan fails, and her stalker attempts to rape her. In having Elizabeth meet up with her assailant again, Dunant is conforming to the dictates of genre: 'After all, it's... part of the myth that the hero gets to meet the bad guy again' ('Rewriting' 1993: 28). As in the seduction scene, Elizabeth's immediate fear is for her life: 'I don't want to die ... Please don't let me die' (328). Rape is presented as a clear alternative to murder: 'Fuck me, but don't kill me' (332). Unlike in the seduction scene, however, Elizabeth's attempts to comfort the intruder fail and he gives way to violence.

Where *Nothing Natural* concludes by asking us to entertain the dangers involved in confronting the reality of fantasy, *Transgressions* concludes by suggesting it is possible, finally, to tell the difference between the real and the imaginary. That difference or distinction is secured in relation to an image of 'real rape'. In the novel's final scene, fiction is used as a way of putting reality firmly into place. As the stalker tries to unbutton his trousers, the text interjects: 'This was the bit you never saw in the movies. Even the most violent of rape scenes stopped short of showing the engorged cock. Instead you got to read the size of the erection from the panic and trauma in the woman's face' (334). If, in order to effect seduction, Elizabeth had to acquire an imaginary penis (her 'shaft of power'), here her surrogate male member becomes a pair of scissors. Holding them up to defend herself, the stalker rams into them and is fatally stabbed. In the best tradition of horror and rape-revenge, the connections between sex and death are writ large: 'His groan was like the one she remembered from his orgasm, rising up from somewhere dark inside him' (335). The feel of his blood on Elizabeth's hand is 'one more appalling intimacy between them' (336).

In the novel's final plot twist, Elizabeth discovers that her assailant was a stalker/rapist and not a serial rapist and murderer. What Elizabeth had earlier dismissed as a statistical improbability – the 'chances of there being two rapists operating in the same five-mile radius of London ... seemed slim' (248) – turns out not to be so unlikely after all. It could well be argued, I think, that one of the more difficult aspects of the novel is the way in which the resolution of the plot appears to offer some sort of apologia for the activities of the solitary rapist. For there is a strange sense in which *Transgressions* brings back a pre-feminist notion of rape as an isolated incident between individuals. When the stalker reveals that he has been watching Elizabeth all night, she realizes that he could not have been responsible for the murder of the woman that occurred some distance away. This also means that he could not have been responsible for the other rapes that have been happening in the area. As he lies dying in Elizabeth's arms, she says: '"It was only me, wasn't it? That's what you meant about choosing me. You never did anything to anybody else, did you? It was always only me"' (337). The novel returns to the idea that his violence was just a cover for his 'pain' (336, 337). Just as she had initially blamed her ex-lover for the strange occurrences in her home, Elizabeth has again blamed the wrong man, erroneously thinking that her 'mad stalker' was a serial rapist when in fact there 'was only one scene to his crime, and only one victim' (340). In the novel's final pages, we learn that another man was responsible for the serial rapes:

> Like many before him, the real Holloway Hammer had turned out to be an otherwise respectable fellow; a freelance car mechanic, married with two kids, living in Hendon and working on a breakdown contract for the AA in the Islington, Holloway area. The kind of job that took him all places at all hours... He'd been playing with his kids when they got to him, setting up a Christmas model garage for his youngest boy, his wife in the kitchen peeling the sprouts for lunch. Just a regular sort of bloke. Hard to imagine his family visiting him in prison.
>
> (340)

The violence of the stalker, along with Elizabeth's complicity in that violence, is displaced onto the serial rapist, the figure who is used to tie up the loose ends of the plot.

Conclusion

By way of wrapping up, I want to consider another definition of 'translation': to renovate, make new from old. How to rework or renovate the story of female victimization and male violence, 'our ultimate gender story', is one of the bigger challenges facing contemporary feminist writers (Clover *Men* 1992: 227). This challenge is particularly acute for women crime writers who are openly caught up in the business of transforming the conventions of genre. The irony, as Dunant sees it, is that 'as the genre of the crime thriller has become definably more misogynistic, so more and more women have been entering it... In many cases, women have picked this form precisely because it has been so male' ('Rewriting' 1993: 28). The question of how to distinguish itself from the masculine form of the genre is a source of intense pleasure, and anxiety, for the female crime writer.

In *Transgressions*, Dunant compares the female translator and her 'small notation[s]' to the 'Renaissance biblical copyists leaving their individual mark on the page' (106). But does *Transgressions* succeed in making new from old? A prevalent danger from the start of the novel, by the story's end the main narrative has become indissociable from the thriller. Though the purpose of including the thriller is to show how a woman writer can fight fantasy with fantasy, *Transgressions* ends up seeming like too much of the same. One is left wondering whether the novel is not its own opponent.

In the wake of her trauma with the stalker, Elizabeth tries to empower the thriller's fictional heroine, Mirka. In fiction that mirrors 'real life', Elizabeth writes a seduction scene for her heroine. 'And so it was that at last Mirka came to learn what it felt like to rub herself up against a country boy and find his farm fingers groping their way into the wetlands of her cunt' (222). There is a certain confusion here as to whether this is the thriller, the main narrative or both: 'The words flowed like genital juices. But still she made Mirka work at it, made her use the slap-slurp sound of sex and her own extravagant groans to cover up the scrape of the knife as she slid it up from the steel tray beside the bed' (222). So accurately do some of its criticisms of the thriller apply to the formulaic narrative action of the last half of *Transgressions* the novel might be referring to itself. But the fact that *Transgressions* openly bares its confusions and contradictions only serves to raise discussion of the power that rape holds for feminism as a fantasy formation. The recurring scenario of rape in feminist crime writing shows the deep fascination with the continuous communication – and erosion – between the boundaries of reality and fantasy.

6

RAPE ON TAPE?

Raw Deal: A Question of Consent

Rape is a perfect crime for film.

Lynn A. Higgins

Whether a contested interaction is rape comes down to whose meaning wins.

Catharine MacKinnon

The discussion of any representation of violence is fraught with difficulties but the representation of rape is especially emotive. This was brought home to me several times during the writing of this book, particularly when I had to think about how to present my research to others, both in casual conversations and in formal academic situations. At one conference, aptly titled 'Dangerous Representations', I delivered a paper on rape and spectatorship in Kathryn Bigelow's film *Strange Days* (1995).[1] I declined to show a clip from the film. One member of the audience asked why. Given that I was focusing on the controversy surrounding the film's graphic rape scene, why did I not show the scene itself? How can one discuss a 'dangerous representation' without first looking at it?

This dilemma will be familiar to those who have the experience of teaching films that include volatile images of sex and violence. My reason for not showing the rape scene was that it would be inappropriate to display such an upsetting scene out of context from the rest of the film. Such a rationale ends up reproducing the debate at the centre of *Strange Days* discussed in Chapter 4, regarding what it means to 'play back' images of sex and violence. While Lenny (Ralph Fiennes) claims that he is fulfilling a public service by peddling virtual reality clips of graphic sex, Mace (Angela Bassett) refuses to watch such clips on the grounds that they are 'porno for wireheads'. In deciding not to screen the rape scene, it might seem that I am implicitly endorsing the view that there is something ethically dubious in screening – and in spectating – a rape clip.[2]

An extraordinary documentary was recently brought to my attention, which raises the stakes to these issues higher still. *Raw Deal: A Question of Consent* (2001) is about an alleged rape that took place in a fraternity house in Florida in 1999. Described as 'one of the most controversial films of the modern day' (Miele 2001),

Raw Deal was a *cause célèbre* at the 2001 Sundance Film Festival. What makes the film so controversial is its inclusion of sexually graphic 8 mm footage of an alleged rape, filmed by the fraternity members involved. With *Raw Deal* the notion of public rape reaches its extreme.

The inclusion of hand-held camera footage puts the documentary at the forefront of a debate about reality cinema and the lengths cinema is willing to go in the quest for authenticity (Smith 2001: 17). *Raw Deal* is part of an emerging tendency in cinema to show 'real' and explicit sex acts. Much has been written recently regarding art house movies that trouble the 'border between the art film and the porn movie' ('The Limits of Sex' 2001) by containing shots of penetrative sex. Films such as Patrice Chereau's *Intimacy* (UK 2001), which includes a shot of the leading actress fellating the leading actor, are noted for the way they place us in 'uncomfortable proximity' to the performers (Falcon 2001). This chimes with Todd McCarthy's *Variety* review of *Raw Deal*: '[It] … makes for an uncomfortable sit, mostly out of embarrassment for the people on such literally naked display' (2001). With *Raw Deal* we find ourselves awkwardly aware of the bodies onscreen but with the significant distinction that – in contrast to fiction films such as *Intimacy* or *Baise-Moi* (Despentes and Trinh Thi 2000) – we are watching real people having violent sex never intended for our eyes, rather than actors performing real sex staged for the camera. We are presented with a 'spectacle caught unawares' (Metz 1999: 96). The raw footage, however, is not 'accidental' like the Abraham Zapruder film of JFK's assassination in 1963 or George Holliday's video recording of the beating of Rodney King by LAPD officers in 1991.[3] The authentic footage found in *Raw Deal* was 'directed' by members of the fraternity of Delta Chi, who anticipated eventually showing the film to other male members of the frat house as a home pornographic video.

On 26 February 1999, Lisa Gier King and another woman were hired to perform as exotic dancers at the University of Florida Delta Chi fraternity. After their performance King returned to party with the men. The next morning she ran out of the house screaming for help. She said she had been raped by one of the fraternity brothers, Mike Yarhaus. Remarkably, the entire incident was captured on videotape. Two of the fraternity members, Leo Yuque and Yarhaus, had two cameras running throughout the night, filming the exotic dancing and the wild party that ensued. The cameras filmed the disputed incident between Yarhaus and King, which some claim was rape, while others insist it was consensual sex.

But what makes this case truly astonishing is that the videotapes of the incident were made available to the general public. When the police watched the tapes, they dropped Yarhaus' rape charge, claiming that the sex shown was 'clearly willing and consensual sexual intercourse' (cited in Bridgewater 1999).[4] Not only did they drop the charges filed by King – they charged her with filing a false report.[5] After pressure from the National Organization of Women, the State Attorney's office decided to circulate the tape publicly as 'state evidence' so that people could 'see for themselves' what happened between Yarhaus and King. With this decision, visual spectacle takes the place of the criminal trial. That is, it is no longer an issue of contemporary trials resembling media spectacles, but rather of spectacle replacing the legal forum completely. The videotapes were released to the public under Florida's Sunshine Law, which supports 'the public's right of access to governmental meetings and records' ('Florida's Government'). Videotapes of the graphic sexual acts between Yarhaus and King could be seen by anyone. Some individuals began selling the videos on the black market for $20. The footage was circulated throughout Florida and, eventually, the world.

As far as the men involved were concerned, the video backed their innocence. As participant Tony Marzullo notes: 'In retrospect…that tape was great. Because that tape saved Mike Yarhaus' ass…No one was considering myself an accessory to rape any more or a proponent for the abuse of women.' But for King's mother, the release of the footage meant that 'anybody could have a private copy of my daughter's rape for their viewing pleasure'.[6] Here, the notion of the rape trial as a 'second rape', as discussed in regard to the New Bedford rape case in Chapter 3, takes on new and disturbing meaning. In this 'public rape trial', in which people are put in the position of judge and jury, the act of alleged violation is endlessly replayed for public – and personal – consumption.

This final chapter examines what it means to have an incident that the female participant called 'rape' turned into a public record – a spectacle of the real. According to *Raw Deal's* director, Billy Corben, the contentious footage was included in his documentary to demonstrate the limitations of film in revealing reality (cited in Walker 2000–01). Corben thus appears to heed the warning that has become especially acute in the wake of the Rodney King video: it is dangerous to assume that 'the preservation and subsequent re-presentation of historical events on film or tape can serve to stabilize or ensure meaning' (Renov 1993: 8). In this regard, *Raw Deal* is part of what Stella Bruzzi identifies as a new breed of documentaries that reflexively examine the negotiation between the image and the real (2000: 6). This chapter explores the contract between the filmmakers of *Raw Deal*, the subject matter of rape, and the film's spectators. For while the film sets out to contest the naïve view that videotapes can capture the real, it is precisely the aura of reality surrounding *Raw Deal* that draws viewers and makes the film so intriguing.

Much of the thrill and the revulsion surrounding this film and its inclusion of authentic video footage concern its mode of address to the spectator. As I have argued throughout this book, rape brings questions of audience involvement in onscreen violence to a crisis point. The spectacle of cinematic rape reveals the potentially troubling elements behind the widespread academic assertion that 'a media text cannot be reduced to a single, fixed and coherent "meaning", but will instead be open to various interpretations by its various audiences' (Selby and Cowdery 1995: 22). For what happens if rape is open to various interpretations? This worry, presumably, is at the heart of the British Board of Film Classification guidelines that insist that 'where the [filmic] portrayal [of rape] eroticises sexual assault, cuts are likely to be required' (cited in Kermode 2002). If there is anything in a film that might lead to the interpretation of rape as erotic or sexual, then that film is an immediate candidate for censorship.

Due largely to feminism's important work on raising public consciousness about sexual violence, scenes in which women are pictured 'enjoying' rape are now culturally outlawed.[7] According to Carol Clover, the trajectory of cinematic representations of rape through the 1970s to the 1980s and 1990s runs: 'from a more or less justifiable male-centred event to an unjustifiable female-centred one; from the deed of a psychopathic creep to the deed of a "normal" man; from an event construed as an act of sex, in which one or both parties is shown to take some pleasure (if only perverse) to an act of violent humiliation' (1992: 140). As noted in Chapter 4, *The Accused* (Kaplan 1988) is responsible for bringing the subject of rape into the mainstream in the late 1980s in a feature film clearly influenced by feminist analyses of sexual violence. More recently, rape has continued to be depicted in mainstream movies, with films like *Strange Days* (1995) and *Boys Don't Cry* (1999) perpetuating discussion about whether showing rape onscreen is moral.

At the beginning of the twenty-first century, we are confronted by a new period in cinematic representations of rape. In the UK, the BBFC has entered a period of relative openness and is re-issuing previously banned rape films such as *Straw Dogs* (Peckinpah 1971) and *I Spit on Your Grave* (Zarchi 1978). As I write this conclusion, a series of new European films featuring ever more graphic and 'authentic' rape scenes has been released. Virginie Despentes and Coralie Trinh Thi's *Baise-Moi* (2000) is a fiction film that includes a graphically realistic rape scene, and features porn actresses who engage in real sex for the camera. To defend the movie, which was banned in France, the film's directors employ feminist arguments regarding the need to show the public the ugliness of rape. Despentes is quoted as saying: 'We didn't invent rape. I've been raped and one of my actresses has been raped … It's horrific, so I don't see why I shouldn't treat it that way' (cited in Ruth Williams 2001). *Baise-Moi* was released in Britain with only one cut. The cut was of a penetration shot in the rape scene that censors felt was problematic because it draws links between sex and violence. 'Its extreme sexual imagery is unmatched elsewhere in the rape scene. Without it, the sequence remains a compelling portrayal of the ugliness and horror of rape. With it, the scene takes on a more explicitly pornographic dimension and is a matter of serious concern' (BBFC classification 26 February 2001).

Gaspar Noe's *Irreversible* (2002), a film that includes a nine-minute rape scene in which a gay pimp anally rapes the female protagonist, was released in Britain without any cuts. The BBFC sought the advice of a clinical forensic psychiatrist who concluded that the film offered a 'harrowing and vivid portrayal of the brutality of rape' ('BBFC passes' 21 October 2002). Significantly, for the BBFC, this meant that the film's depiction of rape was not 'designed to titillate' and therefore was unlikely to promote 'harm' by associating sexual violence with sexual pleasure (ibid.).[8] Particularly interesting for a discussion of *Raw Deal* and the multiple viewing contexts for the video footage, is the BBFC's warning that it might not be so lenient when it comes to the home video release of *Irreversible* 'because video scenes can be replayed repeatedly ('British Board of Film' 26 September 2000).

This concern about scenes of rape being 'replayed repeatedly' is linked to a growing public anxiety regarding the cumulative effects of film (Lebeau 1995: 139).

Moreover, the worry is that when the viewing context for a film is changed from the public space of the cinema to the private space of the home, then the meaning of the images may also change. This was dramatically demonstrated with the public circulation of the amateur videotape of Rodney King's beating by a group of white LAPD officers. Initially, the televised videotape was widely taken as 'proof' of white police brutality and racism. However, as Mike Mashon notes, when the tape shifted into the context of the courtroom, the 'meaning' of the video changed (1993: 9). The defense attorneys replayed the images – rewinding, fast forwarding and freeze framing – to build their argument that the white officers were merely responding to an aggressive black man – that it was in fact the group of armed white police officers, and not the unarmed lone black man, who were under threat (ibid.: 14). In her discussion of the Rodney King videotape, Judith Butler argues that we cannot assume that the video ' "speaks for itself" ' (1993: 17). Rather, it is 'politically imperative to read such videos aggressively, to repeat and publicize such readings' (ibid.).[9]

As an exemplar of cinema's new explicitness of sex and violence, *Raw Deal*: A *Question of Consent* dramatizes the issues surrounding the fraught activity of watching images of rape. It reveals, in the words of Butler, that 'there is no simple recourse to the visible' (ibid.). It looks at what happens when an apparent sexual assault is 'taken out of context and viewed repeatedly' by spectators. The BBFC guidelines discussed above are based on the idea that it is possible to make a distinction between violence and sexuality. In this, it follows a strand of feminist argument that says rape is a crime of violence, not of sex. *Raw Deal*, however, shows that the attempt to separate images of sex from violence is tricky work, if not impossible. It illustrates the confusion in the public domain regarding how to tell the difference between consensual sex and rape and between pornographic spectacle and rape, both in the real world and in the cinema. What are more compelling, and ultimately more conclusive, than the visual footage are the reactions of the spectators to that footage.[10] By representing those spectators and their responses, *Raw Deal* shows us how images of rape initiate struggles over meaning in culture, over who gets to control it and whose interpretation is deemed worthy.

Government under the Sunshine

Following the guidelines set down by Florida's 'Government-in-the-Sunshine Law', which champions open government 'responsible to the needs of the people' ('Florida's Government'), Judge Chester Chance ruled that the videotapes depicting the alleged sexual violation should be made public. The videotapes exposed the 'seedy' and immoral behaviour at the base of the 'code of brotherhood' that constitutes male fraternity societies on American campuses ('Getting off easy' 11 May 1999).

Left unanswered is the question of whose 'needs' are being served by the public release of the tapes. Certainly not the needs of Lisa King or those of her family, who vigorously opposed the state's release of the tapes. And, although Judge Chance declared that the tape did not reveal King as a victim, it is clear that the decision to make the tape public did indeed victimize her.[11] As King is quoted as saying in *Raw Deal*: 'It was absolutely devastating to me that a copy of me being raped and victimized was out in public'. But while some newspaper reports referred to the damage the tape had on King's life, most focused on the damage done to the collective fraternity body. When the videotapes were first released, spokespeople from the University of Florida were quoted as being worried about the tarnishing of the fraternity's image, and were concerned to emphasize 'what is positive about fraternities, such as their civic contributions' (Washington 9 May 1999). The language used here echoes that found in the newspaper reports on the New Bedford rape case, discussed in Chapter 3, in which the rape of a woman became transformed into the rape of a city and in which the Portuguese immigrants who were reported as having done so much for that city were seen as 'damaged' by the rape. One report, for example, written as a follow-up on the incident one year later, concentrated on Delta Chi's efforts to recover its status. 'The members of the fraternity say they have to move beyond the hurt and begin the process that will allow them to become an active fraternity again' (Wise 2002).

In *Fraternity Gang Rape*, anthropologist Peggy Reeves Sanday writes that gang rape is common on university campuses throughout the US. She identifies a pattern:

> The incident begins with drinking or drugs and male conspiracy in finding, trapping or coercing, and sharing a "party girl." A vulnerable young woman, one who is seeking acceptance or who is high on drugs or alcohol, is taken to a room. She may or may not agree to having sex with one man. She then passes out, or she is too weak or scared to protest, and a "train" of men have sex with her.
>
> (1990: 91)

This could well serve as a description of the events that transpired at the Delta Chi fraternity on the night of 26 February 1999. During a wild alcohol fuelled party, Yarhaus and some of his male friends plot to have sex with the 'stripper', the party girl in their midst. A naked and drunken King asks if she can lie down in a room. Yarhaus then wakes her up. What follows is a confused and ambiguous incident, lasting over four hours, in which Yarhaus and King engage in a kind of sexual warfare while two other men watch – and film. It is not a gang rape in so far as the other two men do not have intercourse with King (though it should be noted that Marzullo does engage in sex acts with her), but it is nevertheless a group affair in which the other men participate as spectators.

As noted earlier in this book in regard to both *The Women's Room* and *The Accused*, the figure of the drunk 'party girl' who is sexually threatened by a group of men is a familiar scene repeated across a number of cultural texts. Fraternity rape involving a rowdy group of 'brothers' and a lone vulnerable woman has a mythic status in American culture. Sanday suggests that fraternity gang rape can be viewed as a sociodrama through 'which the brothers vent their interest in one another through the body of a woman' (ibid.: 12). As she writes: 'The woman plays the role of ritual scapegoat who receives the brunt of collective male sexual aggression that would otherwise turn a group of privileged heterosexual males into despised homosexuals' (ibid.: 59). This recalls *Le Lévite d'Ephraim*, as discussed in Chapter 2, in particular the observation that the possibility of homosexual rape leads to heterosexual rape. The woman's body becomes the substitute for the man's, with rape serving as the means of imposing clear lines of sexual difference.

As in Brownmiller's account of gang rape as the site of collective identification between men, Sanday's anthropological analysis of fraternity rape as the 'social building block of male dominance' (ibid.: 186) demonstrates how fraternity gang rape is about extending and confirming the bonds of brotherhood. To borrow Carole Pateman's terms, it is a means of upholding the socio-sexual contract. As Sanday argues: 'Having resorted to abuse as a means to establish their bond to the brotherhood, the newly confirmed brothers resort to abusing others – new generations of pledges and party women – to uphold the original contract and renew their sense of the autonomous power of the brotherhood' (ibid.: 172).

Rape and replay

At the heart of *Raw Deal* is the 8 mm videotape footage shot by the Delta Chi fraternity members. The story of the alleged rape is inseparable from the story of its representation on videotape. The tapes quickly became the object of public fascination upon their release. The Florida State Attorney's Office was bombarded with requests for the video footage, from national news organizations, as well as from the general public. As one male spectator of the footage is quoted as saying in *Raw Deal*: 'Everybody and their mother wanted to see that tape – my parents wanted to see it!'

The decision by the State Attorney's Office to release the videotapes has since been much criticized by media and legal commentators as ethically and legally dubious. In a sense, *Raw Deal* repeats the problematic gesture of publicizing the incident by including the contentious footage as a film within a film. This was the basis of the National Organization of Women's complaint against the documentary.[12] However, *Raw Deal* repeats this gesture with a crucial difference: it annotates the images it shows whereas the legal authorities suggested that the images could 'speak for themselves'. What is interesting and important about *Raw Deal* is that it shows how individuals wrest meaning from images in violent, contradictory and self-serving ways.

Lisa Gier King endorses the documentary. She says *Raw Deal* 'did a better job of investigating this than the police' (cited in Lumenick 25 January 2001). Certainly, the investigation by both the police and the State Attorney's Office was widely viewed as a debacle.[13] *Raw Deal* steps in and takes over where the law left off. As 21-year-old filmmakers, of a similar age to those involved in the incident at Delta Chi, Corben and Spellman said they wanted to find out what happened that night (Walker 2000–01). It is significant that the only time we see the filmmakers in the documentary is when they are attempting, unsuccessfully, to obtain an interview from State Attorney Rod Smith and other individuals from his office. These moments of direct intervention on the part of the filmmakers signal their overt concern with revealing the injustice of the legal system's handling of the case. As with *The Accused*, cinema serves a civic purpose.

Was it rape or was it consensual sex? In dealing with this question, *Raw Deal* is entering into a long-running debate about the problem of determining rape, a charge 'easily to be made and hard to be proved' in the notorious words of Lord Hale (cited in Estrich 1987: 5). *Raw Deal* is to documentary film what Akira Kurosawa's *Rashomon* (1950) is to fiction film: a self-reflexive exploration of the limitations of cinema's truth-telling functions.[14] As Lynn Higgins suggests of *Rashomon*, it is not surprising that this classic filmic examination of the multiplicity of meaning centres on a rape. As Higgins observes: 'A rape defense case can rest on the claim that what occurred was not a rape and so the question is not *who committed* the crime, but *whether a crime occurred at all*' (1991: 307). A 'perfect crime for film', rape dramatizes questions of subjectivity, storytelling, testimony and interpretation (ibid.: 306).

'Welcome to the Argument' read the sign posted on the editing room for *Raw Deal*, where the directors made crucial decisions regarding what images to include and what to leave out. As observed in the press notes for the film: 'Corben and Spellman discovered that they could create great drama by juxtaposing arguments on either side of the case' (Walker 2000–01). *Raw Deal* belongs to the category of documentary film defined by Bill Nichols as 'interactive'. The focus in interactive documentary is on 'the social actors recruited: their comments and responses provide a central part of the film's argument' (Nichols 1991: 44). *Raw Deal* is structured around interviews in which individuals from both sides of the debate address the camera and provide their interpretation of the video footage. Notably, given their presence in other moments of the film, the filmmakers choose not to make themselves visible during the interviews. The interviews are, to borrow Nichols' term, 'pseudomonologues', which 'appear to deliver the thoughts, impressions, feelings, and memories of the individual witness directly to the viewer' (ibid.: 54). Lisa Gier King is interviewed extensively. Though Mike Yarhaus declined to be interviewed, his friend and fellow fraternity member, Tony Marzullo, one of those who engaged in sexual acts with King and who helped to film the incident, offers his interpretation of the incident. The typical structure of *Raw Deal* is as follows: we are given two opposing testimonies, most usually from King and Marzullo, then we are given a visual image from the video footage which either backs up or refutes their claim or shows something more complicated than either viewpoint would allow for. These visual images function as flashbacks to the past. Similar to the structure of *The Accused*, the most graphic visual images of the alleged rape are withheld until the film's concluding scenes. It is noteworthy that *Raw Deal* never shows us the video footage without accompanying commentary either from one of the participants or from one of those involved with the case. There is no voice-over in the film; the interviews form the narrative and the judgement of whether or not a rape occurred is left up to the cinematic audience to decide.

Reviews of the film focus on the challenge it presents to its spectators. In the UK, commissioning editor Adam Barker and legal advisor Prash Naik explain their decision to run *Raw Deal* on Channel 4 as 'an unparalleled opportunity to examine the question of consent... So who is to be believed? You'll have to view the film for yourself and see if you can make a judgment' (28 January 2002). In America, critic Rene Rodriguez states that the film is worthy of interest because of the position it puts viewers in. 'Don't be surprised to find yourself changing your mind again and again', he writes (2002). Corben similarly points to his film's multiplicity of meaning: 'The story has taken on a life of its own. After watching the movie multiple times you can change your mind about what happened' (cited in McDonald 2001). Following the premiere of the film at the Sundance Film Festival in 2001, Corben and Spellman were reported as saying that 'they changed their own minds on the issue of whether King was actually raped by Yarhaus' (cited in Lumenick 25 January 2001). According to Corben, some individuals complained that there was 'not enough of the footage for them to make up their minds whether Lisa was raped or not' (ibid.). After the documentary was screened on Channel 4 in the UK, one American website devoted to the case was bombarded with email messages asking how to obtain the four hours of original footage taken at the Delta Chi fraternity house. It got so out of hand that the website put up the following message: 'These requests seem predicated on the belief that seeing the "rape" on video will prove whether it did indeed take place. Please do not send me any more of these requests' (Delta Chi Rape Allegation Website).

I want to problematize this idea of the visual images serving as 'proof' of whether a crime occurred by turning to feminist discussions of rape law. As Catharine MacKinnon argues, the problem facing the law is how 'to tell the difference between sex (heterosexuality) while rejecting violence (rape). The problem remains what it has always been: telling the difference' (1983: 646). Feminist legal critics such as MacKinnon and Susan Estrich (1987) argue that this problem is compounded by the fact that the law sees things from a male point of view. Concealing this fact, the law proceeds as though it were possible to determine an objective reality in rape cases. Rape law 'uniformly presumes a single underlying reality, not a reality split by divergent meanings, such as those inequality produces' (MacKinnon 1983: 652). For the fact of the matter is that 'women are violated every day by men who have no idea of the meaning of their acts to women. To them, it is sex' (ibid.). MacKinnon reaches the disturbing conclusion that 'the deeper problem is the rape law's assumption that a single, objective state of affairs existed, one which merely needs to be determined by evidence, when many (maybe even most) rapes involve honest men and violated women' (ibid.: 654). Honest men and violated women: this reading of the 'split reality' in rape cases, in which the meaning of what happened is 'gendered to the ground' (ibid.: 655) has deep relevance for a reading of the video footage in *Raw Deal*. Rather than revealing the indeterminacy of meaning, I would suggest that *Raw Deal* ends up illuminating the profoundly split and gendered nature of reality.

'Campus Rape Ignored... Even When There's A Videotape'. This headline from a National Organization of Women (NOW) newsletter expresses disbelief at the authorities' refusal to 'see' what was before their eyes. NOW agreed with the University Police Department that the visual images spoke for themselves, only they argued that what they showed was 'clear-cut' rape. To counter the view that the sex shown was 'clearly consensual', members of NOW drew attention to sections in the tape when the men referred to what was happening as a rape. However, what NOW did not do was discuss other aspects of the tape that depict King in a less than flattering light. One of the strengths of *Raw Deal* is that it doesn't shy away from this. Towards the beginning of the film, it shows us the images of a naked King drinking and performing lap dances for men. It shows her simulating sex with numerous men of the fraternity, as well as with the other female exotic dancer. It is difficult not to make judgements about King – and the dozens of men present – as we watch the footage of the dancing. As these images are shown to us, we are provided with King's comment that it 'was just a regular strip show'. We then hear from Marzullo who describes the show as outrageous and unprofessional, a view the visual images seem to support. Of course, what Marzullo and other commentators on the footage of the dancing rarely remark upon, is the fact that the male behaviour during this show – and indeed throughout the entire evening – is as lewd and unruly as King's. For many individuals, King's exhibitionism during the exotic dancing settles the case. It is not necessary to see any other video footage. In *Raw Deal*, former victim support officer Heather McLeod tells about how she viewed the footage with Assistant State Attorney Bill Cervone and attempted to talk to him about it afterwards, explaining how the sex it shows was not consensual. 'He mostly focused on the dancing scene... As if to say it was her fault. He laughed at me'. Similarly, as Jennifer Baumgardner notes in an article on the case, 'What Does Rape Look Like?', the investigating policewoman Alice Hendon 'was not open to considering King a victim after she saw that the "dancing" consisted of such moves as grabbing a dollar bill out of a supine man's mouth with her vagina' (2000: 23).

Film theorist Christian Metz and his influential discussion of voyeurism and the scopic regime can help us to understand this response to the footage. As Metz suggests: 'Voyeurism... rests on a kind of *fiction*, more or less justified in the order of the real, sometimes institutionalized as in the theatre or striptease, a fiction that stipulates that the object "agrees", that it is therefore exhibitionist' (1999: 810). In the striptease, as in the theatre, the object is 'presumed to consent'. Metz adds that 'desire is presumed to be sufficiently guaranteed by the physical presence of the object: "Since it is there, it must like it" ' (ibid.). For some viewers of the footage from Delta Chi, there is an assumption that the exhibitionism witnessed on the tape is carried over to the later footage of the alleged rape. Here, too, King is 'presumed to consent'. As with the feminist spectators of *The Accused* in Chapter 4, we are dealing with the issue of how spectators see things they already believe. As Frank Tomasulo suggests in regard to the Rodney King videotape, 'People generally do not come to believe things *after* seeing them; they see things only when they *already* believe them – based on their prior *Lebenswelt* and media exposure' (1996: 82).

Some viewers of the explicit footage in *Raw Deal* hold to the 'fiction' of the striptease – that the object has agreed. It is necessary to observe, however, that the film spectator is in a markedly different position to that of the spectator of the striptease. 'The cinema's voyeurism', Metz writes, 'must (of necessity) do without any clear mark of consent on the part of the object' (1999: 811). Because we are not present at the same time and in the same location as those involved, we cannot rely on the fiction of a 'real or supposed consensus with the other' (ibid.). By contrast, 'cinematic voyeurism … is from the outset more strongly established than that of the theater in direct line from the primal scene' (ibid.). The link between spectators at the cinema, and the child of the Freudian primal scene, who '*sees* the amorous play of the parental couple, who are similarly ignorant of it and leave it alone, a pure onlooker whose participation is inconceivable', is well established (ibid.). The primal scene of sex and violence is the preoccupation of many films 'marked by narratives of anxious sexual investigation' (Merck 1993: 206). As noted in Chapter 1 of this book, primal fantasies are seen to provide representations of the enigmas that face the child; the primal scene deals with apprehensive questions concerning the origin of the subject. In his discussion of the primal scene, Freud writes that children 'adopt what may be called a *sadistic view of coition* … as something that the stronger participant is forcibly inflicting on the weaker' (1984: 198). The act, in other words, is perceived as rape. Later, in his 'Wolf Man' case history, Freud notes that the young witness to the spectacle of the primal scene may be confused as to whether the act is painful or pleasurable. There is a fundamental ambivalence written into the primal scene of rape, one that can be linked to the uncertainty that *Raw Deal* plays upon regarding the question of belief, and the spectator's attempt to determine what went on between Yarhaus and King.

'The tapes reveal no positively identifiable acts of rape,' one editorial confidently declared ('Getting off easy' 1999). For some feminists, this uncertainty regarding the visual image is part and parcel of how the male point of view masquerades as objectivity. In *Only Words* MacKinnon quotes from a defense attorney, who said to the jury, as a videotape of a husband's alleged rape of his wife (who was bound and blindfolded) was being played to the court: 'Was that a cry of pain and torture? Or was that a cry of pleasure?' (1994: 83). For MacKinnon, as for other feminists, rape is rape when a woman says so. But historically rape has been viewed as a crime that revolves around two opposing testimonies. So how do you positively identify rape? This is the question that has beleaguered many a jury in a rape trial and this is the quandary *Raw Deal* confronts.[15] As Frances Ferguson has noted, rape is unique insofar as it is a crime that depends on the elucidation of mental states of the two persons – 'the intention of the accused and the consent or nonconsent of the victim' (1987: 88).[16] Visual images of rape cannot reveal the mental states or the motivation of those involved. Speaking of the infamous videotape surveillance images used at the trial of Symbionese Liberation Army captive Patty Hearst, Bill Nichols notes the limitations of these images as 'evidence'. The videotape showed Hearst as a participant in a bank robbery. On the one hand, the prosecution claimed that 'the tape demonstrated that Ms Hearst was an active, willing member of the Army and deserved the same treatment as they did' (1991: 153). On the other hand, the defense pointed to the same images to argue that 'she was an unwilling participant and acted only as a result of threat, coercion, and brainwashing that gave her no viable alternative' (ibid.). The point, as Nichols suggests, is that 'by changing the motivation underlying an action the meaning of the action is radically changed. But a photographic image represents the visible event, not the motivation. Subjectivity eludes its grasp' (ibid.). The arguments used on either side of the Delta Chi incident are similar: either the tapes demonstrate that King was 'active' and 'willing' (at several points in *Raw Deal*, Marzullo and his attorney refer to King as the 'aggressor') or the tapes demonstrate that she was an 'unwilling participant' who was threatened and coerced into having sex (King and victim support officer Heather McLeod point out that Yarhaus was threatening to break her neck if she didn't comply).

Finally, as *Raw Deal* acknowledges, what we do not see may be just as significant as what we do see. According to Marzullo, he fell asleep at eight in the morning. As a printed message towards the end of the documentary tells us: 'At this time, both video cameras were turned off. Lisa claims this is when the violence escalated'.

Public rape

In response to the reactions of people who viewed the videotape and concluded she had not been raped, King offered the following statement: 'The general public doesn't understand [that] rape doesn't always look the way it does in the movies' (cited in Lumenick 25 January 2001). Because they don't see a 'typical Hollywood rape', King says, they think the sex they see is consensual. King's comments resonate with the observation found at the conclusion of *Transgressions*, as discussed in the previous chapter, when Elizabeth is about to be raped by her stalker: 'This was the bit you never saw in the movies' (334). Questions of authenticity, reality and spectacle apply here. As Phyllis Frus notes about the relationship between film and reality: 'The irony is that we get our ideas about what is real from narrative and dramatic constructions, from particular rhetorical devices and cinematic strategies that produce the effect of reality, and we judge the realism or credibility of even nonfictional representations against these conventions' (2001: 227). Our idea of what is real, in other words, comes from the world of representation. It is certainly true that, compared to recent fiction films such as *Baise-Moi* and *Irreversible*, King's alleged rape probably would not count as 'real'. However, if *Raw Deal* were a fiction film, the BBFC would be unlikely to pass it uncut on the grounds that it draws too close a juxtaposition between sex and violence.

What should give some pause for thought, is that the men involved in the incident, the men who insist it was consensual sex, refer to it as 'rape' at least fifteen times during the video footage (Baumgardner 2000: 20). 'It looked like rape', Marzullo says in an interview in *Raw Deal*. 'It was more or less funny. We thought the next day we were going to put this tape in and sit on the couch with a bunch of people and just laugh our asses off.' Throughout the incident with King the fraternity brothers were highly conscious of the fact they were filming. Indeed, Corben and Spellman are not the only filmmakers we see in *Raw Deal*. The fraternity men framed the evening – from start to finish – as a representation. This was a factor that King's attorney, Craig de Thomasis, repeatedly tried to draw attention to: 'The tape was produced, directed and narrated by those Lisa claims victimized her. It's not Lisa King's representation' (cited in Colavecchio 1999).

This issue of ownership of the representation becomes more complex as the tape is transmitted in a variety of contexts. Hidden in the frat house, the tape was a dirty home video. The videotape then moved out into the realm of the law where it functioned as 'evidence', not of King's rape but of her mendacity in the eyes of the law. From its function as 'evidence' in the legal setting it then shifted out into the wider public domain. Why the massive interest in the raw footage? Most people claimed to be merely curious: 'I wanted to see what the big deal is. Everyone is talking about it' (cited in Washington 1999). King points to more disturbing implications: 'You can take this tape home and make copies of it ... You can sit around with your buddies, you can do whatever you want with it'. In *Raw Deal* King's worry about the uses to which the tape will be put is juxtaposed with the comments of one man who says he decided to get a beer keg and have a party of 45 or 50 people over at his house to watch the tape. NOW later reported that 'a man offered it for sale on the internet as a "Live frat rape tape"'. The video footage then ends up in Spellman and Corben's documentary, screened at a film festival. This documentary is screened one year later at 11 p.m. on Channel 4 television in the UK with digital blurring concealing the close-up shots of genitals. This televised debut of the film in turn leads to more requests for the copies of the original footage filmed in the Delta Chi fraternity. And so the public circulation of the raw footage continues.

What *Raw Deal* makes apparent is that, for the men, the representation of the event is part of the event. 'Soon to be released on DVD', jokes Yarhaus as he surreptitiously films a naked Marzullo and King in the hot tub outside. Though King is clearly aware of the camera at certain moments in the night, it is also apparent that there are many times when she has no idea she is being filmed.[17] At one stage in the evening the men even consider the possibilities of selling the video footage over the internet. At several points, Yarhaus speaks to the camera and says that his 'mission' is to 'take the prostitute to bed'. Before King and her fellow dancer even arrive at the frat house, men are quoted on camera as saying that it is Yarhaus' intention to 'fuck prostitutes'. To King and her attorney, this was evidence of premeditation.

The filming of the night – from the strip show through to the incident between Yarhaus and King – functions as a kind of 'trophy' of the men's prowess. To quote MacKinnon: 'Taking photographs is part of the ritual of some abusive sex' (1994: 19). With *Raw Deal* and its inclusion of the video footage from Delta Chi, we return to Mark Seltzer's notion of 'spectacular violence' discussed in Chapter 3 in regard to the feminist debate on the relationship between reality and representation. Spectacular violence, according to Seltzer, is 'violence inseparable from its reproduction as spectacle' (1998: 186). Relevant to a reading of the Delta Chi footage, is Seltzer's contention that it is important to see 'fantasy or intention not as *the cause of an act but as part of an act*' (ibid.: 187). The fraternity brothers' fantasies and intentions surrounding King are a significant part of the action that followed. While some people suggested that the men would not have filmed the incident if it were a crime, the point is that the filming of the incident – its display as a representation – was intimately bound up with the incident itself.

Where the police concluded that the tape shows consensual sex, *Raw Deal* provides us with the comments of Marzullo on the raw footage as he directly addresses the group of male spectators he imagines watching it the next day: 'Probably one of the more exciting evenings – in the history of Delta Chi, that is, the raping of a white trash crackhead bitch. Please observe.' At another juncture in the tape we find the following address to the camera:

> *Yuque*: 'This is what you call …'
> *Marzullo*: 'Rape.'
> *Yuque*: 'Dirty white trash.'
> *Marzullo*: 'Rape.'
> *Yuque*: 'Crack whore.'
> *Marzullo*: 'Rape. Please observe. Let's see what's going on.'

But while they use the word 'rape', the men appear to make an important distinction between what went on between Yarhaus and King and 'real rape'. As an exasperated Marzullo asks in his interview for *Raw Deal*: 'What kind of rape is this?' Marzullo continually complains that King did not show the physical or verbal resistance one associates with rape.

Although the filmmakers resist taking an explicit stand on the video images at the heart of their documentary, it is nevertheless possible to discern a particular slant in their presentation of the footage. A close analysis of *Raw Deal* suggests that Corben and Spellman choose images that back up King's story more than they refute it. As one witness recounts how the investigating police officers believed King was lying, *Raw Deal* provides us with flashes of the tape that show Yarhaus acting in an aggressive manner – pulling a naked and struggling King across the floor. As King and members of her family give testimony, there are continual flashes of footage showing King violently struggling with Yarhaus. And while the video footage included towards the beginning of the film apparently supports Marzullo's testimony, as the film continues the images shown tend to shore up the testimony of King.

King notes that at one point, as she was struggling to escape Yarhaus's grasp, Yuque jumped on her back and pinned her down. Marzullo denies that this ever happened. We are then provided with a visual image from the raw footage that shows Yuque pinning her down on top of Yarhaus. This image is followed by Marzullo's testimony: 'At no time did I think this woman was being raped.' I contend that this statement is most likely true and that is what is so profoundly disturbing about it. The men's apparent inability to tell the difference between consensual sex and rape is linked, I would suggest, to King's occupation as an exotic dancer and their perception of her as a 'whore'. As MacKinnon argues: 'The law of rape divides the world of women into spheres of consent according to how much say we are legally presumed to have over sexual access to us by various categories of men' (1983: 648). According to this division, 'good girls, like children, are unconsenting, virginal, rapable; bad girls, like wives, are consenting, whores, unrapable' (ibid.). King is the unrapable 'whore' whom the men on the videotape hold in contempt.

Raw Deal illustrates that the sexual hatred the men hold for King is inseparably linked to their disdain for her socio-economic background. In her study on frat rape, Sanday writes that fraternity parties play an important role in 'reaffirming the men's position in a privileged social hierarchy' (1990: 37). Oftentimes, the young men select ' "sleazy women" from other schools, whom they need not face on campus the next day. They dominate these women by denigrating them for being willing to have sex. The women are described as inferior – "low-class", "cheap", or "slutty", – or they are dehumanized with animalistic terms' (ibid.). The individuals involved in the incident at Delta Chi are all white, but the men continually draw attention to King's status as 'white trash' to position her as the ' "bad" other' and thus affirm their own perceived worth as ' "good" whites' (Newitz 1997: 136). Repeatedly throughout the video footage King is referred to as 'white trash', a 'crack whore', a 'dirty rotten whore', a 'prostitute', a 'bitch'. During his interview in *Raw Deal* Marzullo makes plain his feelings on King who he continually describes as 'trash'. He says that he typically dates women from the 'upper echelon of society' and says that he considers King to be 'bottom of the barrel'.

As many commentators point out, King is far from the 'ideal victim' of the traditional rape script (Baumgardner 2000: 23). As the police noted, and as the makers of *Raw Deal* include as information in their film, she has appeared on several American TV talk shows, including Jerry Springer and Sally Jessy Raphael. Amphetamines were found in her bloodstream the day after the incident at Delta Chi.[18] On the video footage of the alleged rape, we see an intoxicated and naked King engaging in crude banter with Yarhaus, slapping her vagina, taunting him and deriding his masculinity. According to Marzullo, this was mere 'role playing', part of the consensual sexual game Yarhaus and King were playing. King, on the other hand, says that it was her attempt to fight back against rape. She says she 'fought him with' [her] attitude' ... Because I knew it was a power control issue. He was trying to degrade me so I degraded him.' This attempt to turn the tables on the man is reminiscent of Dunant's fictional heroine's efforts to fight back against her stalker, as discussed in the previous chapter. It is a statement that also resonates more generally with feminist literature on women's self defence. As Jennifer Baumgardner concludes in her article on the case:

> From a feminist point of view, King's behavior on the tape once the alleged rape began – taunting the men, using sarcasm, acting like a badass – could be construed as strategic. In model-mugging and self-defense courses, women are taught to do whatever they have to do to de-escalate the situation and often the worst thing a victim can do is act like the perpetrator has power. The feminist analysis of rape says that "rape is a crime of power" and, furthermore, that rape almost never looks like a stranger in the bushes attacking a fair maiden.
>
> (2000: 23)

In her attempt to manoeuvre herself out of the role of victim, King does indeed use many of the strategies suggested by feminist activists on rape. In the video footage, King has the role of the 'wisecracking, scolding, and bossy woman' whom feminist theorist Sharon Marcus says may have the potential to 'disrupt the grammar of rape' (1992: 396). For those attempting to determine the 'truth' of the incident, some of the most difficult scenes in the film concern King's bargaining with Yarhaus, in which she lets him perform certain sex acts and not others, in which she lets him shave her pubic hair and she shaves his, and in which she engages in sex acts with Marzullo (according to King, in an attempt to escape from Yarhaus). King says that she did anything she could to avoid penetration. As one doctor from a rape crisis centre is quoted as saying in *Raw Deal*: 'What I saw in this video was Lisa trying to maintain control but finally being forced and the control taken away from her'.

'The spectacle is not a collection of images; rather, it is a social relationship between people that is mediated by images', writes Guy Debord in *Society of the Spectacle* (1995: 12). One of the most fascinating aspects of *Raw Deal* concerns how the filmmakers use the techniques of cinema to expose the terms of the 'social relationship' between various individuals involved with the case, as it is 'mediated by images'. Near the conclusion of *Raw Deal* the filmmakers employ their editing skills to stage a dialogue between King and Marzullo. While we do not hear the question asked by the interviewer, each individual is evidently asked what he or she would like to say to the other:

> *King*: 'Why didn't you help me?'
> *Marzullo*: 'You didn't ask me for help Lisa. And you didn't need it.'
> *King*: 'You knew I was incapable of fighting with everything I had. You
> knew what he was doing, why he was doing it and you could have
> helped.'
> *Marzullo*: 'You're a liar. That's all you are, is a liar.'

These are the two intransigent views that *Raw Deal* leaves us with, the two polarized perspectives that the spectator is apparently asked to 'choose' between. As I have argued, however, it may not simply be a matter of 'choosing' between the two opposed points of view. What seems undeniable, finally, is that King believes she was raped and Marzullo believes she wasn't. If we follow MacKinnon's argument, the disturbing possibility we must confront is that it is possible for both views to be true. Heather McLeod, a former victim support officer who is quoted extensively in *Raw Deal*, concludes that King 'got a really crap deal', a quotation that echoes the title of the film. While critics have praised Corben and Spellman for their objectivity, the film does in fact present a forceful argument: all parties involved in the incident got a 'raw deal'. The film argues that King, as well as the men involved, were let down by the 'system'.

There is an unnerving moment near the end of *Raw Deal*, which concludes with the 'conclusion' of the raw video footage. Loud dance music plays in the background as Marzullo turns towards the camera: 'She's now left the building. And I would say that concludes the Delta Chi porno extravaganza. Thank you. Special thanks to Brother Yuque and Mike Yarhaus for being gracious enough to let us use his camera and filming and fucking a crackhead bitch... Thank you and good night.' How are we implicated in this final address to the spectator? I began this chapter by noting that *Raw Deal* dramatizes difficult questions surrounding the activity of watching spectacles of rape. It dramatizes them, but does it solve them? What are the ethics, finally, of watching *Raw Deal*? Corben and Spellman agonized over whether to include the raw video footage in their documentary. Their decision to do so is predicated on the idea that in showing the video footage, and more importantly, the spectator response to the footage, they call into question the visual as the 'sure ground of evidence' (Butler 1993: 17). Moreover, in rehearsing the images and putting them in a critical context, they are able to illustrate how sexual violence is the site of a cultural struggle over meaning and its ownership.

Importantly, the filmmakers obtained King's consent. This was influential in Channel 4's decision to screen the documentary. As Adam Barker and Prash Naik, the men who decided to show the film on Channel 4, note: 'Before we could proceed we needed to satisfy ourselves that the filmmakers had acted responsibly in gaining King's informed consent. In the UK it is an offence to publish any matters which are likely to lead to the identification of a rape complainant' (28 January 2002). While King did not give her consent to the legal ruling to have the initial tapes released she 'willingly participated' in *Raw Deal* in an attempt to set the record straight (ibid.). But even though King may have approved of the documentary, the question of consent does not go away. The uncomfortable fact of the matter is that the images that appear in *Raw Deal* can still be put to uses that would exceed King's consent. As Ferguson notes in her discussion of pornography, 'Not even the consent of pornographic performers can insure that [the] subsequent uses [of pornography] will reenact such consent' (1995: 689). What, then, of the viewer who consents to watch *Raw Deal*?

Many critics have noted that *Raw Deal* is a film that leaves you feeling sullied. According to *Variety* the film may be 'compulsively watchable' in the 'manner of a train derailment', but it does leave you feeling distinctly uneasy (McCarthy 2001). Ethically, there is no way out when watching *Raw Deal*. If you believe King, then you are left in a very uncomfortable position: in the final minutes of the film you are watching a woman get raped. If you believe Marzullo, then you are watching home-made pornography never intended for your eyes. This latter position is perhaps easier in terms of the cognitive 'reward' it provides: it is easier to believe that such things don't take place, it is better to believe that you did not just see a rape in the raw.

Conclusion

With its emphasis on questions of interpretation, meaning and representation, *Raw Deal: A Question of Consent* brings together many of the themes I have explored throughout this book. One of my central arguments has been that it is necessary to unlock restrictive debates about whether images of sexualized violence promote 'pleasure' or 'horror', in order to explore how contested images of rape bring to light public fantasies of gender, power, ethnicity and class in contemporary culture. As a disturbing example of an alleged 'public rape', the video footage of the Delta Chi incident exposes the association between sexualized violence and visual technology in dramatic fashion. But as shocking and as graphic as *Raw Deal* is, it is only a particularly acute example of what I have noted in regard to all the representations I have discussed: in its treatment as a public event that concerns the community, the depiction of an alleged rape draws arresting attention to the ambivalence of spectatorship, and the question of our complicity and participation in scenes of violence.

The publicity surrounding stories of rape does not show any signs of abating. It is thus imperative to examine the role that cultural narratives of rape play in public life, underpinning ideas about the workings of the body politic. Public fantasies of rape will continue to provoke, constantly forcing us to reconsider and reevaluate the way we think about our role in relation to the text.

NOTES

INTRODUCTION

1 Thanks to Barbara Leckie for drawing my attention to this controversy.
2 See Alcoff and Gray (1993) for a sensitive discussion of survivor discourse and the 'strategic metaphor of "breaking the silence"' (261).
3 For a brilliant critique of Masson's argument see Jacqueline Rose's *Sexuality in the Field of Vision* (1986) and 'Where Does the Misery Come From?: Psychoanalysis, Feminism and the Event' in *Why War? – Psychoanalysis, Politics, and the Return to Melanie Klein* (1989).
4 As bell hooks notes: 'By cleverly calling no attention to the work of powerful feminist thinkers who have continually critiqued the very excesses she names (Judith Butler, Audre Lorde, Kimberlé Crenshaw, and Diana Fuss, to name a few) Roiphe makes it appear that her ideas offer a new and fresh alternative to feminist dogmatism' (1994: 104).
5 Brownmiller is regularly evoked in discussions of rape across a number of disciplines, most recently that of evolutionary biology. In *A Natural History of Rape: Biological Bases of Sexual Coercion* (2000), Randy Thornhill and Craig Palmer put forth the contentious argument that rape is a 'mechanism for spreading genes that is as much a part of the natural landscape of sexual behaviour as courtship and flirting' (Concar 2000: 45). What's interesting is that Thornhill and Palmer feel it is necessary to construct their argument about rape and evolution in opposition to Brownmiller's 'social science explanation of rape' (their phrase). See Brownmiller's response (2000) to Thornhill and Palmer.

1 ORIGIN STORIES: RAPE, FANTASY AND THE FOUNDATIONS OF FEMINISM

1 Noting 'how little emphasis nineteenth-century feminists placed on rape *per se*', Ellen Carol Dubois and Linda Gordon argue there is a 'parallel construction between the nineteenth-century focus on prostitution and the modern emphasis on rape as the quintessential sexual terror' (1989: 32).
2 Norman Podhoretz (1991) coins this phrase in a scathing critical review of feminist writing on sexual violence.
3 All quotations from *Against Our Will: Men, Women and Rape* (1991) will be taken from this edition.
4 As Brownmiller recounts, the anti-rape movement changed the way rape was handled by the authorities. In 1976, a year after the publication of *Against Our Will*, 'four hundred rape crisis centers were in place around the country ... Changes in the law took place just as swiftly. In one year, 1975, thirty states overhauled their rape laws to make them more equitable to victims. Between 1970, when the feminist movement first started to talk about rape, and 1979, when the militance had receded, every state in the union went

through a serious re-evaluation of its rape codes and made significant adjustments. Hospital procedures and police attitudes were transformed as well. The revolution in thinking about rape was profound' (1999: 253).

5 See Elizabeth Cowie's discussion of the rape fantasy in 'Pornography and fantasy: Psychoanalytic perspectives' (1992). As Cowie notes, 'It is a profoundly passive fantasy, and apparently found as commonly in men as in women; in its benign form it absolves the subject from the guilt and responsibility of his or her desire, which appears to come from outside, apparently imposed, but in which the subject will be pleasured' (142).

6 It should be stressed that it is not my intention to provide an overview of feminist literature on rape. Rather, the selected texts typify what I consider to be significant questions about rape and feminism.

7 As I was writing this chapter, I came across Deborah Horvitz's (2000) *Literary Trauma: Sadism, Memory and Sexual Violence in American Women's Fiction*. Horvitz includes an excellent analysis of *Corregidora* and *Bastard Out of Carolina* as novels that investigate the need to return to, and incorporate, one's past history of sexual trauma. While I see a similarly important convergence between the two novels my interest is more specifically focused on how these texts raise noteworthy questions for feminism regarding rape and fantasy.

8 The irony, as several critics argue, is that for a book credited with 'putting rape back into history', *Against Our Will* is a fundamentally ahistorical work (Porter 1986: 216). As Heidi Hartmann and Ellen Ross write: 'Although Brownmiller draws evidence from the past, she does not treat rape as a changing social force, as a dynamic in the social, sexual and legal contexts of specific societies' (1978: 932).

9 Maria Lauret (1994) provides an important overview of what she calls 'feminist fictions of subjectivity', in which 'we can see the construction of a new script – that of "how I became a feminist" – at work' (100). Lauret offers a thoughtful analysis of a variety of first-person feminist novels including Doris Lessing's *The Golden Notebook*, Erica Jong's *Fear of Flying*, and Marilyn French's *The Women's Room*.

10 Criticizing Brownmiller's biological determinism, Winifred Woodhull (1988) argues that she 'inadvertently presents women as primordially disempowered', confirming 'the very assumption her book sets out to invalidate' (171).

11 *The Fountainhead* (1943) plays a significant role in feminist discussions of 'rape myths' in the 1970s. Brownmiller also discusses the rape scene in Rand's novel, denouncing it for its romanticization of rape (1991: 313). Rand, like Helene Deutsch, is treated as a 'traitor to her own sex' (ibid.: 315).

12 See bell hooks (1982) Angela Davis (1983) and Jacquelyn Dowd Hall (1983).

13 Crenshaw's influential concept of intersectionality examines the intersections of race and gender and disrupts 'tendencies to see race and gender as exclusive or separable categories' (1993: 114).

14 In Brownmiller's text, the analogies between black oppression and female oppression, as several critics have pointed out, are problematic in so far as they efface the question of how rape is a crime involving race as well as gender. Brownmiller falls into what Jacquelyn Dowd Hall describes as 'the error of radical feminist writing that misconstrues the realities of racism in the effort to illuminate sexual subordination' (1983: 331). However, as Dowd Hall also observes, this is not to say that the links between racism and sexual subordination, and between lynching and rape, should not be explored. In a stimulating discussion of the links between feminist political discourse and black political movements, Maria Lauret similarly suggests that 'what has become obscured by [the] guilt-ridden rejection of a discursive alignment of the plight of women with that of African-Americans is the common history of the Black movements of the 1960s and Women's Liberation' (124). See Lauret's *Liberating Literature* (1994) for an important and suggestive discussion of the links between black and feminist political movements.

15 See Diana Russell (1975) *The Politics of Rape*, a collection of victims' responses to sexual assault published in the same year as *Against Our Will*. Russell's study includes chapters entitled, 'The Rape of a White Radical' and 'Reverse Racism and Rape'. Both chapters are designed to explore the question: 'Is it racist for a white woman raped by a black man to be more wary of black men and angry toward them afterward?' (163) Remarkably, Russell answers this question as follows: 'If some black men see rape of white women as an act of revenge or as a justifiable expression of hostility towards whites, I think it is equally realistic for white women to be less trusting of black men than many of them are' (180).

16 It is interesting to note that the description of this rape is included in Elizabeth Stanko (1985) *Intimate Intrusions: Women's Experience of Male Violence*. Stanko includes a page-long description of the rape in a wider discussion of women's real-life traumatic experiences of sexual violence. Nowhere does she indicate that Chris's rape is 'fictional'. Stanko writes: 'Disarmed by threats, Chris ... searches for ways to avoid her rape, and ultimately to stay alive. Such is the experience of raped women' (46).

17 My thinking on the role that the black woman plays in French's novel is inspired by Toni Morrison's brilliant reflections on 'symbolic figurations of blackness' in American literature in *Playing in the Dark* (1993: xi).

18 Davis suggests that 'one of the major weaknesses of Susan Brownmiller's study on rape is its absolute disregard of Black women's pioneering efforts in the anti-lynching movement' (1983: 195). In failing to include the important work of women such as Ida B Wells, and Mary Church Terrell, Davis argues that Brownmiller misses an opportunity to theorize the relationship between race, gender and rape. In her recent memoirs, Brownmiller implicitly responds to criticism of this kind by including discussion of the work by black feminists on rape in the 1970s. However, it is worth noting that Brownmiller's inclusion of this work still does not alter her perception of race and gender. I would argue that this is due to her continuing failure to think about how feminism discursively constructs images of rape.

19 Brownmiller includes *Corregidora* on her website (SusanBrownmiller.com) as a recommended novel: 'So many great novels by black women were published in the seventies. I'm ashamed to say that I didn't get around to reading *Corregidora* until last year ... I think it's one of the most powerful books I've ever read.'

20 See Toni Morrison's *The Bluest Eye* (1970). Morrison's Pulitzer Prize winning novel contains a scene in which the central black male character, Cholly Breedlove, is sexually humiliated and symbolically 'raped' by white men. Morrison explicitly links the sexual violation of the black man to his own sexual violation of his daughter. See Morrison's discussion of the connection between these two scenes in her 'Afterword' to the 1993 Penguin edition of the novel.

21 All quotations are taken from Dorothy Allison (1993) *Bastard Out of Carolina*, London: Flamingo.

22 In his study, *The Politics of the Family*, RD Laing suggests that the 'family as a shared fantasy image is usually a container of some kind *in* which all members of the family feel themselves to be, and *for* which image all members of the family may feel each should sacrifice themselves' (1969: 9).

23 Allison's use of storytelling as a space of self-preservation accords with Freud's recognition of the role that fiction plays in relation to death: 'In the realm of fiction we find the plurality of lives which we need. We die with the hero with whom we have identified ourselves; yet we survive him, and are ready to die again just as safely with another hero' (Freud, cited in Weber: 97). See Samuel Weber's (De Vries and Weber 1997) on Freud's understanding of the relation between death and fiction in 'Wartime', pp. 80–105.

24 Carole Vance (1984), for example, frames the 'juxtaposition of pleasure and danger' as perspectives a woman may 'choose at different points in her life' (431).

25 For a good account of the feminist 'sex wars' see Ruby Rich (1986).

26 In *Two or Three Things I Know For Sure* (1996), an autobiographical exploration of the issue of sexual violence, published a year after *Bastard Out of Carolina*, Allison theorizes the activity of storytelling. She writes about the taboo of trying to tell two stories at the same time: 'Two or three things I know, but this is the one I am not supposed to talk about, how it comes together – sex and violence, love and hatred. I'm not ever supposed to put together the two halves of my life – the man who walked across my childhood and the life I have made for myself... I'm not supposed to talk about sex like that, not about weapons or hatred or violence, and never to put them in the context of sexual desire' (45, 47).

27 In 1996 Anjelica Huston directed the film version of *Bastard Out of Carolina*. While Allison has said she was generally pleased with the way the film dealt with the violent scenes, she has also registered her disappointment that 'all of the places in which Bone Boatwright has agency were gone'. See interview with Laura Miller (1998).

28 As Elizabeth Cowie (1992) notes in her discussion of fantasy: 'The delays, diversions and obstacles in a story are all means to postponing the ending. They mark a pleasure in the happening and continuing to happen of the scene, of how the consummation will come about, not the act itself' (137).

2 BODY POLITICS: ROUSSEAU'S *LE LÉVITE D'EPHRAIM*

1 For an important discussion of wartime rape, see *Mass Rape: The War Against Women in Bosnia-Herzegovina* (1994).

2 There is fierce debate in Rousseau studies regarding the date of the composition of the *Essay*. See Jacques Derrida (1974) *Of Grammatology*. In his cogent discussion of 'The Initial Debate and the Composition of the Essay', Derrida cites a long note from Pierre Maurice Masson regarding the chronology of the *Essay*. Here is the relevant excerpt: 'In 1754, the *Essay* on languages was a long note to the second *Discourse*; in 1761, it became an independent dissertation, augmented and corrected... Finally, in 1763, this dissertation, revised for one last time, was divided into chapters' (1974: 194). The *Lévite* was composed in 1762.

3 Similar to the way Brownmiller has been taken to task for the sweeping quality of her historical narrative of rape, Pateman has been criticized for what Lori Chamberlain calls the 'epic nature' of her work. For the lively criticism that has developed on *The Sexual Contract* see Lori Chamberlain (1991); Margaret Whitford (1991); Chantal Mouffe (1992); Wendy Brown (1995); and Moira Gatens (1996).

4 This is beginning to change. My work must situate itself in relation to an emerging body of writing on the *Lévite*. See Judith Still (1989) Susan Jackson (1992) and Peggy Kamuf (1988). More recently, Elizabeth Wingrove (1998) explores how performance is central to Rousseau's account of masculinity and femininity in the *Lévite*. These engaging studies provide important insights into the depiction of sexual difference in the *Lévite*. None of the above articles, however, reads the story specifically for its depiction of rape.

5 De Man notes in passing: 'In the *Essay on the Origin of Languages* all examples destined to illustrate the "natural" language of man are acts of violence' (1979: 140). He then refers the reader to the relevant section in the *Essay*. As he explains in a footnote: 'Rousseau mentions the threatening gifts sent by the king of the Scythians to King Darius and especially the Old Testament story (Judges) of the Levite from Ephraim who sent the body of his murdered wife, cut in twelve pieces, to the Tribes of Israel to spur them on to revenge. The same theme is taken up in the later story *Le Lévite d'Ephraim*' (ibid.: 140).

6 It is important, however, not to fall into the trap of grouping these 'white male fictions' together in an ahistorical manner. To do so would be to ignore the fact that each text comes from different historical and social periods and employs different representational strategies.

7 My thinking on the structure of Rousseau's tale of social origins is informed by Mikkel Borch-Jacobsen's excellent analysis of Freud's myth of social origins in *The Freudian Subject* (1988) and *The Emotional Tie: Psychoanalysis, Mimesis and Effect* (1992).

8 All quotations are taken from *Le Lévite d'Ephraim* in *Oeuvres Complètes de Jean-Jacques Rousseau Volume II* (eds) B Gagnebin and M Raymond, Pléaide Paris, Gallimard 1959–69. All translations from *Le Lévite* are mine.

9 In Claude Lévi-Strauss's classic structural account of the origins of the masculine social alliance, the prohibition of incest is a rule that has less to do with barring marriage with the mother, sister or daughter, 'than as a rule obliging the mother, sister or daughter to be given to others' (1969: 481). The reason men marry other men's sisters instead of their own, is because they want to gain a brother-in-law.

10 For a detailed discussion of how the representation of hospitality in the *Lévite* relates to Rousseau's account of his flight into exile in the *Confessions* see Peggy Kamuf (1988) and Susan Jackson (1992).

11 There are several interesting essays that explore the role rape plays in the founding stories of republics. In particular, see Nancy J Vickers (1986), Patricia Klindienst Joplin (1991) and Coppélia Kahn (1991).

12 See Derrida (1981). In his discussion of Socrates and the *pharmakon*, Derrida notes the contradictory way in which the drug is turned into a remedy, the poison into a counter-poison (125).

13 In her analysis of the myth of Lucretia and Judges 19, Mieke Bal notes that discussions of the allegorical use of the raped woman ignore critical questions. They do not, for instance, 'explain the choice of vehicle for tenor' (1991: 84).

14 Peggy Kamuf (1988) asks a similar question in her reading of the *Lévite*: 'what might it mean that the need or desire for a living or animated writing... takes as its model the mutilation and dispersion of a woman's dead body?' (95). Linking this question to her wider examination of the concept of the signature in Rousseau's body of writing, Kamuf writes that the 'dispersed body of the girl... is a written contract which all the brothers sign... finding their support on the forever silent body which serves as their means of writing' (97–98).

15 In fact, the story is mentioned once in *Of Grammatology* but only in a long quotation that Derrida cites from Pierre Masson: 'About 1763, [Rousseau] wished to bring together in one small volume three short works that he had in hand: *L'imitation theatrale, Essay on the Origin of Languages, Le Lévite d'Ephraim.* The collection was never published' (cited in Derrida 1974: 194).

16 Peggy Kamuf (1988); Judith Still (1989); and Susan Jackson (1992) all draw upon Derrida's reading of Rousseau in *Of Grammatology* yet none question Derrida's curious omission of the story from his reading of the *Essay*.

17 As several critics have noted, there is an obvious resemblance between the father–daughter conflict in *Le Lévite* and that contained in Rousseau's literary classic *Julie or La Nouvelle Héloise* (Kavanagh 1983; Still 1989; Jackson 1992). In both texts, the daughter sacrifices herself on behalf of her father, forsaking her lover and agreeing to wed the man of her father's choice.

18 For useful discussions of Rousseau's theories on gender and public life, see Jean Bethke Elshtain's *Public Man, Private Woman: Women in Social and Political Thought* (1981) and Joan Landes' *Women and the Public Sphere in the Age of the French Revolution* (1988).

19 See René Girard on the figure of the scapegoat in *Violence and the Sacred* (1978) and Derrida on the idea of the *pharmakon* in 'Plato's Pharmacy' in *Dissemination* (1981). Andrew J McKenna's discussion of Girard's notion of the 'surrogate victim' serves as a helpful gloss on the plot of the *Lévite*: 'It is the essential function of sacrifice to contain violence by investing it in a scapegoat whose expulsion unites a community in driving out one of its marginal members' (1996: 233).

3 'RAPE IS NOT A SPECTATOR SPORT': THE NEW BEDFORD 'BIG DAN'S' GANG RAPE

1 Following other feminists who have written on the New Bedford rape case (Rosen 1985, Bumiller 1990, Benedict 1992), I have decided not to use the victim's name. Though the woman's name became widely available during the trial, the exposure of her identity remains a matter of intense dispute. For an excellent discussion of the debate on naming rape victims see Katha Pollitt (1991).

2 Benedict's *Virgin or Vamp: How the Press Covers Sex Crimes* (1992) is an invaluable source book for anyone interested in major American rape trials of the past three decades.

3 Felman is concerned with the issues of witnessing and testifying in relation to the Holocaust. Though one should be careful not to merge the Holocaust with other traumatic experiences, deliberations on the representation of the Holocaust hold importance for a feminist interrogation of the difficulty of representing rape.

4 It is interesting that here the vilified community is the Portuguese. As noted in Chapter 1 in regard to *Corregidora*, Portugal was a colonial power and a nation of slave owners. In this case, however, the Portuguese-Americans are the ethnic minority.

5 See Kimberle Crenshaw's (1993) discussion of the Anita Hill–Clarence Thomas sexual harassment hearings. Crenshaw discusses how Hill was cast as a 'de-raced – that is, white – woman' by the feminist movement as well as by the black community (415). According to Crenshaw, the hearings offer 'a stark illustration' of how the 'opposition between narratives of rape and of lynching' work to disempower the black woman (405).

6 Jenny Sharpe's important essay 'The Unspeakable Limits of Rape: Colonial Violence and Counter-Insurgency' (1991), an analysis of colonial discourse and EM Forster's *A Passage to India*, influences my reading of how the media depicted the Portuguese women's response to the rape. As Sharpe observes, in Mutiny narratives the rape of Indian women is never acknowledged. 'What happens to Indian women when subjected to the "tender mercies" of British soldiers is predictably missing from this report. In the place of that absent narrative, we have representations of Indian women inciting mutineers to rape and torture' (1991: 231).

7 In a sociological essay that focuses on why the women of New Bedford turned against the raped woman, Lynn Chancer writes: 'Anti-Portuguese prejudice was commonly recognized and accepted by the community as a whole, but sexual oppression was not. For the women as well as the men in the community, ethnic loyalty was legitimate and built into the fabric of daily understanding. Feminist loyalties, based on a sense of sexual oppression were not' (1987: 255).

8 Both Ellen Israel Rosen (1985) and Lynn Chancer (1987) consider the Portuguese community's response to the rape and explore why a large segment of the community was hostile to the rape victim. More recently, the case has been analysed from the perspective of critical legal theory. Feminist legal theorists Kristin Bumiller (1990) and Lisa Cuklanz (1996) provide readings of the case from the point of view of feminist law reform.

9 Though the feminist literature on the case draws attention to the fact that the Big Dan's case was televised, it is only in the most cursory of ways. Kristin Bumiller, for example, relegates the information to a footnote: 'The entire trial was videotaped and televised by a local New Bedford public television station' (1990: 141).

10 Books outlining the history of CNN tend to exclude the Big Dan's rape trial. See Dan M. Flournoy (1992) and Dan M Flournoy and Robert K Stewart (1997). Source books on television also neglect the rape trial. See Anthony Smith (ed.) (1995) and Horace Newcomb (ed.) (1997).

11 It is possible to obtain taped segments of the trial from the Harvard Law School Library audio–visual department. In addition to being televised by CNN, the trial was also aired by several other cable outlets in America.

12 I am indebted to Frances Ferguson (1987) for this idea of rape as a vehicle for inaugurating new representational modes. Ferguson's essay provides an excellent discussion

of how Samuel Richardson uses rape to inaugurate one of the 'first full attempts at a psychological novel' – *Clarissa* (98).

13 This question is the title of Alice Henry's article (1988) on the subject in *Feminism and Censorship: The Current Debate*.

14 See Robin Morgan (1980) for a good overview of the anti-pornography movement's arguments regarding the connections between pornography and rape.

15 See Mandy Merck (1992) for a discussion of the impact of the MacKinnon–Dworkin ordinance in Britain.

16 See *Women Against Censorship* (1985) for a collection of feminist responses to the MacKinnon–Dworkin Minneapolis city ordinance.

17 Diamond's concluding emphasis on the 'positive' aspects of pornography is consistent with other critiques of the anti-pornography position. In the same anthology, Lisa Duggan *et al.* defend pornography on the grounds that it 'serves some social functions, which benefit women: it advocates sexual adventure, sex outside of marriage, sex for no reason other than pleasure, casual sex, anonymous sex, group sex, voyeuristic sex, illegal sex, public sex' (1985: 145). Somewhere along the way, a question about the relationship between violence and spectacle goes missing.

18 Remarkably, Hentoff's comment (1994), which refers to Carlin Romano's controversial review of MacKinnon's *Only Words*, discussed in the first chapter of this book, connects MacKinnon's theories of pornography and representation to the Levite of Ephraim. While Hentoff refers to the biblical Levite story to criticize the censorious nature of MacKinnon's arguments, my view is that there is more to this connection than meets the eye. It is MacKinnon's concern with the way in which rape operates as public spectacle, I would argue, that makes her theories on spectatorship and violence relevant to a discussion of the 'horror show' of a woman's rape and dismemberment.

19 See Wendy Brown (1990).

20 MacKinnon's interest in the speech–act theory of JL Austin (1975) unexpectedly connects her to the work of feminist poststructuralists like Judith Butler. Despite MacKinnon's marginalization as a 'radical feminist', it is very interesting to note the way in which her work is regularly taken up by poststructuralist feminism. Critic Naomi Morgenstern has recently asked whether Dworkin and MacKinnon 'represent poststructuralist feminist theory's Other, its haunting doubled double' (1997: 44). For an example of poststructuralism's engagement with MacKinnon, see Morgenstern (1997) and Judith Butler (1995).

21 There is an extensive body of writing on *Only Words*. See Carlin Romano (1993); Bernard Williams (1994); Phil Cox (1994); Parveen Adams and Mark Cousins (1995); Naomi Morgenstern (1997).

22 MacKinnon compares the relation between rape and visual technology to the relation between the lynching of black men and photography: 'In this country, nothing has at once expressed racial hatred and effectuated racial subordination more effectively than the murder and hanging of a mutilated body, usually of a Black man. Photographs were sometimes taken of the body and sold, to extend its message and the pleasure of viewing it' (1994: 23). On the role that communications technology played in lynching see Jacquelyn Dowd Hall (1983); Robyn Wiegman (1993); David Marriott (1996); and Jacqueline Goldsby (1996). My argument concerning the role that representation plays in rape is informed by this engaging body of work; in particular, the idea that the 'representation of racial violence is part of the social experience of the event' (Goldsby 1996: 274).

23 It should be noted that MacKinnon is familiar with the New Bedford rape case. In *Feminism Unmodified*, she quotes Edward Harrington, one of the defense attorneys from the New Bedford case: 'If you're living with a man, what are you doing running around the streets getting raped' (1987: 145)? For Judith Butler's post-structuralist take on the same quotation see the conclusion to 'Contingent Foundations' (1992).

24 Unless otherwise specified, the following quotations are taken from the transcript of the inquiry, US Senate Hearing (1984, 24 April).

25 Pina testified that the extensive press interest in the case intimidated the rape victim. The trial proceeded only when a ruling was passed which allowed the television cameras to be in the courtroom but which refused to let them film the raped woman: 'When the victim took the stand they would not photograph her, they would photograph the walls of the room, or the defense counsel, the prosecution, but not the victim. The victim's voice was allowed on the air, and that was it' (cited in US Senate Hearing 1984: 5).

26 Comerford's essay looks at the televised rape trial as a 'critical site of gender construction' (1997: 231). Though she quotes extensively from the Senate Hearing on the Big Dan's rape trial, she does not actually discuss the trial itself. In this respect, it is interesting that the Big Dan's case emerges as the archetypal trial in her account.

4 'THEY DID WORSE THAN NOTHING': RAPE AND SPECTATORSHIP IN *THE ACCUSED*

1 To say *The Accused* is Hollywood's first feature-length film on rape is not to suggest that there are not mainstream films, prior to 1988, that deal with the subject. In fact, rape is arguably bound up with the very origins of cinema and plays a prominent role in founding films such as DW Griffith's *Birth of a Nation* (1915). But *The Accused* remains unique as the culminating product of over two decades of feminist consciousness-raising on rape.

2 In *The Accused* the rape takes place on a pinball machine not a pool table. Decorated with a picture of a half dressed 'sexy' woman being 'slam-dunked' through a basketball hoop, the pinball machine is part of the film's critique of rape as male sport (Clover 1992).

3 I am grateful to Percy Walton for alerting me to the film's omission of the ethnic tensions involved in the real-life case.

4 Promotional slogan taken from the rental video box of *The Accused*.

5 James Snead (1991) employs the term 'constitutive omissions' in his absorbing examination of the hidden sub-plots in *King Kong* (1933).

6 *Women Viewing Violence* claims to 'bring together two separate issues for the first time: the feminist concern with representations and their consumption by women and the wholly separate study of domestic and sexual violence' (Schlesinger *et al.* 1992: 127). The study of sexual violence has been bound up with the feminist concern with representation – and vice versa – from the start, but the study nonetheless makes a very valuable contribution to research on audience reception. Especially important is its focus on the 'experience of violence and on ethnicity as the major determinants of varying interpretations of media representations of violence against women' (ibid.: 42).

7 *Crimewatch UK*, broadcast on prime time television since 1984, is one of the UK's longest running 'reality' television shows with an audience of 11.5 million. See John Sears (1995) and Philip Schlesinger (1992).

8 Ruby Rich (1983) uses the phrase in relation to the controversial feminist anti-pornography documentary, *Not a Love Story: A Film About Pornography* (Klein, Canada, 1981). *Not a Love Story* explores how the pornography industry exploits women and promotes an idea of sexual violence as erotic and titillating. While the film's stated goal is to advocate censorship of pornographic images it nonetheless includes those graphic images in an attempt to show how harmful pornography is. In her critique of the film, Rich describes it as 'a kind of snuff movie for an antisnuff crowd' (58). The problem is that rather than exploring questions of voyeurism and point of view, the 'filmmakers seem unquestioningly to accept and deploy traditional cinematic practices' (59). Although *The Accused* appears to tackle the question of point of view, it, too, can be said to exploit its graphic subject matter. Like *Not a Love Story*, *The Accused* wants us to be horrified at the images of sexual violence it shows us, even though the camera

arguably puts us in a voyeuristic position and fails to show us the scene from the woman's point of view.

9 Faludi sees *The Accused* as Lansing's attempt to 'polish up her feminist credentials' after *Fatal Attraction*. According to Faludi, *The Accused* should be 'mourned as a depressing artefact of the times – because it tells us only how much ground women have already lost. By the end of the 1980s a film that simply opposed the mauling of a young woman could be passed off as a daring feminist statement' (1992: 170).

10 My exploration of what happens when a real event is turned into cinema owes a great debt to Vicky Lebeau who helped me to think through the idea of cinema as cure and whose work on violence and spectatorship provided the inspiration for this chapter. See Lebeau's 'Lost Angels: *River's Edge* and social spectatorship' in *Lost Angels: Psychoanalysis and Cinema* (1995).

11 As Mary Ann Doane (1987) notes in her discussion of the 1940s cycle of woman's films: 'In films addressed to women, spectatorial pleasure is often indissociable from pain' (16).

12 This misreading is perpetuated in recent examinations of the film. See, for example, Julia Hallam and Margaret Marshment (2000). The rape sequence, they suggest, is 'situated at the end of the film as part of Foster's testimony' (113).

13 Cuklanz's *Rape on Trial: How the Mass Media Construct Legal Reform and Social Change* (1996) is an important and insightful examination of famous rape trials and the popular representation of rape in the mass media. Cuklanz is very sensitive to ethnic and racial issues; that is why her misreading of the rape scene is all the more suggestive.

14 For another example of this erasure see Susan Jeffords' (1994) interesting discussion of *The Accused*. In spite of her concern to explore the white man as a heroic fantasy figure of justice, nowhere does Jeffords consider the raped woman as white – she is simply the raped woman.

15 Walker foregrounds 'nonrealist' trauma films that emphasize 'non-linearity, fragmentation, nonsynchronous sound, repetition, rapid editing and strange angles' (214). While the films I discuss are realist, they can still be classed as trauma cinema, I believe, on the grounds that they are dealing with rape and the traumatic past.

16 Rodney King, a black motorist, was beaten by a group of white officers from the LAPD. The incident was captured on a home video camera by George Holliday, a white man who lived in a nearby apartment. Despite the fact that the incident was captured on video, the police officers were acquitted when the case went to trial, a verdict that resulted in the LA riots. *Strange Days* invokes the King incident as part of its interrogation of millennial fears and fantasies regarding virtual reality technology and spectatorship.

17 Bigelow uses new technology in the form of a special lightweight compact camera in order to render the playback clips as realistic as possible. The rape clip, according to Bigelow, is the scene that brings out the full 'intensity' and visceral impact of this new technology. See Bigelow's comments on the rape playback in her interview with Dave Gardetta (1995).

18 Several reviewers have drawn comparisons between *Strange Days* and Michael Powell's *Peeping Tom* (1960), a film in which a professional cinematographer kills the women he films with an extendable spike on his camera. The camera also has a mirror on it so that the women are forced to view their own terror at the moment of death. Like Bigelow's film, *Peeping Tom* met with critical outrage, ruining Powell's career as a director as a consequence. But in recent years the film has become widely recognized as a classic 'metafilm', an honour that, some argue, may some day be bestowed upon *Strange Days*.

19 See Christopher Goodwin (1996) 'Has Hollywood Gone Too Far?' *The Sunday Times*, 10 March.

20 Not everyone, of course, vilified the film and its director. Joan Smith (1996), for instance, compares *Strange Days* to *The Accused* and praises the former for its innovative attempt to deal with the 'problem of point-of-view' (199). Where female terror in *The Accused*

'carries an erotic charge', Smith suggests that *Strange Days* forces the (male) audience to identify with the woman's suffering (200, 204).

21 See Gabe Elias' compelling discussion of *Strange Days* as a feminist film (www. KathrynBigelow.com). According to Elias, the narrative punishes the character of Faith for her 'desire to be watched'. As he argues, 'Faith's desire to insert herself into the objective position of *Strange Day's* violent gaze is one that this feminist text finds repulsive and ultimately self-destructive'.

22 See my further discussion of the Freudian primal scene in Chapter 6 on *Raw Deal: A Question of Consent*.

23 To date, there appears to be little or no controversy in feminist circles regarding *Boys'* depiction of rape. Instead, criticism has centred on a love scene between Brandon and Lana that occurs after the rape. As Judith Halberstam asks: 'Why would Brandon want to have sex within hours of a rape?' (297) See *Screen* 2001, 42(3) and other articles included in the *Boys Don't Cry* (2001) debate in *Screen*. See also Rachel Swan (2001).

24 There is another disturbing link between the two films. Just as *The Accused* elides the ethnic conflict that embroiled the actual case, so *Boys Don't Cry* omits the story of Philip Devine, the African American man who was murdered alongside Brandon Teena and Lisa Lambert. According to Judith Halberstam, 'Peirce claimed that this subplot would have complicated her film and made it too cumbersome – but race is a narrative trajectory that is absolutely central to the meaning of the Brandon Teena murder' (2001: 298).

25 See Susan Muska and Greta Olafsdottir's documentary *The Brandon Teena Story* (1998), which includes the taped recording of the interrogation.

26 The phrase is from Eve Kosofsky Sedgwick (1985).

27 The quotation is from Cheyney Ryan (1996: 24). Though Ryan does not discuss rape, her fascinating reading of the classic Western yields a number of interesting points of comparison. Of particular interest is her concern with a seemingly circular structure of violence in which 'the violence that founds "civilization" (and the legal order at its heart) is one that at the same time problematizes the whole distinction between "civilization" and its Other' (37–38).

5 'MORE INTIMATE THAN VIOLENCE': SARAH DUNANT'S *TRANSGRESSIONS*

1 As Naomi Morgenstern (1997) notes in a provocative examination of what she calls 'pornogothic feminism', the novel is difficult to classify. 'Is *Mercy* fiction? Is it *just* fiction? Is it a political manifesto? Is it a confession?' (40) According to Morgenstern, *Mercy* is a 'novel that thematizes fiction's power: literature becomes a place for doing everything and anything' (41).

2 See Dworkin's dispute with novelist John Irving over the causal relationship between fictional and real violence. In a letter to the editor in The *New York Times* (1992) Dworkin states: 'I have written (in my novels *Ice and Fire* and *Mercy*) about a woman raped by two men sequentially, the first aggressor routed by the second one, to whom the woman, near dead, submits; he bites viciously and repeatedly into her genitals. When I wrote it, someone had already done it – to me. My imagination can barely grasp my real life'. The interesting question that arises is: why write about it as fiction if fiction is barely adequate? Dworkin does not, to my knowledge, ever fully confront the implications of this question.

3 Unless otherwise specified, all quotations are from Sarah Dunant's *Transgressions* (1997) London: Virago.

4 See Priscilla Walton and Manina Jones (1999) *Detective Agency: Women Rewriting the Hard-boiled Tradition* for an excellent discussion of violence and the 'resistant female body' (179) in female detective fiction.

6 RAPE ON TAPE? *RAW DEAL: A QUESTION OF CONSENT*

1 Thanks to those who organized the 'Dangerous Representations' conference at the University of Sussex in June 2001. I am grateful for the helpful comments and questions raised by the audience at the reading of my paper.

2 As Michele Aaron helpfully suggested, at the 'Spectacle of the Real' conference, Brunel University (2003), these kinds of issues regarding the politics of displaying the image point towards the possibility of an ethical spectatorship.

3 See Stella Bruzzi (2000) for a discussion of 'film as accidental record' (13).

4 As several news reports point out, the officer, Alice Hendon, who made the determination that the incident was 'clearly consensual' was female.

5 This charge against King was eventually dropped. The State Attorney's Office said that it did not want to discourage other rape victims from coming forward to report their assault. It is important to note that the men involved were never charged with rape. As Jennifer Baumgardner reports, 'King and six of the fraternity members were charged with misdemeanors – dancing without a license for her and assignation (gathering for the purpose of lewdness) for the guys' (2000: 22). The fraternity members were allowed to return to Delta Chi in 2000.

6 Unless otherwise indicated, all quotations are from *Raw Deal: A Question of Consent* (Corben, US, 2001).

7 See Linda Williams (1999) *Hard Core: Power, Pleasure, and the 'Frenzy of the Visible'*. As Williams suggests, even in hard-core porn, 'enjoyment-of-rape scenarios became increasingly unacceptable in the 1980s and the 1990s' (166).

8 It would appear that many audience members agree with the BBFC that *Irreversible* does not titillate. BBC News reported that 'at the 2002 Cannes Film Festival, about 250 people walked out of a screening, with some needing medical treatment to get over the shock of the movie' ('"Rape Film"' 21 October 2002).

9 My reading of *Raw Deal*, and the circulation of the video footage it contains, is influenced by the remarkable body of critical work on the Rodney King video. See Mike Mashon (1993); Frank Tomasulo (1996); and the essays included in (ed.) Robert Gooding-Williams, *Reading Rodney King, Reading Urban Uprising* (1993).

10 As Frank Tomasulo suggests in his reading of the Rodney King video footage, 'although the subjective states of mind of *the participants* may not have been amenable to video dissection, the subjectivity of *the spectators of the videotape* is relevant to the issue at hand' (1996: 82).

11 It should be noted, too, that the men involved were far from happy about the release of the tape. In *Raw Deal*, Marzullo speaks of his grave 'embarrassment' about being exposed in the tape. He states that he is particularly upset that he should be seen hanging out 'with this white trash woman'.

12 *Raw Deal* strongly criticizes Smith's handling of the case and his decision to release the video footage as a public record. At the end of the film it is reported that 'State Attorney Rod Smith was elected to the Florida State Senate. His first responsibility was to aid in the investigation of improprieties in the 2000 Presidential election.'

13 As Corben explains: 'Campus NOW had lost a big fight to keep the tapes from being made public, and they felt that we would be exploiting King using the tapes in a movie' (cited in Walker 2001). Corben and Spellman made repeated requests for NOW to appear in *Raw Deal*; the organization said they would only do so if their demands for a cash fee, a percentage of the film's future profits, and approval of the title and final cut were met. Understandably, Corben and Spellman declined.

14 *Rashomon*, which is structured through flashbacks, tells the story of a woman's rape and a man's murder. The viewer is provided with many different perspectives of the incident. For interesting discussions of the film's complex narration and its undermining of the idea of truth, see Richie (1987) and Fleishman (1992).

15 This is an important point of divergence between *Raw Deal* and the theory of MacKinnon. In her discussion of pornography, MacKinnon takes what Parveen Adams and Mark Cousins describe as a 'fundamentalist stand' (1995: 93) on the issue of representation and the question of how individuals respond to images. As Deborah Philips usefully pointed out to me, at the 'Spectacle of the Real' conference, Brunel University (2003), this sort of fundamentalism regarding the uses and consequences of visual materials would seem to fly in the face of *Raw Deal's* attempt to open up a debate about the politics of visual images.

16 For a compelling discussion of the issue of consent in rape cases see Frances Ferguson (1987).

17 When King reported the rape she told the police officers that there had been video cameras running during the evening, prompting the police to search for the tapes that were hidden behind a picture in a fraternity house bedroom.

18 King admits that she was highly intoxicated on the night in question. Ironically, this should make the issue of consent a moot point because, according to the law, when a woman is under the influence of alcohol or drugs she is incapable of giving consent. As noted in a printed message in *Raw Deal*, the men were drinking heavily on the evening in question and, according to King, were also taking drugs. They were never tested. The results of the medical examination given to King the next morning were lost and never made public.

BIBLIOGRAPHY

'A Dozen Who Made a Difference' (1976) *Time*, 5 January: 20.

Adams, Parveen and Mark Cousins (1995) 'The Truth on Assault', October (71; Winter): 93–102.

Agus, Carole (1986) 'Requiem for a Rape Victim', *Newsday*, 30 December.

Alcoff, Linda and Laura Gray (1993) 'Survivor Discourse: Transgression or Recuperation?' *Signs: Journal of Women in Culture and Society*, 18(2): 260–290.

Allison, Dorothy (1993) *Bastard Out of Carolina*, London: Flamingo.

——(1995) *Skin: Talking About Sex, Class and Literature*, London: Pandora Press.

——(1995) *Trash: Stories and Poems*, London: Flamingo.

——(1996) *Two or Three Things I Know for Sure*, London: Flamingo.

Amir, Menachem (1971) *Patterns in Forcible Rape*, Chicago: UP.

Angelo, Bonnie (1994) 'Assault by Paragraph', *Time*, 17 January: 37.

Appio, I (1989) 'Review of *The Accused*', in T Milne (ed.) *The Time Out Film Guide*, Harmondsworth: Penguin.

Ashbrook, Penny (1989) 'Rape on Screen', *SpareRib*, April: 37–39.

Austin, JL (1975) *How to Do Things with Words*, Cambridge: Harvard University Press.

Baker, Houston (1991) *Workings of the Spirit: The Poetics of Afro-American Women's Writing*, Chicago: The University of Chicago Press.

Bal, Mieke (1986) 'The Bible as Literature: A Critical Escape', *Diacritics*, Winter: 71–79.

——(1988) 'The Rape of Narrative and the Narrative of Rape: Speech Act and Body Language in Judges', in Elaine Scarry (ed.) *Literature and the Body: Essays on Populations and Persons*, Baltimore/London: Johns Hopkins University Press.

——(1991) *Reading 'Rembrandt'. Beyond the Word-Image Opposition*, The Northrop Frye Lectures in Literary Theory, Cambridge: Cambridge University Press.

Barker, Adam and Prash Naik (2002) 'A Question of Consent', *The Guardian*, 28 January: 10.

Barker, Martin (1984) 'Nasty Politics or Video Nasties?' in *The Video Nasties: Freedom and Censorship in the Media*, London: Pluto Press.

'Bar Crowd Cheers as Woman is Raped' (1983) *Boston Herald*, 9 March.

Barnett, Pamela (1998) 'Figurations of Rape and the Supernatural in *Beloved*' in Carl Plasa (ed.) *Icon Critical Guides: Beloved*, Cambridge: Icon.

'Barroom Rape Trial Hears of Failed Call' (1984) *New York Times*, 8 March.

Baumgardner, Jennifer (2000) 'What Does Rape Look Like?' *The Nation*, 3 January: 20–23.

'BBFC passes IRREVERSIBLE uncut for adult cinema audiences', Online. Available HTTP: http://www.bbfc.co.uk/website/2000About.nsf/News/$first?OpenDocument&AutoFra … (accessed 3 November 2002).

'BBFC classification of *Baise Moi*', Online. Available HTTP: http.www.bbfc.co.uk/_
802568b8005a70f7.nsf/0/c3a3b912c781167d802569ff003f7... (accessed 3 November
2002).

Beck, Melinda and Marsha Zabarsky (1984) 'Rape Trial: "Justice Crucified"?' *Newsweek*,
2 April.

Benedict, Helen (1992) *Virgin or Vamp: How the Press Covers Sex Crimes*, New York/Oxford:
Oxford University Press.

Bennett, Catherine (1994) 'A Prophet and Porn', *The Observer*, 28 May.

Berlant, Lauren (1991) 'National Brands/National Body: *Imitation of Life*', in Hortense
J Spillers (ed.) *Comparative American Identities: Race, Sex, and Nationality in the Modern Text*,
New York and London: Routledge, 110–138.

Bersani, Leo (1987) 'Is the Rectum a Grave?' October, 43: 197–222.

'Big Dan's Tavern' (1984) *National Review*, 20 April: 20.

Blakely, Mary Kay (1983) 'New Bedford Gang Rape: Who Were the Men?' *Ms*. July:
51–101.

Bondebjerg, Ib (1996) 'Public discourse/private fascination: hybridization in "true-life-story"
genres', *Media, Culture & Society*, 18: 27–45.

Borch-Jacobsen, Mikkel (1988) *The Freudian Subject* (transl. Catherine Porter), Stanford:
Stanford University Press.

——(1992) *The Emotional Tie: Psychoanalysis, Mimesis, and Affect* (transl. Douglas Brick *et al.*),
Stanford: Stanford University Press.

Boston Herald, 10 March 1983.

Boston Herald, 26 March 1983.

Bowers, Elisabeth (1990) *Ladies Night*, London: Virago.

Bridgewater, Florida A (1999) 'Stripper Arrested, Delta Chi Suspended', *Gainseville Sun*,
Online. Available HTTP: http://www.mindspring.com/~krypto/March%202, %201999%
20Sun.html (accessed 7 May 2002).

'British Board of Film Classification New Guidelines allow the depiction of consensual sexual
SM' (2000) Online. Available HTTP: http.www.spannertrust.org/press/bbfcguidelines.asp
(accessed 3 November 2002).

Bronfen, Elisabeth (1992) *Over Her Dead Body. Death, Femininity and the Aesthetic*,
Manchester: Manchester University Press.

Brown, Wendy (1990) 'Consciousness Razing', *The Nation*, 8/15 January: 61–64.

——(1995) *States of Injury: Power and Freedom in Late Modernity*, Princeton: Princeton
University Press.

Brownmiller, Susan (1991) *Against Our Will: Men, Women and Rape*, London: Penguin. First
published in 1975.

——(1993) 'Making Female Bodies the Battlefield', in Alexandra Stiglmayer (ed.) *Mass
Rape: The War Against Women in Bosnia-Heregovina* (transl. Marion Faber), Lincoln and
London: University of Nebraska Press.

——(1999) *In Our Time: Memoir of a Revolution*, New York: The Dial Press.

——(2000) 'Rape on the Brain', *feminista!* Volume 3.9, Online. Available: HTTP:
http://www.feminista.com/v3n9/brownmiller.html (accessed 15 January 2002).

——'On the Bookshelf'. Online. Available: HTTP: http://www.susanbrownmiller.com/
html/what_I_ve_been_reading.html (accessed 16 September 2002).

Bruzzi, Stella (1994) 'Trial by Television: *Court TV* and Dramatising Reality', *Critical Survey*,
6(2).

——(1999) 'A Civil Action', Film Review, in *Sight and Sound*, April.

Bruzzi, Stella (2000) *New Documentary: A Critical Introduction*, London/New York: Routledge.

Bumiller, Kristin (1990) 'Fallen Angels: The Representation of Violence Against Women in Legal Culture', *International Journal of the Sociology of Law*, 18: 125–142.

Burgin, Victor (1986) 'Preface', in V Burgin, J Donald and C Kaplan (eds) *Formations of Fantasy*, London/New York: Methuen.

——(1992) 'Fantasy', in Elizabeth Wright (ed.) *Feminism and Psychoanalysis: A Critical Dictionary*, Oxford: Basil Blackwell.

Butler, Judith (1992) 'Contingent Foundations', in Judith Butler and Joan Scott (eds) *Feminists Theorize the Political*, New York: Routledge, 3–21.

——(1993) 'Endangered/Endangering: Schematic Racism and White Paranoia', in Robert Gooding-Williams (ed.) *Reading Rodney King, Reading Urban Uprising*, New York/London: Routledge.

Butterfield, Fox (1984) 'Trial of Six Starts Today in Pool Table Rape in Massachusetts', *New York Times*, 5 February.

Cameron, James (1996) *Strange Days*, screenplay, London: Penguin.

Campbell, Beatrix (1989) 'The Accused On Release', *Marxism Today*, March: 42–43.

Canetti, Elias (1984) *Crowds and Power* (transl. Carol Stewart), New York: Noonday.

Caputi, Jane (1988) *The Age of the Sex Crime*, London: The Women's Press.

Card, Claudia (1996) 'Rape as a Weapon of War', *Hypatia*, 11(4): 5–18.

Caruth, Cathy (ed.) (1995) 'Trauma and Experience', in *Trauma: Explorations in Memory*, Baltimore/London: The Johns Hopkins University Press.

Castle, Terry (1982) *Clarissa's Ciphers. Meaning & Disruption in Richardson's 'Clarissa'*, Ithaca and London: Cornell University Press.

Chamberlain, Lori (1991) 'Consent After Liberalism? A Review Essay of Catharine MacKinnon's *Toward a Feminist Theory of the State* and Carole Pateman's *The Sexual Contract*', *Genders*, 11: 105–125.

Chancer, Lynn S (1987) 'New Bedford, Massachusetts, March 6, 1983–March 22, 1984: The "Before and After" of a Group Rape', *Gender & Society*, 1(3): 239–260.

Chrisafis, Angelique (2002) 'Why should we be Regularly Exposed to Graphic Scenes of Murder, but be Spared Rape?', *The Guardian*, 23 October.

Clark, Anna (1987) *Women's Silence, Men's Violence: Sexual Assault in England 1770–1845*, London: Pandora Press.

Clendinen, Dudley (1983) 'Barroom Rape Shames Town of Proud Heritage', *New York Times*, 17 March.

Clover, Carol (1992) 'Getting Even: Rape and Revenge in "I Spit on Your Grave" and "The Accused" ', *Sight and Sound*, May: 16–18.

——(1992) *Men, Women and Chainsaws*, London: British Film Institute.

——(1993) 'Introduction', in Pamela Church Gibson and Roma Gibson (eds) *Dirty Looks: Women, Pornography, Power*, Gibson, London: bfi publishing.

Colavecchio, Shannon (1999) 'Video Shows Seedy Side of Greek Life, Initiation', *Independent Florida Alligator*, Online. Available HTTP: http://www.mindspring.com/~ krypto/May%2011,%201999%20Alligator2.html (accessed 9 May 2002).

Comerford, Lynn (1997) 'Channel Surfing for Rape and Resistance on Court TV', in M Huspek (ed.) *Transgressing Discourses: Communication and the Voice of Other*, New York: State University of New York Press.

Concar, David (2000) 'Opinion Interview', *New Scientist*, 19 February: 45–47.

Cook, Pam (1989) 'The Accused', *Monthly Film Bulletin*, 56: 35–36.

Cook, Pam (1998) 'No Fixed Address: The Women's Picture from *Outrage* to *Blue Steel*', in Steve Neale and Murray Smith (eds) *Contemporary Popular Cinema* London/New York: Routledge, 229–246.

Cope, Karin (1992) 'Sadomasochism' in Elizabeth Wright (ed.) *Feminism and Psychoanalysis: A Critical Dictionary*, Oxford: Basil Blackwell.

Corliss, Richard (1988) 'Bad Women and Brutal Men', *Time*, 21 November: 127.

Coward, Rosalind and Linda Semple (1989) 'Tracking Down the Past: Women and Detective Fiction', in Helen Carr (ed.) *From My Guy to Sci-Fi: Genre and Women's Writing in the Postmodern World*, London: Pandora.

Cowie, Elizabeth (1990) 'Woman as Sign', in Parveen Adams and Elizabeth Cowie (eds) *The Woman in Question: m/f*, London: Verso.

——(1992) 'Pornography and Fantasy: Psychoanalytic Perspectives', in Lynne Segal and Mary McIntosh (eds) *Sex Exposed: Sexuality and the Pornography Debate*, London: Virago Press, 132–325.

——(1997) 'Fantasia', in *Representing the Woman: Cinema and Psychoanalysis*, Basingstoke: MacMillan.

Cox, Phil (1994) '"Speech" And Some of Its Wounds', *Diacritics*, 24(1): 63–77.

Creed, Barbara (1993) *The Monstrous Feminine: Film, Feminism, and Psychoanalysis*, London: Routledge.

Cranston, Maurice (1968) 'Introduction' to Jean Jacques Rousseau's *The Social Contract*, Harmondsworth: Penguin.

Crenshaw, Kimberle (1993) 'Whose Story Is It, Anyway? Feminist and Antiracist Appropriations of Anita Hill', in Toni Morrison (ed.) *Race-ing Justice, En-gendering Power. Essays on Anita Hill, Clarence Thomas, and the Construction of Social Reality*, London: Chatto, 402–440.

Cuklanz, Lisa M (1996) *Rape on Trial. How the Mass Media Construct Legal Reform and Social Change*, Philadelphia: University of Pennsylvania Press.

Dahlgren, Peter (1995) *Television and the Public Sphere: Citizenship, Democracy, and the Media*, London: Sage Publications.

Davis, Angela (1983) *Women, Race and Class*, New York: Random House.

Debord, Guy (1995) *Society of the Spectacle* (transl. Donald Nicholson-Smith), New York: Zone Books.

De Man, Paul (1979) *Allegories of Reading*, New Haven: Yale University Press.

——(1983) *Blindness and Insight: Essays in the Rhetoric of Contemporary Criticism*, London: Methuen. First published in 1971.

Derrida, Jacques (1974) *Of Grammatology* (transl. Gayatri Chakravorty Spivak), Baltimore and London: The Johns Hopkins University Press.

——(1981) *Dissemination* (transl. Barbara Johnson), London: The Athlone Press.

——(1987) *The Post Card* (transl. Alan Bass), Chicago: Chicago University Press.

——(1988) 'Structure, Sign and Play in the Discourse of the Human Sciences', in David Lodge (ed.) *Modern Criticism and Theory: A Reader*, London and New York: Longman.

De Vries, Hent and Samuel Weber (eds) (1997) *Violence, Identity, and Self Determination*, Stanford: Stanford University Press.

Diamond, Sara (1985) 'Pornography: Image and Reality', in Varda Burstyn (ed.) *Women Against Censorship*, Vancouver/Toronto: Douglas McIntyre, 40–57.

Diski, Jenny (1990) *Nothing Natural*, London: Minerva.

Doane, Mary Ann (1988) 'Women's Stake: Filming the Female Body', in Constance Penley (ed.) *Feminism Film Theory*, New York/London: Routledge, 216–228.

Doane, Mary Ann (1987) *The Desire to Desire: The Woman's Film of the 1940s*, Basingstoke: MacMillan.

——(1991) *Femmes Fatales: Feminism, Film Theory, Psychoanalysis*, New York: Routledge.

Donovan, Robert J and Ray Scherer (1992) *Unsilent Revolution: Television News and American Public Life, 1948–91*, New York: Cambridge University Press.

Dowd Hall, Jacqueline (1983) '"The Mind That Burns in Each Body": Women, Rape, and Racial Violence', in Ann Snitow, Christine Stansell and Sharon Thompson (eds) *Powers of Desire: The Politics of Sexuality*, New York: Monthly Review Press, New Feminist Library, 328–349.

Dubois, Ellen Carol and Linda Gordon (1989) 'Seeking Ecstasy on the Battlefield: Danger and Pleasure in Nineteenth-century Feminist Sexual Thought', in Carole S Vance (ed.) *Pleasure and Danger: Exploring Female Sexuality*, London: Pandora.

Duggan, Lisa, Nan Hunter and Carole Vance (1985) 'False Promises: Feminist Anti-pornography in the U.S.', in Varda Burstyn (ed.) *Women Against Censorship*, Vancouver/Toronto: Douglas McIntyre, 130–151.

Dunant, Sarah (1988) *Snow Storms in a Hot Climate*, London: Methuen.

——(1993) 'Rewriting the Detectives', *The Guardian*, 29 June: 28.

——(1993) *Fatlands*, London: Hamish Hamilton.

——(ed.) (1994) *War of the Words: The Political Correctness Debates*, London: Virago.

——(1997) *Transgressions*, London: Virago.

——(1997) 'Rape: My Side of the Story', *The Observer*, 1 June.

Dworkin, Andrea (1981) *Pornography: Men Possessing Women*, The Women's Press.

——(1987) *Intercourse*, London: Secker & Warburg.

——(1990) *Mercy*, London: Secker & Warburg.

——(1992) 'Letter to the Editor', *New York Times Book Review*, 3 May.

Dyer, Richard (1988) 'White', in *Screen*, The Last 'Special Issue' on Race? 29(4; Autumn).

Eagleton, Terry (1982) *The Rape of Clarissa: Writing, Sexuality, and Class Struggle in Samuel Richardson*, Oxford: Basil Blackwell.

Elias, Gabe, Online. Available: HTTP: http://www.kathrynbigelow.com/articles/gabe (accessed 16 September 2002).

Elshtain, Jean Bethke (1981) *Public Man, Private Woman: Women in Social and Political Thought*, Princeton: Princeton University Press.

Estrich, Susan (1987) *Real Rape*, Cambridge: Harvard University Press.

Falcon, Richard (2001) 'Last Tango in Lewisham', *Sight and Sound*, Online. Available HTTP: http://www.bfi.org.uk/sightandsound/2001_07/sex.html (accessed 4 July 2002).

Faludi, Susan (1992) *Backlash: The Undeclared War Against Women*, London: Chatto.

Felman, Shoshana (1982) 'Turning the Screw of Interpretation', *Literature and Psychoanalysis: The Question of Reading Otherwise*, Baltimore and London: The Johns Hopkins University Press.

——(1991) 'Film as Witness: Claude Lanzmann's *Shoah*, "Literature and the Ethical Question"', *Yale French Studies*, 79: 90–103.

Ferguson, Frances (1987) 'Rape and the Rise of the Novel', *Representations*, 20: 88–112.

——(1995) 'Pornography: The Theory', *Critical Inquiry*, 21: 670–694.

Fetterley, Judith (1978) *The Resisting Reader: A Feminist Approach to American Fiction*, Bloomington: Indiana University Press.

Fiedler, Leslie (1967) *Love and Death in the American Novel*, London: Paladin.

Fiske, John (1994) *Media Matters: Everyday Culture and Political Change*, Minneapolis: University of Minnesota Press.

Fleck, Patrice (1990) 'The Silencing of Women in the Hollywood "Feminist" Film: *The Accused*', *Post-Script-Essays-In-Film-And The Humanities*, 9(3): 49–55.

Fleishman, A. (1992) *Narrated Film: Storytelling Situations in Cinema History*, Baltimore/London: The Johns Hopkins University Press.

Fletcher, John (1995) 'Primal Scenes and the Female Gothic: *Rebecca* and *Gaslight*', *Screen*, 36(4).

—— (1986) 'Poetry, Gender and Primal Fantasy', in V Burgin, J Donald and C Kaplan (eds) *Formations of Fantasy*, London/New York: Routledge.

'Florida's Government in the Sunshine Law', Florida Attorney General, Online. Available HTTP: http//legal.firn.edu/sunshine/general.html (accessed 1 February 2002).

Flournoy, Dan M (1992) *CNN World Report: Ted Turner's International News Coup*, Academia: Research Monograph 9.

Flournoy, Dan M and Robert K Stewart (1997) *CNN: Making News in the Global Market*, Luton: University of Luton Press.

Foreman, Jonathan 'The Tragic Life and Death of a Boy Trapped in a Girl's Body', *The New York Post*, Online. Available: HTTP: http://www.nypost.com/movies/9775.htm (accessed 25 August 2002).

Forrester, John (1986) 'Rape, Seduction and Psychoanalysis', in Sylvana Tomaselli and Roy Porter (eds) *Rape*, Oxford: Basil Blackwell.

Francke, Lizzie (1997) 'Virtual Fears', *Sight and Sound*, 12: 6–9.

Friedberg, Anne (1993) *Window Shopping: Cinema and the Postmodern*, Berkeley: University of California Press.

French, Karl (1996) *Screen Violence*, London: Bloomsbury.

French, Marilyn (1997) *The Women's Room*, London: Virago. First published 1977.

Freud, Sigmund (1984) 'On the Sexual Theories of Children' in Angela Richards (ed.) *On Sexuality*, The Pelican Freud Library, vol. 7 (transl. James Strachey). First published in 1908.

—— (1979) 'From the History of an Infantile Neurosis', in *Case Histories II* Pelican Freud Library, vol. 9, Harmondsworth. First published in 1918.

Frus, Phyllis (2001) 'Documenting Domestic Violence in American Films', in David J. Slocum (ed.) *Violence and American Cinema*, New York/London: Routledge.

Fuchs, Cindy (1989) 'The Accused', *Cineaste*, 17(1): 26–28.

Fuller, Graham (1995) 'Big bad Bigelow'; Interview, Online. Available HTTP: http://www.kathrynbigelow.com/articles/interview.html (accessed 16 September 2002).

Gaitskill, Mary (1994) 'On Not Being A Victim: Sex, Rape, and the Trouble with Following Rules', *Harper's*, March: 35–44.

Garber, Marjorie, Jann Matlock and Rebecca Walkowitz (eds) (1993) *Media Spectacles*, New York/London: Routledge.

Gardetta, Dave (1995) 'A Mind's Eye for Mayhem; Director Kathryn Bigelow; Pulling Audience into the Picture', Online. Available HTTP: http://www.kathrynbigelow.com/articles/washpost.html (accessed 16 September 2002).

Gatens, Moira (1996) *Imaginary Bodies: Ethics, Power and Corporeality*, London/New York: Routledge.

Gerrard, Nicci (1997) 'In Front of the Children', in Karl French (ed.) *Screen Violence*, London: Bloomsbury.

—— (1994) 'Battlefield of the Body Politic', *The Observer*, 19 June.

'Getting off easy' (1999), in *Independent Florida Alligator*, Online. Available HTTP: http://www.mindspring.com/~krypto/May%2011,%201999%20AlligatorEd.html (accessed 9 May 2002).

Gilbert, Harriett (1992) 'So Long as it's not Sex and Violence: Andrea Dworkin's Mercy,' in Lynne Segal and Mary McIntosh (eds) *Sex Exposed: Sexuality and the Pornography Debate*, London, Virago, 216–229.

Girard, René (1978) *Violence and the Sacred* (transl. Patrick Gregory), Baltimore: Johns Hopkins University Press.

Goldbsy, Jacqueline (1996) 'The High and Low Tech of It: The Meaning of Lynching and the Death of Emmett Till', *The Yale Journal of Criticism*, 9.2: 245–282.

Gomery, Douglas (1997) 'Cable News Network' in Horace Newcomb (ed.) *Encyclopedia of Television*, vol. I, Chicago and London: Fitzroy Dearborn Publishers, 271–272.

Gooding-Williams, Robert (ed.) (1993) *Reading Rodney King, Reading Urban Uprising*, New York/London: Routledge.

Goodwin, Christopher (1996) 'Has Hollywood Gone Too Far?' *The Sunday Times*, 10 March.

Griffin, Susan (1982) *Made From This Earth. Selections from her Writing, 1967–1982*, London: The Women's Press.

Gristwood, Sarah (1996) 'Lights, Camera, Lots of Action: Only One Woman in Hollywood Specialises in Thrillers', *The Independent*, 25 February.

Halberstam, Judith (2001) 'The Transgender Gaze in *Boys Don't Cry*', *Screen*, 42(3).

Hallam, Julia with Margaret Marshment (2000) *Realism and Popular Cinema*, Manchester and New York: Manchester University Press.

Halperin, David M (1990) *One Hundred Years of Homosexuality: And Other Essays on Greek Love*, New York/London: Routledge.

Hart, Lynda (1994) *Fatal Women: Lesbian Sexuality and the Mark of Aggression*, London: Routledge.

Hartmann, Heidi and Ellen Ross (1978) 'Comment on "On Writing the History of Rape"', *Signs: Journal of Women in Culture and Society*, 3(4): 931–935.

Hazen, Helen (1983) *Endless Rapture: Rape, Romance, and the Female Imagination*, New York: Scribner's.

Hengehold, Laura (1994) 'An Immodest Proposal: Foucault, Hysterization, and the "Second Rape"', *Hypatia*, 9(3; Summer): 88–107.

Henry, Alice (1988) 'Does Viewing Pornography Lead Men To Rape?' in Gail Chester and Julienne Dickey (eds) *Feminism and Censorship: The Current Debate*, Dorset: Prism Press.

Henry, William III (1984) 'When News Becomes Voyeurism', *Time*, 26 March.

Hentoff, Nat (1994) 'The Public Rape of Catharine MacKinnon', *The Village Voice*, 4 January: 16–17.

Herman, Dianne F (1989) 'The Rape Culture', in *Women: A Feminist Perspective*, Mountain View, California: Mayfield Publishing Co.

Herman, Judith (1992) *Trauma and Recovery*, New York: BasicBooks.

Higgins, Lynn (1991) 'Screen/Memory: Rape and Its Alibis in *Last Year at Marienbad*', in Higgins and Silver (eds) *Rape and Representation*, London/New York: Columbia University Press, 303–321.

Higgins, Lynn and Brenda Silver (eds) (1991) 'Introduction: Rereading Rape,' in *Rape and Representation*, London/New York: Columbia University Press.

hooks, bell (1982) *Ain't I A Woman: Black Women and Feminism*, London/Winchester: Pluto Press.

—— (1994) *Outlaw Culture: Resisting Representations*, New York/London: Routledge.

—— (1996) *Reel to Real: Race, Sex, and Class at the Movies*, New York/London: Routledge.

Hutchings, Vicky (1997) 'If you find Slugs too Arousing, Read this', *New Statesman*, 11 July: 49.

Irving, John (1992) 'Pornography and the New Puritans', *New York Times Book Review*, 29 March.

Jackson, Kevin (1996) 'Film: What you See is What you Get', *The Independent*, 3 March.

Jackson, Susan (1992) *Rousseau's Occasional Autobiographies*, Columbus: Ohio State University Press.

Jeffords, Susan (1991) 'Rape and the New World Order', *Cultural Critique* Fall: 203–215.

——(1994) *Hard Bodies: Hollywood Masculinity in the Reagan Years*, New Brunswick, NJ: Rutgers University Press.

Johnson, Barbara (1995) 'Writing', in Frank Lentricchia and Thomas McLaughlin (eds) *Critical Terms for Literary Study*, Chicago and London: The University of Chicago Press, 39–49.

Jones, DB (1989) 'Book Review', *Journal of Film and Video*, 41(4; Winter): 75–79.

Jones, Gayl (1988) *Corregidora*, London: Camden Press. First published in 1975.

——(1985) Interview in Claudia Tate (ed.) *Black Women Writers At Work*, Harpenden: Oldcastle Books.

Joplin, Klindienst, Patricia (1991) 'The Voice of the Shuttle Is Ours', in Lynn Higgins and Brenda Silver (eds) *Rape and Representation*, London/NY: Routledge, 35–64.

Kahn, Coppélia (1991) '*Lucrece*: The Sexual Politics of Subjectivity', in Lynn Higgins and Brenda Silver (eds) *Rape and Representation*, New York and London: Columbia University Press, 141–159.

Kamuf, Peggy (1988) *Signature Pieces. On the Institution of Authorship*, Ithaca and London: Cornell University Press.

Kaplan, David A (1991) 'Remove That Blue Dot: A *Newsweek* Writer Argues for Naming Names', *Newsweek*, 16 December: 26.

Kappeler, Susanne (1986) *The Pornography of Representation*, Cambridge: Polity Press.

'Kathryn Bigelow Makes a "Wake–up Call" About the Coming of the Millenium' (1995) *Boston Globe*, Online. Available HTTP: http://www.kathrynbigelow.com/Articles/ boston.html (accessed 16 September 2002).

Kavanagh, Thomas (1982) 'Rousseau's *Lévite d'Ephraim*: Dream, Text, and Synthesis', *Eighteenth-Century Studies*, 16.2: 141–161.

Kaveney, Roz (1991) 'Review Article: Dworkin's *Mercy*', *Feminist Review*, 38: 79–85.

Kermode, Mark (2001) 'Left on the Shelf', in *Sight and Sound,* Online. Available HTTP: http://www.bfi.org.uk/sightandsound/2001_07/sex.html (accessed 4 July 2002).

Kipnis, Laura (1992) '(Male) Desire and (Female) Disgust: Reading *Hustler*', in Lawrence Grossberg, Cary Nelson and Paula Treichler (eds) *Cultural Studies*, New York/London: Routledge, 373–391.

——(1996) *Bound and Gagged: Pornography and the Politics of Fantasy in America*, New York: Grove.

Landes, Joan (1988) *Women and the Public Sphere in the Age of the French Revolution*, Ithaca and London: Cornell University Press.

Laing, RD (1969) *The Politics of the Family*, Massey Lectures, CBC Enterprises, Montreal.

Laplanche, Jean and JB Pontalis (1986) 'Fantasy and the Origins of Sexuality', in V Burgin, J Donald and C Kaplan (eds), *Formations of Fantasy*, London: Methuen: 11–30. First published in 1964.

——(1988) *The Language of Psychoanalysis*, London: The Institute of Psychoanalysis, Karnac Books.

Laub, Dori (1992) *Testimony: Crises of Witnessing in Literature, Psychoanalysis, and History*, Shoshana Felman and Laub (eds), London: Routledge, 57–76.

Lauret, Maria (1994) *Liberating Literature. Feminist Fiction in America*, London and New York: Routledge.

Lebeau, Vicky (1995) *Lost Angels: Psychoanalysis and Cinema*, London: Routledge.

——(2001) *Psychoanalysis and Cinema: The Play of Shadows*. London/New York: Wallflower Press.

Lederer, Laura (ed.) (1980) *Take Back the Night: Women on Pornography*, New York: William Morrow.

Leigh, Danny (2000) 'Boy Wonder'; Interview with Kimberley Peirce, *Sight and Sound*, March.

Leith, Sam (1997) 'Misogyny and Machismo, Horror and Hard-boiled Brutality. Why is it Men who Get to have all the Fun?' *The Observer*, 15 June: 1.

Lévi-Strauss, Claude (1969) *The Elementary Structures of Kinship* (transl. J Bell, J Von Sturmer and R Needham), Boston: Beacon Press. First published in 1949.

Lukacher, Ned (1986) *Primal Scenes: Literature, Philosophy, Psychoanalysis*, Ithaca: Cornell University Press.

Lumenick, Lou (2001) '"Rape" Documentary Leaves 'Em Reel-ing; Frat-Sex Footage Aids Probe of Unprosecuted Fla. Scandal', *New York Post*, Online. Available HTTP: http://www.mindspring.com/~krpto/nyp012502a.html (accessed 7 April 2002).

——(2001) '"Raw Deal" Furor Prompts Bidding Frenzy', Online. Available HTTP: http://www.pagesix.com/sundance09.htm (accessed 14 March 2002).

Lyttle, John (1996) 'Controversy is a Trick of the Trade', *The Independent*, 8 June.

MacCannell, Juliet Flower (1991) *The Regime of the Brother: After the Patriarchy*, London/ New York: Routledge.

McCarthy, Todd (2001). 'Raw Deal: a Question of Consent', *Variety.com*, Online. Available HTTP: www.variety.com/index.asp?layout=review&reviewid=VE1117797244&categoryi... (accessed 6 June 2002).

McDonald, Kathy A (2001) 'Controversial "Deal" Invites Heated Debate', *Variety*, Online. Available HTTP: http://web6.infotrac.galegroup.com/itw/infomark/518/824/23463983w6/purl=rc1_EAIM... (accessed 6 June 2002).

MacGregor, Brent (1997) *Live, Direct and Biased? Making Television New in the Satellite Age*, London and New York: Arnold, a member of The Hodder Headline Group.

MacGregor, Henry (1997) 'Women on Top', letter to the editor, *The Sunday Times*, 15 June.

McKenna, Andrew J (1996) 'Public Execution', in John Denvir (ed.) *Legal Reelism: Movies as Legal Texts*, Urbana and Chicago: University of Illinois Press.

MacKinnon, Catharine (1983) 'Feminism, Marxism, Method, and the State: Toward Feminist Jurisprudence,' *Signs: Journal of Women in Culture and Society*, 8: 635–658.

——(1987) *Feminism Unmodified: Discourses on Life and Law*, Cambridge/London: Harvard University Press.

——(1993) 'Turning Rape into Pornography: Postmodern Genocide', in Alexandra Stiglmayer (ed.) *Mass Rape: The War against Women in Bosnia-Herzegovina*, Lincoln and London: University of Nebraska Press, 73–81.

——(1994) *Only Words*, London: HarperCollins.

Marcus, Sharon (1992) 'Fighting Bodies, Fighting Words: A Theory and Politics of Rape Prevention', in Judith Butler and Joan Scott (eds) *Feminists Theorize the Political*, New York and London: Routledge, 385–403.

Marriott, David (1996) 'Bordering On: The Black Penis', *Textual Practice*, 10(1): 9–28.

Mars-Jones, Adam (1996) 'To be Other than We Are: Strange Days', *The Independent*, 29 February.

——(1989) 'Unmoving Violation', *The Independent*, 16 February.

Marshall, David (1988) *The Surprising Effects of Sympathy. Marivaux, Diderot, Rousseau, and Mary Shelley*, Chicago and London: The University of Chicago Press.

Mashon, Mike (1993) 'Losing Control: Popular Reception (s) of the Rodney King Video', *Wide Angle*, 15(2; April): 7–18.

Mass Rape: The War against Women in Bosnia-Herzegovina (1994) Alexandra Stiglmayer (ed.). Lincoln and London: University of Nebraska Press.

Masson, Jeffrey (1992) *The Assault on Truth: Freud and Child Sexual Abuse*, Hammersmith: Fontana.

Matlock, Jann (1993) 'Scandals of Naming: The Blue Blob, Identity, and Gender in the William Kennedy Smith Case', in Marjorie Garber, Jann Matlock and Rebecca Walkowitz (eds) *Media Spectacles*, London/New York: Routledge, 137–159.

Mayne, Judith (1988) 'The Female Audience and the Feminist Critic', in Janet Todd (ed.) *Women and Film*, New York/London: Holmes and Meier.

Megan, Carolyn E (1994) 'Moving Toward the Truth, Interview with Dorothy Allison', *The Kenyon Review*, Fall: 75.

Merck, Mandy (1993) *Perversions: Deviant Readings by Mandy Merck*, London: Virago Press.

——(1992) 'From Minneapolis to Westminster', in Lynne Segal and Mary McIntosh (eds) *Sex Exposed: Sexuality and the Pornography Debate*, London: Virago, 50–63.

——(2000) 'Bedtime', *Women: A Cultural Review*, 11(3): 252–261.

Metz, Christian (1999) 'Identification, Mirror', in Leo Braudy and Marshall Cohen (eds) *Film Theory and Criticism: Introductory Readings*, New York/Oxford: Oxford University Press.

Miele, Anthony (2001) 'Raw Deal: A Question of Consent', Online. Available HTTP: http://www.filmthreat.com/Reviews.asp?Fil=ReviewsOne.inc&Id=1653 (accessed 14 March 2002).

Miller, Laura (2000) 'The Salon Interview – Dorothy Allison', Online. Available HTTP: http://archive.salon.com/books/int/1998/03/cov_so_31intb2.html... (accessed 1 November 2002).

Millett, Kate (1977) *Sexual Politics*, London: Virago. First published in 1970.

Minsky, Terry (1984) 'For Many Spectators At the Big Dan's Trial, The Verdict Is In', *Boston Globe*, 1 March.

Mitchell, Juliet (1974) *Psychoanalysis and Feminism*, Middlesex: Penguin Books.

Mitchell, WJT (1995) 'Representation', in Frank Lentricchia and Thomas McLaughlin (eds) *Critical Terms for Literary Study*, Chicago and London: The University of Chicago Press, 11–22.

Moore, Susanna (1995) *In The Cut*, London: Picador.

——(1989) 'Asking for it?', *New Statesman & Society*, 17 February: 16–17.

Morgan, Robin (1980) 'Theory and Practice: Pornography and Rape', in Laura Lederer (ed.) *Take Back the Night: Women on Pornography*, New York: William Morrow, 134–140.

Morgenstern, Naomi (1997) "There is Nothing Else Like This": Sex and Citation in Pornogothic Feminism', in Thomas Foster, Carol Siegel and Ellen E Berry (eds) *Sex Positives? The Cultural Politics of Dissident Sexualities*, a special issue of *Genders*, 25: 39–67.

Morley, John (1888) *Rousseau*, London: MacMillan.

Morrison, Toni (1993) *Playing in the Dark: Whiteness and the Literary Imagination*, London: Picador.

——(1993) *The Bluest Eye*, London: Penguin. First published in 1970.

Mouffe, Chantal (1992) 'Feminism, Citizenship, and Radical Democratic Politics', in Judith Butler and Joan Scott (eds) *Feminists Theorize the Political*, New York: Routledge.

Mulvey, Laura (1999) 'Visual Pleasure and Narrative Cinema', in Leo Braudy and Marshall Cohen (eds) *Film Theory and Criticism*, Fifth edition, New York/London: Routledge. First published in 1975.

Munt, Sally (1994) *Murder By the Book? Feminism and the Crime Novel*, London and New York: Routledge.

Nathan, Ian (1996) 'No Retreat, No Surrender', *Empire*, Online. Available: HTTP: http://www.kathrynbigelow.com/articles/empire1.html (accessed 16 September 2002).

Neely, Barbara (1992) *Blanche on the Lam*, New York: Penguin.

Neely, Barbara (2000) *Blanche Passes Go*, New York: Penguin.

Neustatter, Angela (1997) 'Fear and Loathing: A Rape Victim who Seduces her Attacker? What can Sarah Dunant have been Thinking of when she Included *that* Scene in her new Novel?, *The Guardian*, 27 May.

Newcomb, Horace (ed.) (1997) *The Encyclopedia of Television*, Chicago: Fitzroy Dearborn/Museum of Broadcast Communications.

Newitz, Annalee (1997) 'White Savagery and Humiliation, Or A New Racial Consciousness in the Media', in Matt Wray and Annalee Newitz (eds) *White Trash: Race and Class in America*, New York/London: Routledge, 131–154.

Newitz, Annalee and Mark Wray (eds) (1997) 'Introduction' to *White Trash: Race and Class in America*, New York and London: Routledge, 1–12.

Newman, Jenny (ed.) (1988) 'Introduction', *The Faber Book of Seductions*, London: Faber.

Nichols, Bill (1991) *Representing Reality: Issues and Concepts in Documentary*, Bloomington: Indiana University Press.

'One Director's Reality Check' (1995) *Chicago Tribune*, Online. Available HTTP: http://www.kathrynbigelow.com/articles/chi4.html (accessed 16 September 2002).

Pateman, Carole (1988) *The Sexual Contract*, Cambridge: Polity Press.

Peterson, Karla (1995) 'Director joins boys' club – and it only costs her compassion', *San Diego Union Tribune,* Online. Available HTTP: http://www.kathrynbigelow.com/articles/diego.html (accessed 16 September 2002).

Pitchford, Nicola (1997) 'Reading Feminism's Pornography Conflict: Implications for Post-modernist Reading Strategies', in Thomas Foster, Carol Siegel and Ellen E Berry (eds) *Sex Positives? The Cultural Politics of Dissident Sexualities*, a special issue of *Genders*, 25: 3–37.

Plaza, Monique (1981) 'Our Damages and Their Compensation. Rape: The Will Not to Know of Michel Foucault', *Feminist Issues*: 25–35.

Plummer, Ken (1995) *Telling Sexual Stories: Power, Change, and Social Worlds*, London: Routledge.

Podhoretz, Norman (1991) 'Rape in Feminist Eyes', *Commentary*, 10/9.

Pollitt, Katha (1991) 'Naming and Blaming: Media Goes Wilding in Palm Beach', *The Nation*, 24 June: 847–852.

Porlock, Harvey (1997) 'Sarah Dunant's Novel has got a lot of Knickers in a Twist', *The Sunday Times*, 15 June.

Pornography and Sexual Violence: Evidence of the Links (1988) The complete transcript of Public Hearings on Ordinances to Add Pornography as Discrimination Against Women: Minneapolis City Council, Government Operations Committee, 12 and 13, December 1983, London: Everywoman.

Porter, Roy (1986) 'Rape – does it have a Historical Meaning?' in Sylvana Tomaselli and Roy Porter (eds) *Rape*, Oxford: Basil Blackwell, 57–83.

Portman, Jamie (1995) 'Strange Days for a Female Director under Attack for her Style', *Vancouver Sun*, Online. Available: HTTP: http://www.kathryn.bigelow.com/Articles/vsun.html (accessed 16 September 2002).

Press, Aric (1983) 'The Duties of a Bystander', *Newsweek*, 28 March: 79.

Projansky, Sarah (2001) *Watching Rape: Film and Television in Postfeminist Culture*, New York/London: New York University Press.

Rangel, Jesus (1984) 'Rape Trial Keeps Massachusetts Area on an Emotional Edge', *New York Times*, 4 March.

——(1984) 'Rape Trial is Monitored By a Women's Coalition', *New York Times*, 8 March.

Rangel, Jesus (1984) 'Portuguese Immigrants Fear Rape Case May Set Back Gains', *New York Times*, 16 March.

' "Rape film" released uncut' in *BBC News*, Online. Available HTTP: http://news.bbc.co.uk/1/low/entertainment/film/2346769.stm (accessed 24 October 2002).

'Rape war crime verdict welcomed' in CNN.Com./World, Online. Available HTTP: http://www.cnn.com/2001/WORLD/europe/02/23/hague.trial/ (accessed 15 December 2002).

Rascaroli, Laura (1997) 'Steel in the Gaze: On POV and the Discourse of Vision in Kathryn Bigelow's Cinema', *Screen*, 38(3; Autumn): 232–246.

Read, Jacinda (2000) *The New Avengers: Feminism, Femininity and the Rape-Revenge Cycle*, Manchester/New York: Manchester University Press.

Reddy, Maureen T (1988) *Sisters in Crime*, New York: Frederick Ungar.

Renov, Michael (ed.) (1993) *Theorizing Documentary*, New York/London: Routledge.

Rich, Ruby (1983) 'Anti-Porn: Soft Issue, Hard World: Not A Love Story, A Film About Pornography', *Feminist Review*, 13 (February): 56–68.

——(1986) 'Review Essay: Feminism and Sexuality in the 1980s', *Feminist Studies*, 3: 525–561.

——(1993) 'Never a Victim: Jodie Foster, A New Kind of Female Hero', in Pam Cook and Philip Dodd (eds) *Women in Film: A Sight and Sound Reader*, London: Scarlet Press, 50–61.

Richie, Donald (ed.) (1987) *Rashomon: Akira Kurosawa, Director*, New Brunswick and London: Rutgers University Press.

Riggs, Larry W. and Paula Willoquet (1989) 'Up Against The Looking Glass! Heterosexual Rape as Homosexual Epiphany in *The Accused*', *Film Quarterly*, 4: 214–223.

Roiphe, Katie (1993) *The Morning After: Sex, Fear, and Feminism*, London: Hamish Hamilton.

Rodriguez, Rene (2002). ' "Raw Deal" is Disturbing, Utterly Absorbing', in *The Miami Herald*, Online. Available HTTP: www.miami.com/mld.miamiherald/entertainment/columnists/rene_rodriguez/2540 ... (accessed 9 April 2002).

Romano, Carlin (1993) 'Between the Motion and the Act', *The Nation*, 15 November: 562–570.

Rooney, Ellen (1983) 'Criticism and the Subject of Sexual Violence', *Modern Language Notes*, 98(5): 1269–1277.

——(1991) ' "A Little More Than Persuading": Tess and the Subject of Sexual Violence', in Lynn Higgins and Brenda Silver (eds) *Rape and Representation*, London/New York: Routledge.

Rose, Jacqueline (1986) *Sexuality in the Field of Vision*, London: Verso.

——(1989) 'Where Does the Misery Come From?: Psychoanalysis, Feminism and the Event,' in R Feldstein and J Roof (eds) *Feminism and Psychoanalysis*, Ithaca: Cornell University Press.

——(1993) *Why War? – Psychoanalysis, Politics, and the Return to Melanie Klein*, Oxford: Blackwell Press.

——(1996) *States of Fantasy*, Oxford: Clarendon Press.

——(1998) 'The Case of Peter Pan', in Henry Jenkins (ed.) *The Children's Culture Reader*, New York: New York University Press.

Rosen, Ellen Israel (1985) 'The New Bedford Rape Trial', *Dissent*, 32: 207–11.

Rosen, Marjorie (1988) 'The Accused' in *Ms*. (November).

Rousseau, Jean-Jacques (1959–69) *Le Lévite d'Ephraim*, in B Gagnebin and M Raymond (eds) *Oeuvres complètes de Jean-Jacques Rousseau*, vol. II, Paris: Gallimard. First published in 1781.

——(1960) *Politics and the Arts. Letter to M'Alembert on the Theatre* (transl. Alan Bloom), Ithaca, New York: Cornell University Press. First published in 1758.

Rousseau, Jean-Jacques (1964) *The First and Second Discourses* (ed. Roger D Masters, transl. Roger D and Judith R Masters), New York: St. Martin's Press. First published in 1750.

——(1968) *The Social Contract* (transl. Maurice Cranston), Harmondsworth: Penguin. First published in 1761.

——(1979) *Emile or On Education* (transl. Alan Bloom), London: Penguin. First published in 1761.

——(1990) *Essay on the Origin of Languages*, in *The First and Second Discourses, Together with the Replies to Critics and Essay on the Origin of Languages* (selected and transl. by Victor Gourevitch), New York: Harper Torchbooks. First published in 1763.

——(1996) *The Confessions* (ed. Tom Griffith), Wordsworth Classics of World Literature, Hertfordshire: Wordsworth Editions Limited. First published in 1781.

——(1997) *Julie, or the New Heloise* (eds Roger D Masters and Christopher Kelly, transl. Philip Stewart and Jean Vache), in *The Collected Writings of Rousseau*, Dartmouth College: University of New England Press. First published in 1760.

Russell, Diana (1975) *The Politics of Rape*, New York: Stein and Day.

Ruth Williams, Linda (2001) 'Sick Sisters: Is the Violent *Baise-moi* an Issue Drama or Pure Exploitation', in *Sight and Sound*, Online. Available HTTP: http://www.bfi.org.uk/sightandsound/2001_07/sex.html (accessed 4 July 2002).

Ryan, Cheyney (1996) 'Print the Legend: Violence and Recognition in *The Man Who Shot Liberty Valance*' in John Denvir (ed.) *Legal Reelism: Movies as Legal Texts*, Urbana/Chicago: University of Illinois Press.

Sanday, Peggy Reeves (1990) *Fraternity Gang Rape: Sex, Brotherhood, and Privilege on Campus*, New York City: New York University Press.

Schlesinger, Philip, R Emerson Dobash, Russell P Dobash and C Kay Weaver (1992) *Women Viewing Violence*, London: bfi publishing.

Scott, Ann (1996) *Real Events Revisited: Fantasy, Memory, and Psychoanalysis*, London: Virago.

Sears, John (1995) '*Crimewatch* and the Rhetoric of Versimilitude', *Critical Survey*, 7(1): 51–58.

Segal, Lynne (1993) 'Does Pornography Cause Violence? The Search for Evidence', in Pamela Church Gibson and Roma Gibson (eds) *Dirty Looks: Women, Pornography, Power*, London: bfi publishing, 5–21.

Sedgwick, Eve Kosofsky (1985) *Between Men: English Literature and Male Homosocial Desire*, New York: Columbia University Press.

Segal, Lynne (1993) 'Sweet Sorrows, Painful Pleasures: Pornography and the Perils of Heterosexual Desire', in Lynne Segal and Mary McIntosh (eds) *Sex Exposed: Sexuality and the Pornography Debate*, New Jersey: Rutgers University Press.

Selby, Keith and Ron Cowdery (1995) *How to Study Television* Hampshire: Palgrave.

Seltzer, Mark (1998) *Serial Killers: Death and Life in America's Wound Culture*, New York/London: Routledge.

Sharpe, Jenny (1991) 'The Unspeakable Limits of Rape: Colonial Violence and Counter Insurgency', *Genders*, 10: 25–42.

Shorter, Edward (1977) 'On Writing the History of Rape', *Signs: Journal of Women in Culture and Society*, 3(2): 471–482.

Silverman, Kaja (1992) *Male Subjectivity at the Margins*, New York/London: Routledge.

Simons, Madeleine Anjubault (1972) *Amitié et Passion: Rousseau et Sauttersheim*, Geneve: Librairie Droz.

Smart, Carol (1989) *Feminism and the Power of Law*, London: Routledge.

Smeeth, Mary and Susanne Kappeler (1990) 'Mercy: A New Novel By Andrea Dworkin', *Sparerib*, 27.

Smith, Adam (2001) 'Raw Footage: A Question of Consent', *Empire*, May: 17.

Smith, Anthony (ed.) (1995) *Television: An International History*, Oxford: Oxford University Press.

Smith, Joan (1996) 'The Movies, Me and Violence,' in Karl French (ed.) *Screen Violence*, London: Bloomsbury.

—— (1997) 'A Woman's Right to Choose', *The Sunday Times*, 8 June.

Smith, Valerie (1990) '"Split Affinities": The Case of Interracial Rape', in Marianne Hirsch and Evelyn Fox Keller (eds) *Conflicts in Feminism*, New York/London Routledge, 271–287.

Snead, James (1991) 'Spectatorship and capture in *King Kong*: the guilty look', *Critical Quarterly*, 33(1) 53–69.

Snitow, Ann (1985) 'Retrenchment Versus Transformation: The Politics of the Anti-pornography Movement', in Varda Burstyn (ed.) *Women Against Censorship*, Vancouver/Toronto: Douglas McIntyre, 107–120.

Soggin, Albert J (1987) *Judges: A Commentary*, London: SCM Press, Ltd.

Sontag, Susan (1977) *On Photography*, London: Penguin.

Spillers, Hortense (1987) 'Mama's Baby, Papa's Maybe: An American Grammar Book', *Diacritics* (Summer): 65–81.

Stanko, Elizabeth (1985) *Intimate Intrusions: Women's Experience of Male Violence*, London and New York: Routledge.

Starobinski, Jean (1979) 'Rousseau's Happy Days', *New Literary History: A Journal of Theory and Interpretation*, 11: 147–66.

Starr, Mark (1983) 'Gang Rape: The Legal Attack', *Newsweek*, 12 March.

Steiner, Wendy (1991) 'Declaring War on Men', review of *Mercy*, by Andrea Dworkin, *New York Times Book Review*, 15 September: 7.

Stewart, Leah (2001) *The Body of a Girl*, London: Piatkus.

Still, Judith (1989) 'Rousseau's *Lévite d'Ephraim*: The Imposition of Meaning (on Women)', *French Studies: A Quarterly Review*, 12–30.

Suleiman Rubin, Susan (ed.) (1986) *Subversive Intent: Gender, Politics, and the AvantGarde*, Cambridge/London: Harvard University Press.

Swan, Rachel (2001) 'Boys Don't Cry', *Film Quarterly*, 54(3).

Tanner, Tony (1979) *Adultery in the Novel*, Baltimore: Johns Hopkins.

Tasker, Yvonne (1998) *Working Girls: Gender and Sexuality in Popular Cinema*, London/New York: Routledge.

—— (1999) 'Bigger than Life', *Sight and Sound*, May.

'Tears of Two Rapists' (1984) *Boston Herald*, 23 March.

'The Accused' (1988) *Variety*, 19 October, 14.

'The Crime That Tarnished a Town' (1984) *Time*, 5 March.

'The Limits of Sex' (July 2001) in *Sight and Sound*, Online. Available HTTP: www.bfi.org.uk/sightandsound/2001_07/sex.html (accessed 4 July 2002).

'The Tavern Rape: Cheers and No Help' (1983) *Newsweek*, 21 March.

Todorov, Tzvetan (1988) 'The Typology of Detective Fiction', in David Lodge (ed.) *Modern Criticism and Theory: A Reader*, London and New York: Longman: 158–165. First published in 1966.

Tomaselli, Sylvana (1986) 'Introduction', in Tomaselli and Roy Porter (eds) *Rape*, Oxford: Basil Blackwell.

Tomasulo, Frank P. (1996) '"I'll see it when I Believe it": Rodney King and the Prison-House of Video', in Vivian Sobchack (ed.) *The Persistence of History: Cinema, Television, and the Modern Event*, New York and London: Routledge.

Trible, Phyllis (1984) *Texts of Terror: Literary Feminist Readings of Biblical Narratives*, Philadelphia: Fortress Press.

Turim, Maureen (1989) *Flashbacks in Film: Memory and History*, New York and London: Routledge.

US Senate Hearing (1984, 24 April). United States Ninety-Eighth Congress hearing before the Sub-committee on Criminal Law of the Committee on the Judiciary United States. Impact of Media Coverage of Rape Trials. Second session on Oversight on the Effect of Publicity On the Victims in Rape Cases, and the Right of the Press to Have Access to Such Proceedings. Washington: US Government Printing Office.

Vance, Carole S. (ed.) (1992) 'Pleasure and Danger: Towards a Politics of Sexuality' in *Pleasure and Danger: Exploring Female Sexuality*, London: Pandora.

——(1992) 'More Danger, More Pleasure: A Decade after the Barnard Sexuality Conference', in *Pleasure and Danger: Exploring Female Sexuality*, London: Pandora.

Vickers, Nancy J. (1986) 'This Heraldry in Lucrece' Face', in Susan Rubin Suleiman (ed.) *The Female Body in Western Culture: Contemporary Perspectives*, Cambridge: Harvard University Press.

'Virtual Vision' (1996) *Daily Yomiuri*, Online. Available: HTTP: http://www.kathryn-bigelow.com/articles/yom.html (accessed 16 September 2002).

Walker, Alice (1982) *You Can't Keep a Good Woman Down*. London: The Women's Press.

Walker, Janet (2001) 'Trauma Cinema: False Memories and True Experience', *Screen*, 42(2).

Walker, Jeremy (2000–01). Press notes on *Raw Deal* prepared before Sundance 2001.

Walker, Melissa (1991) *Black Women's Novels in the Wake of the Civil Rights Movement 1966–89*, New Haven and London: Yale University Press.

Walton, Priscilla L and Manina Jones (1999) *Detective Agency: Women Rewriting the Hard-Boiled Tradition*, Berkeley: University of California Press.

Warner, William (1983) 'Reading Rape: Marxist–Feminist Figurations of the Literal,' *Diacritics*, Winter: 12–32.

——(1979) *Reading Clarissa: The Struggles of Interpretation*, New Haven: Yale University Press.

Washington, Ray (1999) 'UF awaits Fallout from Videotape Release' in *Gainseville Sun*, Online. Available HTTP: http://www.mindspring.com/~krypto/May%209,%201999%20Sun2. html (accessed 7 May 2002).

Whitford, Margaret (1991) *Luce Irigaray: Philosophy in the Feminine*, London and New York: Routledge.

——(1992) 'Rape: Political Perspectives', in Elizabeth Wright (ed.) *Feminism and Psychoanalysis: A Critical Dictionary*, Oxford: Basil Blackwell.

Wiegand, Chris 'Raw Deal: A Question of Consent', Online. Available HTTP: http:www.box-office.com/scripts/fiw.dll?GetReview?&where=Name&terms=Raw+Deal (accessed 9 April 2002).

Wiegman, Robyn (1993) 'The Anatomy of Lynching', in John C Fout and Maura Shaw Tantillo (eds) *American Sexual Politics: Sex, Gender, and Race since the Civil War*, Chicago: University of Chicago Press, pp. 223–245.

Williams, Bernard (1994) 'Drawing Lines', Review of Only Words by Catharine A MacKinnon, *London Review of Books*, 16.9 (12 May): 9–10.

Williams, Linda (1984) 'When the Woman Looks', in Mary Ann Doane, Patrici Mellencamp and Linda Williams (eds) *Re-Vision: Essays in Feminist Film Criticism*, The American Film Institute, University Publications of America.

Williams, Linda (1999) *Hard Core: Power, Pleasure, and the 'Frenzy of the Visible'*, Berkeley: University of California Press.

Wilson, Barbara (1986) *Sisters of the Road*, London: Virago.

—— (1994a) *Murder in the Collective*, London: Virago. First published in 1984.

—— (1994b) 'The Outside Edge: Lesbian Mysteries', in Liz Gibbs (ed.) *Daring to Dissent: Lesbian Culture from Margin to Mainstream*, London: Cassell.

Wilson, Elizabeth (1982) 'Interview with Andrea Dworkin', *Feminist Review*, 11: 23–29.

Wingrove, Elizabeth (1998) 'Republican Romance', *Representations*, 63, Summer.

Wise, Lawrence 'A Year Later, Delta Chi Striving to Recover Status', in *Independent Florida Alligator* Online. Available HTTP: http.www.mindspring.com/~krypto/Mar%202, %202000%20Alligator.html (accessed 9 May 2002).

'Witness Continues to Verify Account of a Barroom Rape' (1984) *New York Times*, 5 March: B13.

Woodhull, Winifred (1988) 'Sexuality, Power, and the Question of Rape', in Irene Diamond and Lee Quinby (eds) *Feminism and Foucault*, Boston: Northeastern University Press, 167–176.

'Words Are All I Have' (1993) The Letter's Page, *The Nation*, 27 December: 786–787.

Žižek, Slavoj (1989) *The Sublime Object of Ideology*, London/New York: Verso.

Zoglin, Richard (1991) 'Justice Faces a Screen Test', *Time*, 17 June: 62.

INDEX